IN HITLER'S SHADOW

IN HITLER'S SHADOW

WEST GERMAN HISTORIANS
AND THE ATTEMPT TO ESCAPE
FROM THE NAZI PAST

RICHARD J. EVANS

PANTHEON BOOKS
NEW YORK

LIBRARY OF CONGRESS CATALOGING-IN-PUBLICATION DATA

Evans, Richard J.
  In Hitler's shadow.
  Bibliography: p.
  Includes index.
  1. Germany—History—1933–1945—Historiography.
2. Historiography—Germany (West) I. Title.
DD256.5.E92 1989 943.086 88-43239
ISBN 0-394-57686-1

Book Design by Anne Scatto

Manufactured in the United States of America

First Edition

CONTENTS

LIST OF MAPS

PREFACE

Fifty years after the outbreak of World War II, is it time to forgive the Germans? Now that most of those who carried out the crimes of Nazism are dead, should the younger West Germans who constitute the majority of the Federal Republic's population today learn to be proud of their country rather than being ashamed of it? Have the memories of Germany's twentieth-century misdeeds been distorted by the legacy of wartime propaganda? Has the moment arrived when we should take a broader and more balanced view, and accept that the evil of Nazism, terrible though it was, did not significantly differ from other evils which have plagued our troubled time, from the Gulag Archipelago to the killing fields of Cambodia?

Over the past few years, these questions have aroused an impassioned debate both within West Germany and outside, as a substantial number of West German historians have argued in various ways that the answer to all of them should be "yes." This book is an attempt to lay out the fundamental issues in this sometimes angry and convoluted discussion, and to reach as balanced an assessment of them as possible. It is not a polemical book. Polemics, though they can have a useful function in bringing a problem to public attention, tend to obscure the central issues in a controversy, and the aim of winning debating points too easily leads to a lack of fairness and discrimination in the weapons used. Nor is it an account of personalities, though a certain amount of background detail has been provided on some of the principal antagonists in the debate. The purpose of this book is to discuss the issues in the light of what we know about the historical events upon which they touch. To help the reader unfamiliar with this controversy, it also attempts to give an account of the political context in which the debate has arisen, and to point to some of the implications for German and European politics as the twentieth century draws to a close.

Writing a book such as this involves a measure of moral judgment which is difficult for an author born, as I was, after the Second World War, to apply. Like so many Europeans of my generation, and unlike so many people in the generation of my parents, I have lived a peaceful life that so far has been free of the curse of war and destruction that was visited with such terrible intensity upon Europe in the half century before my birth. Nothing would be more arrogant or facile than for me to lay down moral imperatives for people who faced decisions and situations with which, thankfully, I have never been confronted. For me, as for the rest of my generation and its successors, this is history rather than living memory or experience.

But one of the historian's most important tools is historical imagination, the ability to bridge the gap between past and present, and to look at historical events in all their complexity and with all their troubling lack of finality. In the debate which is the subject of this book, the exercise of historical imagination also, inevitably, becomes an exercise in moral judgment. With all due consideration for the situation of those involved, therefore, I have not felt able to avoid the issue of what was the morally right thing to do in the circumstances of the Second World War. I like to think that I would have done what was morally right myself had I been faced with these circumstances. But I can never be sure. This book, therefore, is not written in a combative spirit. I have tried as far as possible to avoid expressions of outrage or anger, to eschew violent denunciations of the views of those with whom I disagree, to summarize and quote the historians concerned as fully and fairly as I can, and to steer clear of speculations as to the personal motives of the leading figures in the debate. This has not always been easy. But if historians cannot respect each other, there is little hope of their being able to respect the past which is their chosen subject.

The opportunity to think about the issues involved in the present controversy came in January 1987, when the editors of the *Journal of Modern History* asked me to write a review article on the debate. The article appeared as "The New Nationalism and the Old History: Perspectives on the West German *Historikerstreit*," in volume 59 of the *Journal of Modern History* (December 1987), pp. 761–97. I am grateful to the editors for having asked me to write it, and for the care with which they and their staff went through the editing and production process. Portions of that article appear in the present book, and I am indebted to the University of Chicago Press for allowing me to reproduce them. I have not changed my mind on the central issues since finishing the article in July 1987, but inevitably the vast outpouring of books and essays in the debate since then has altered my perspectives on the problems under discussion, broadened my view on some, and sharpened my focus on others. So when Professor Arno J. Mayer of Princeton University suggested I turn the article into a book, I welcomed the opportunity to think these questions through again. I would like here to express my thanks to him, and to my editor at Pantheon Books, André Schiffrin, for having encouraged me to undertake the task. I am also grateful to the friends and colleagues in Britain, the United States, and the Federal Republic of Germany who have kept me supplied with references and materials—in particular to Hans-Ulrich Wehler, whose bibliographical updates have (I hope) enabled me to take account in this book of everything that appeared in the debate up to the end of 1988.

A number of audiences listened patiently to my views on the controversy as they developed, and provided valuable criticisms and suggestions: I am especially grateful in this connection to the German History Society, the Association for the Study of German Politics, the Max Weber Centre for Applied German Studies at the University of Liverpool, the University of Exeter, the Graduate Seminar in German History at the University of East Anglia, the Mellon Seminar on Nationalism at Princeton University, and the Graduate Seminar in International History at the London School of Economics. A special word of thanks goes to Marie Mactavish for typing the manuscript under considerable pressure of time. Richard Bessel, Ian Kershaw, Arno Mayer, and Jeremy Noakes have put me greatly in their debt by reading the typescript on very short notice and suggesting numerous improvements. The sole responsibility for the book's contents is, of course, mine.

RICHARD J. EVANS
NORWICH, ENGLAND
FEBRUARY 1989

IN HITLER'S SHADOW

CHAPTER ONE

THE BURDEN OF GUILT

I

Half a century has now passed since the outbreak of the most destructive war the world has ever known. On September 1, 1939, German troops invaded Poland. The Second World War had begun. Six years later, when it was over, humanity began to count the cost. Some 50 million people had died as a direct consequence of the war. Untold suffering and cruelty had been deliberately visited upon many millions more who survived. Vast areas of Europe and the Far East had been devastated. Innumerable cities had been reduced to rubble. The face of global politics had been altered beyond recognition. Countries had shifted their boundaries; nationalities and ethnic minorities had changed their domicile, dispersed, or lost their independence. The sheer scale of the devastation wrought by the conflict was almost beyond comprehension.[1] Yet as the victorious troops of the wartime Allies picked their way across the ruins of defeated Germany, they were still shocked by what they found.

On April 4, 1945, for example, as the Fourth U.S. Armored Division entered the small town of Ohrdruf, near Gotha (now

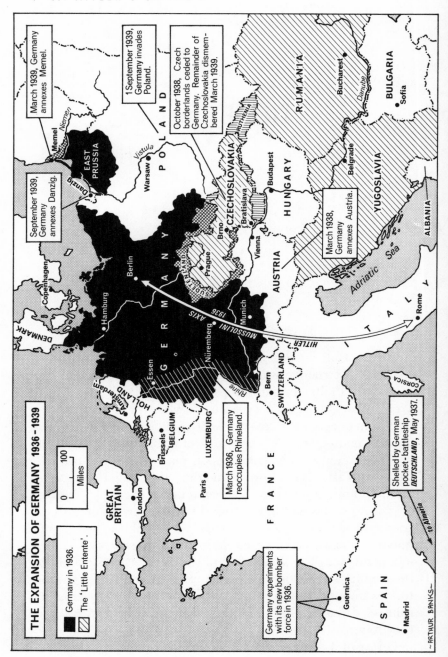

THE EXPANSION OF GERMANY 1936–1939

■ Germany in 1936.
▨ The 'Little Entente'.

0 100
Miles

March 1939, Germany annexes Memel.

1 September 1939, Germany invades Poland.

October 1938, Czech borderlands ceded to Germany. Remainder of Czechoslovakia dismembered March 1939.

September 1939, Germany annexes Danzig.

March 1938, Germany annexes Austria.

March 1936, Germany reoccupies Rhineland.

Shelled by German pocket-battleship *DEUTSCHLAND*, May 1937.

Germany experiments with its new bomber force in 1936.

DENMARK
Copenhagen
EAST PRUSSIA
Memel
Niemen
Danzig
Vistula
Warsaw
P O L A N D
Hamburg
Berlin
G E R M A N Y
Essen
Nüremberg
Munich
SUDETENLAND
Prague
Brno
Bratislava
CZECHOSLOVAKIA
Ruthenia
Vienna
AUSTRIA
HUNGARY
Budapest
RUMANIA
Bucharest
Danube
BULGARIA
Sofia
Belgrade
YUGOSLAVIA
ALBANIA
Adriatic Sea
Rome
I T A L Y
AXIS 1936
MUSSOLINI 1936
HITLER
Bern
SWITZERLAND
Rhine
HOLLAND
Amsterdam
BELGIUM
Brussels
LUXEMBURG
Paris
F R A N C E
GREAT BRITAIN
London
SPAIN
Madrid
Guernica
to Almeria
CORSICA

~ARTHUR BANKS~

in the German Democratic Republic), some Polish refugees led them to a Nazi labor camp located just outside the town. The camp guards and officials had recently gone, but some of the 10,000 men they had incarcerated as slave laborers remained.[2] As General Omar Bradley walked with fellow generals George Patton and Dwight D. Eisenhower through the camp, he became numb with shock. "The smell of death overwhelmed us even before we passed through the stockade," he recalled later. "More than 3,200 naked, emaciated bodies had been flung into shallow graves. Others lay in the streets where they had fallen. Lice crawled over the yellowed skin of their sharp, bony frames." Farther on, they came to a shed piled with bodies, and another containing instruments of torture. Hardened as they were to death, the generals were unprepared for this experience. Patton became physically ill. Eisenhower subsequently ordered all nearby units to visit the camp to see for themselves.[3] Meanwhile, other U.S. forces were discovering even worse conditions elsewhere. A sense of outrage spread through the Army. As one GI, Austrian-born, said later, "My fellow GI's, most of them American born, had no particular feeling for fighting the Germans. They also thought that any stories they had read in the paper, or that I had told them out of first-hand experience were either not true or at least exaggerated. And it did not sink in, what this was all about," he recalled, describing their first encounter with German atrocities, "until we got into Nordhausen." Here, in a series of camps used to house 12,000 slave laborers engaged in building rocket factories, they found piles of skeletal corpses, amid which the living were still lying, weak, lice-ridden, starving, and apathetic. "Many of the boys I am talking about now," recalled another GI present at the scene, "—these were tough soldiers, these were combat men who had been all the way through on the invasion—were ill and vomiting, just at the sight of this."[4]

If public opinion found such accounts hard to believe,[5] the limits of understanding were pushed even further by the revelations that soon came from other, much bigger camps. As conditions in centers such as Auschwitz and Belsen, liberated by Allied troops, became known, it grew clear that the Germans had been engaged in a deliberate program of extermination, affecting to some extent many different groups, from criminals and prostitutes to Gypsies and Jehovah's Witnesses, but applied most systematically and comprehensively to Europe's Jews. From all over occupied Europe, millions of Jews had been shipped off to the camps and gassed to death in conditions of unspeakable brutality and inhumanity.[6] Some had been subjected to cruel medical experiments by camp doctors, injected with fatal diseases, frozen, put into pressure chambers, or otherwise used as guinea pigs in acutely painful operations, without benefit of anaesthetics, and without any necessity for medical research.[7] Others had been effectively worked to death as slave laborers.[8] Altogether, when records could be traced, it emerged that between 5 and 6 million Jews had been deliberately murdered by the Nazis. Such was the enormity of this crime that many refused to believe it at the time. Even while it was occurring, Jewish agencies outside occupied Europe, despite being presented with eyewitness accounts, found it hard to accept.[9]

Gradually, over the years, the contours and dimensions of this massive history of cruelty, murder, and genocide have become clearer. Those who survived have been persuaded to record their experiences for posterity, on tape, on film, or in writing. Major collections of this material now exist in several countries; some of it has been used in Claude Lanzmann's epic film *Shoah*. A great deal of it has been made available in documentary collections and compilations.[10] Just as important, however, is the fact that in the final phases of the war, Allied forces managed to secure vast collections of Nazi, German government, and military records. Several tons of this official paperwork were shipped to the United States. Teams of researchers set to work to try and delineate the outlines and details of Nazi crimes and identify those responsible for them. In the Nuremberg Trials, held in 1946, shortly after the end of the war, the surviving leading figures in the regime were charged with a wide range of crimes against peace and humanity. The evidence presented at the court subsequently filled many stout volumes.[11] Scores of smaller trials of less prominent war criminals were also held. Finally, historians began to gain access not only to the captured documents, but also to the vastly greater quantities of documentation lying in German archives, in government buildings, or in private possession.[12]

This mass of documentary and eyewitness evidence has established the nature and scale of Nazi crimes beyond any reasonable doubt. These crimes had begun even before the war had started. Nazism's immediate roots lay in the aftermath of German defeat in the First World War. Widespread feelings of aggrieved national pride were nourished by the compromises and failures of the Weimar Republic, above all in the chaos of the postwar inflation. Falling quickly under the dominance of Adolf Hitler, the National Socialist, or Nazi, movement attempted a violent takeover of the provincial government in Bavaria in 1923. It was repulsed. But ten years later, on January 30, 1933, Hitler was appointed chancellor and head of government in Berlin. His movement had gained mass support during the years of the economic Depression, starting in 1929. By 1932, with 37 percent of the votes, representing the support of over 13 million adult Germans, it was by far the largest political movement in the country. It differed from a conventional political party in several respects. It wanted the destruction of democracy and its replacement by a dictatorship under Hitler. It preached a gospel of hatred against the republic, the trade unions, socialists, pacifists, Communists, and Jews. It backed this up with the strong-arm tactics of its paramilitary wing, the uniformed, brown-shirted storm troopers who broke up opponents' meetings and attacked, and sometimes murdered, political enemies.[13] Hitler may have been appointed chancellor legally in 1933. But the processes by which the Nazis then proceeded to establish their power were often highly illegal. When the Nazis took power in Prussia (the largest state in Germany, covering over half its area) by a decree of February 6, 1933, they violated the ruling of the German Supreme Court over the legitimate control of the government in Prussia, which still formally belonged to the left-wing Social Democratic Party, illegally removed from office by a conservative coup the previous year. Many aspects of the Nazis' arrest and maltreatment of their opponents in early 1933 were thus illegal in more senses than one.[14]

Once installed in government, the Nazis quickly outmaneuvered their conservative coalition partners and established a one-party dictatorship. They called it the Third Reich and predicted it would last for a thousand years, like its medieval predecessor. Non-Nazi organizations (apart from the churches) were banned. Thousands of opponents of the Nazis were thrown into concentration camps, where they were brutally mishandled; many were summarily executed. The Nazis immediately set about implementing their anti-Semitic policies. A boycott of Jewish businesses was staged in 1933. According to the 1935 Nuremberg Laws, Jews were not allowed to marry Gentiles. They were effectively removed from their jobs and increasingly isolated from the rest of German society.[15] Above all, Hitler and his fellow Nazis began preparing for war. They took Germany out of the League of Nations—the predecessor of the present-day United Nations—and began to rearm. In 1936, they remilitarized the Rhineland. In 1938, German troops marched into Austria. The country was incorporated into the Third Reich without resistance. Later the same year, in the Munich Agreement, Britain and France, who were now expressing concern about Hitler's plans, accepted the forcible cession of a large part of Czechoslovakia to Germany. This was the Sudetenland, home of a substantial German-speaking population. In the spring of 1939, the Nazis effectively took over the rest of Czechoslovakia. There had long been international reservations about the failure of the Treaty of Versailles, after World War I, to agree to national self-determination for the Germans. So Britain and France had so far accepted Nazi expansionism because it mainly involved annexing German-speaking areas which had at one stage or another shown some enthusiasm for this step. Now, however, it was becoming clear that Hitler was after non-German lands as well.[16]

When the Nazis invaded Poland in September 1939, Britain and France therefore declared war. There was, it is true, relatively little they could do to help the Poles. Shortly before, on August 23, Hitler had reached an agreement with Russian dictator Josef Stalin. This was the Nazi-Soviet Pact, a nonaggression treaty which provided that the Soviets would take over the eastern part of Poland while the Germans annexed the western portion. Both sides now occupied their respective parts of the country, and an uneasy border between the two was agreed to. With the East secure, the Germans now turned to the West, and in a series of lightning attacks *(Blitzkriege)* in 1940, conquered France, Belgium, Holland, Denmark, and Norway. Having established domination in the West, Hitler turned again to the East. On June 22, 1941, German Army units launched an all-out assault on the Soviet Union, in "Operation Barbarossa," which drove back the Russians and inflicted heavy losses. The terrain proved too vast, the Soviet resistance too stubborn, and Russian resources too deep for the *Blitzkrieg* strategy to succeed this time. In the winter of 1941–42 and the following spring, German troops became bogged down; and by the next winter, above all in the battle of Stalingrad, they began to suffer serious reverses. In the West, the British were holding out against Nazi bombing raids and, with increasing U.S. help, increased their war production and maintained their supplies. In December 1941, Hitler declared war on the United States. Before long, American resources were beginning to tilt the balance decisively against the Germans and their allies, notably the Italians, who defected in 1943. And German defeats in North Africa had now opened the way for the invasion of Sicily.[17]

The Nazis were meanwhile implementing increasingly radical policies of genocide and extermination. From January 1940, they had been engaged in the mass murder of the inmates of mental hospitals in Germany itself. This "euthanasia program" was temporarily halted, reduced to smaller dimensions, and forced underground by the protests of the Catholic Church. In Poland, following the Nazi invasion, Jews were herded into ghettos, where conditions became increasingly harsh. When German troops entered Russia in 1941, they were followed by death squads, part of Himmler's black-uniformed SS. These were the so-called *Einsatzgruppen,* up to one thousand strong, who now embarked upon mass executions of hundreds of thousands of Jews, possibly as many as 2 million in all. Later on in the same year the "Final Solution" was extended to the whole of German-occupied Europe. Plans were laid to set up the extermination machinery, and deportations began in the autumn. From December 1941, killing operations began at Chelmno, in Poland, and by the spring of 1942 a number of special extermination camps were in full swing, systematically gassing to death trainloads of Jews transported from all over Europe, amid scenes of appalling cruelty and inhumanity. The policy of genocide continued uninterrupted almost until the victorious Russians were at the camp gates. In the chaos of evacuation, thousands more prisoners died, or were killed, on the "death marches" of the surviving camp inmates away from the advancing Red Army. As British, American, and other Allied troops came from the West following the Normandy landings in 1944, and their Soviet allies entered Germany from the East, it was above all the discovery of the concentration camps that damned the Germans in their eyes and convinced them that this was no ordinary war that they had been fighting.[18]

II

In the last months of the war and the first months of peace, the American, British, and Soviet leaders met with their allies to discuss what should be done to reach a lasting peace settlement. They decided that the eastern boundary of Germany should be moved westward, and the German population left behind it in the East should be deported to the other side. Millions of ethnic Germans were thrown out of their homes and forcibly deported from Russia and Poland, as well as from Yugoslavia, Czechoslovakia, and other parts of Eastern Europe; large numbers of them were maltreated, mishandled, or murdered in the process.[19] What remained of Germany was divided into four zones of occupation. By 1949, the Soviet zone had become the German Democratic Republic (East Germany) and the three western zones the Federal Republic of Germany (West Germany). The old capital, Berlin, which was situated roughly in the center of the Soviet zone, was divided into four sectors. An attempt by the Soviets to force the Western Allies out in 1948 was foiled by the "Berlin airlift," in which essential supplies were flown in by plane. In 1961, the East Germans walled off West Berlin, thus completing the isolation of the German Democratic Republic begun by the sealing of its border with the West in 1952. Some 2.2 million East Germans had fled to the West before this event; now the flow was reduced to a trickle. East Germans who continued to try to escape the Communist dictatorship now faced bullets and minefields if they attempted to cross the border illegally.[20]

In the immediate postwar years, Germans were consumed by the needs of survival and reconstruction. But the rift in relations between the Soviet Union and its former Western allies in the fight against Hitler, which reached a peak in the Berlin airlift and quickly spread to other international flashpoints, began to change Western policy. After the war, extensive trials of war criminals, denazification, and reeducation had aimed to eliminate the evil of Nazism and its adherents from public life in the western zones as well as in the East. As the emerging Cold War began to make it more important to prop up West Germany and turn it into a bulwark against the perceived threat of Soviet Communism, priorities started to change. Money was poured into West Germany under the Marshall Plan. Former Nazis and war criminals were now given remittance on their sentences or let off prosecution altogether. Attempts to pursue Nazi criminals not yet brought to justice were abandoned or shelved.[21] The Western Allies gave strong support to the policies of the elected West German government led by Christian Democratic politician Konrad Adenauer, which held office through the 1950s and, under Adenauer's successors Ludwig Erhard and Kurt Georg Kiesinger, all the way up to 1969.

During these years, West Germany not only recovered from wartime damage and the postwar crisis, but became one of the world's richest and most prosperous nations. The "economic miracle" gave the West German economy an enviable stability and strength. Yet this was achieved not least on the basis of trying to forget about the past. Very little was said about Nazism. Next to nothing was taught about it in the schools. The Nazi affiliations of major figures in the economy were never mentioned. Even in politics, there was no great stigma attached to a Nazi background, so long as this did not become the embarrassing object of public debate. The Christian Democratic hegemony of the Adenauer years sought to unite West Germans on the basis of the traditional, Christian, conservative values which it believed the Nazis had overturned. Critical enquiry into the German past was discouraged.[22] Nazism was regarded as an accident, a combination of the weaknesses of modern democracy and their exploitation by the unique, demonic genius of Hitler. Hitler was portrayed as a determined fanatic, whose ideas were more Austrian or European than German, and who planned from the start to launch a world war and exterminate the Jews. The enormities of Nazism's crimes were admitted, and denounced, but they were attributed mainly to Hitler himself, who in turn was presented as the essence of a thoroughly modern dictator. Extensive reparations were made to Israel as part of the *Wiedergutmachung* ("putting things right") process, but this served more as a substitute for German self-examination than as a spur to it.[23]

If Hitler's regime was comparable in this view to anything at all, it was to that other "totalitarian" state, Stalinist Russia.[24] But opinions were divided on this point. One of the central problems of maintaining the theory that Nazism and Stalinism were two sides of the same "totalitarian" coin lay in the fact that no serious commentator at this time was prepared to argue that Hitler's genocidal anti-Semitism had any real counterpart anywhere else in the world. West Germans were prepared to denounce the attempted extermination of the Jews, and all the horrors that went with the name "Auschwitz." But this served to some extent as a means of putting off contemplating Nazism's lesser crimes, which had either been committed, often with conservative complicity, throughout the Third Reich's existence, or been carried on outside the extermination camps, in the rest of occupied Europe, during the war. There was little mention of the "euthanasia program," for example, while the German Army was portrayed in the writings of the time mostly as an honorable military force composed of decent soldiers who had had little to do with Nazism.[25] In this way, conservatives in the postwar years sought to rescue a degree of national self-respect which the Germans could use in the process of reconstruction. Meanwhile, East Germany's Communist regime and its historians faced up to the Nazi past by identifying with the Communist resistance to Nazism, whose dimensions and importance, though considerable, they greatly overestimated. War memorials and museums in the East and literature published there tended to suggest that Nazism's crimes had been committed by those who lived in the west, or had fled there during the period before the building of the Berlin Wall in 1961.

By the second half of the 1960s, there were signs that this postwar era was coming to a close. A new generation of West Germans was growing up. Confronted with a wall of silence from their elders, they wanted to find out for themselves the truth about the Nazi past. Neither they nor the young university historians and teachers who sympathized with them were willing to be fobbed off with references to the demonic genius of Hitler, or by morally vehement but intellectually vacuous denunciations of Auschwitz. This was one of the sources of tension that fueled the student radicalism of 1968. But it also reflected a more general change of mood in West Germany. Already in 1966 the conservative government had been replaced by a "Grand Coalition" in which the Social Democrats came into office for the first time. From 1969 onward, under the leadership first of Willy Brandt and then of Helmut Schmidt, the Social Democrats ruled the Federal Republic in coalition with the small, liberal Free Democratic Party, and the conservative Christian Democrats were in opposition. This change of political leadership was accompanied, as sometimes happens, by far-reaching changes in intellectual life as well. Following Willy Brandt's plea that the Germans should "dare more democracy," historians, publicists, and teachers began to take the business of mastering the past much more seriously.[26]

The signal for a more determined confrontation with the German past had already been given at the trial of leading SS man Adolf Eichmann in Israel in 1960 and at the Auschwitz Trials in Germany in 1964. New sources were becoming available including the captured Nazi documents, now returned to Germany, thus making genuine and serious research much easier than in the immediate aftermath of the war. By the 1970s, numerous major scholarly studies were appearing which left no doubt about the scale and scope of Nazi crimes: studies of Nazi foreign policy and of the extermination camps, the seizure of power, the suppression of opposition, and the complicity of the conservative elites in the early years of the Third Reich. Younger historians vigorously attacked the previous concentration on Hitler as a unique, demonic individual who had planned everything from the start. Instead, the historians generally associated with this "Social-liberal" West German regime in the 1970s traced back the origins of Nazism deep into the German past, to the militarism of Prussia, the authoritarianism of Bismarck, the adventurism of Wilhelm II; to the anti-Semitic political parties of pre-1914 years; to the absence of democracy in Germany before 1918. "More democracy" in German history, it was argued, might have helped prevent the reversion to a dictatorship in 1933.[27]

In the process of coming to terms with the Nazi past, German politicians also began to overcome old hesitations and taboos. During the Cold War of the 1950s and early 1960s, the conservatives, encouraged by Washington, had been adamant in refusing to recognize the legitimacy either of the division of Germany or of the boundary changes brought about at the end of the war. Now, however, Social Democratic Chancellor Willy Brandt signed a series of agreements with the Soviet-bloc countries which helped reduce tension in Central Europe and eased the pressure on West Berlin. The price which he paid lay not only in a tacit acceptance of the new map of Europe; it lay also in an explicit acknowledgment of the burden of Germany's guilt. In a famous gesture, Brandt fell to his knees at the memorial to the Jewish victims of the Warsaw ghetto in Poland, an act which was widely understood to symbolize Germany's obeisance before its historical victims.[28] Back in the Federal Republic, newspapers, magazines, radio, and television, all competed to bring the crimes of Nazism before their audience. As the students of 1968 became the teachers of the 1970s, serious and honest treatment of the Third Reich in German schools and universities became more usual. Of course, this process had its limits. Many war criminals still went unpunished. Many ex-Nazis remained in positions of power and authority. Many writers and historians resisted the new mood of ruthless confrontation with the German past. But of the existence of such a mood at the time, there can be no serious doubt.[29]

III

In 1983, Germans marked the fiftieth anniversary of the Nazi seizure of power with an overwhelming flood of books, newspaper articles, magazine series, television programs, exhibitions, and conferences.[30] Rarely can a historical event of such negative significance have been given such widespread publicity. Yet voices were now beginning to be raised doubting the wisdom of all this. As so often, isolated forerunners had already made themselves heard. In 1978, a major controversy had been caused by the publication of *History of the Germans* by Hellmut Diwald, professor of medieval history at Erlangen University.[31] Diwald argued that the Germans' past had been "morally disqualified" since 1945, "devalued, destroyed, and taken away from them."[32] He sought to restore it in a massive, popular history that began with the present and worked its way back through the past, ending with the establishment of the Holy Roman Empire of the German Nation, the original "thousand-year Reich," in 919. That the book worked back from what was, implicitly, a defeated and disgraced present to a glorious and famous past, was not the least of its problems. Hostile comment was aroused above all by the fact that while Diwald wrote a great deal about the brutal expulsion of the German population from Eastern Europe at the end of the Second World War, he wasted little more than two pages on the crimes and atrocities perpetrated by the Nazis, above all against the Jews. Amid widespread calls for the book to be pulped, the publishers persuaded Diwald to rewrite the offending pages. The book is still in print, but its reputation among serious historians is nil. Even conservatives were shocked by the attempt to minimize the significance of Auschwitz, and the conservative daily newspaper *Frankfurter Allgemeine Zeitung* printed a review by Karl Otmar von Aretin, a historian not known for his political radicalism, which described the book as "confused and stupid."[33]

Diwald was unfortunate in his timing. A few years later, his reception might have been very different. For in 1982 the Social-liberal era came to an end. The Free Democratic Party switched back to form a coalition with the conservative Christian Democrats, and Helmut Schmidt was replaced as chancellor by Helmut Kohl. With the electorate's seal of approval in 1983, confirmed in the elections of 1987, the new government settled down to a prolonged period in power, backed by the defeat of the Social Democrats in a number of provincial elections. As had happened a decade and a half before, the new change in political climate was accompanied by a change of intellectual mood. Encouraged by the new government, its publicity machine, and its appointments policy, conservative intellectuals now began to seize the initiative back from the liberals and Social Democrats. This was the so-called *Tendenzwende*, the "change of tack" in which the achievements of the

1970s were to be denied and reversed on all fronts. Spurred on by the new note of patriotism struck by the Reagan presidency in the United States, Chancellor Kohl's government now began to strike a patriotic chord itself.

The moment for a renewal of German patriotism was opportune. The sharp deterioration in East-West relations which accompanied the Soviet invasion of Afghanistan and the "evil empire" speech of President Ronald Reagan meant that, for the NATO allies, strengthening West Germany's determination to stand up to the East became more important. The West German Army had to be given back pride in its tradition and confidence in its mission in order to help it confront the East German forces across the Communist border. The West Germans now had to be assured that they were trusted allies. For both the American and the West German governments, this meant drawing a line between the present and the past. As the U.S. ambassador to the Federal Republic commented, it was time for the West Germans to free themselves from the "tragedy of the period 1933–45" and gain self-confidence through a greater concentration on the more positive aspects of the German past. A suitable moment seemed to present itself in 1985 on the occasion of the fortieth anniversary of Germany's unconditional surrender to Allied forces at the end of the Second World War. Plans were accordingly laid to turn the event into a celebration of the Western Alliance; and President Reagan agreed to mark the occasion by visiting West Germany and holding a special ceremony to commemorate the end of the war in the small southern German town of Bitburg, in the vicinity of a major American military base.

Reagan's intention was to lay a wreath at the town's military cemetery "in a spirit of reconciliation, in a spirit of forty years of peace, in a spirit of economic and military compatibility." Reacting to protests that there were numerous graves of Himmler's Waffen-SS men as well as of ordinary soldiers at Bitburg, Reagan declared that "those young men are victims of Nazism also. . . . They were victims, just as surely as the victims in the concentration camps." He refused even to balance the visit by going to a concentration camp, on the grounds that, as he said, the Germans "have a guilt feeling that's been imposed on them, and I just think it's unneces-

sary." "I feel very strongly," he added, "that . . . instead of
re-awakening the memories . . . we should observe this day as
the day when, forty years ago, peace began." Only in the face
of mounting protests from many ethnic, religious, and political
groups in the United States—expressed most dramatically by
Elie Wiesel's impassioned personal plea to Reagan ("That
place, Mr. President, is not your place. Your place is with the
victims of the SS")—did the president agree to go to the Bergen-Belsen concentration camp as well as to Bitburg cemetery. But the wreath-laying went ahead.[34]

Reagan earned a good deal of ridicule for his statements
during the Bitburg affair: a French newspaper gave him an "F
in history,"[35] while Arthur Schlesinger, Jr., commented acidly
that "Mr. Reagan in fact is the only American president who
was of military age during the Second World War and saw no
service overseas. He fought the war on the film lots of Holly-
wood, slept in his own bed every night and apparently got many
of his ideas of what happened from subsequent study of the
Reader's Digest."[36] But the truth about the visit is not so simple.
In fact, it was West German Chancellor Kohl, at a meeting with
the president in Washington on November 30, 1984, who suggested that Reagan visit a German military cemetery. As journalist Timothy Garton Ash commented, "The Bitburg debacle
was essentially of his making; and it was certainly Kohl who
kept the President to his foolish promise." Subsequently, Kohl
lent his support to the ethnic German expellees from Silesia by
attending their congress and publicly endorsing the German
state boundaries of 1937, which of course include about a third
of Poland. As he spoke, banners were unfolded in the audito-
rium saying "Silesia Stays German."[37] With characteristic op-
portunism, Chancellor Kohl showed a different face, during a
state visit by the president of Israel, when he declared that the
Nazi "genocide in its cold, inhuman planning and deathly effi-
ciency was unique in the history of mankind. . . . We never want
to forget the Nazi crimes. We shall also resist every attempt to
suppress or play them down." In a much-debated national address, West German President Richard von Weizsäcker did his
best to repair the damage and rightly earned widespread respect, nationally and internationally, by urging Germans to
"face up to the truth."[38] But although a conservative, Weiz-

säcker has a fairly neutral role as the Federal Republic's head of state, and stands to a large extent aloof from the daily realities of the political scene.[39]

His voice, that of a moderate and self-critical German consciousness, has been increasingly drowned by a groundswell of strident nationalism on the right. Chancellor Kohl has reflected this tide of opinion in a variety of ways. He aroused a good deal of comment, for example, when he said that he considered himself freed from guilt by virtue of his youth, being the "first Federal Chancellor of the post-Hitler generation." His belief in the similarity of Communism and Nazism caused a minor international storm when it found expression in his comparison of Soviet Communist Party General Secretary Gorbachev and Nazi propaganda chief Josef Goebbels in a notorious interview printed in *Newsweek*.[40]

The interest of the Kohl government in lightening the burden of German guilt has been reflected in many statements by its supporters in the press, who have (among other things) defended Austrian President Kurt Waldheim and urged Jews to be tactful in their dealings with Germans.[41] The Kohl government has decided to encourage greater and more positive historical consciousness by building a German Historical Museum in Berlin and a House of the History of the Federal Republic in Bonn. The Berlin museum will, it seems, concentrate on presenting a national past in basically chronological form, though the original conception has reportedly been somewhat watered down in the planning process.[42] The Bonn museum will present the history of West Germany according to political principles (the Adenauer years, the Grand Coalition, etc.), largely ignoring social and economic developments, which ought in any case to be periodized according to rather different criteria. Apparently, the Third Reich will more or less be omitted from consideration.[43] Conservative historians predominate on the official commissions set up to establish these museums. As Martin Broszat, director of West Germany's Munich-based Institute of Contemporary History, has commented, the Federal government selected as its advisers "a small group of historians . . . who certainly cannot be seen as representative of historical scholarship and research on contemporary history in the Federal Republic either from their political or from their scholarly standpoint."[44] It remains to be seen how far the museums will try and use the past to build a new and positive sense of German national identity. Some of the objections to the museums have undoubtedly been exaggerated, and a few have been downright silly.[45] But it is to be feared that the picture they present of West Germany's long-term and short-term past will be a partial picture—a picture with many or most of the problems left out.

All this has been backed up by a growing chorus of opinion on the political right, declaring that the time has come for the West Germans to stop feeling guilty about the past and start feeling proud of themselves once more. In the words of the late Bavarian Minister-President Franz Josef Strauss, the Germans should get off their knees and learn to "walk tall" again. "That means," he added, "saying yes to the idea that we have been born German, and not letting the vision of a great German past be blocked by the sight-screens of those accursed twelve years between 1933 and 1945." In Strauss's view, it was at last time for Germany to "emerge from the shadow of the Third Reich" and "become a normal nation again." "German history," he warned, "cannot be presented as an endless chain of mistakes and crimes."[46] Former West German President and Head of State Karl Carstens added his voice to the chorus calling for more "patriotism." He urged a return to "the old patriotic tradition," cleansed of its deformation by the Nazis. He regretted that—in his words—"the generation that is now reaching adulthood simply doesn't want to believe that many of the National Socialist regime's terrible deeds were not known to the majority of Germans of that time."[47] Christian Democratic federal parliamentary floor leader Alfred Dregger has also been outspoken in arguing that the Germans should not be ashamed of their past. And these views have received strong backing from the leading conservative daily newspaper, the *Frankfurter Allgemeine Zeitung*, which in the mid-1980s began printing a long series of articles questioning the thesis of German guilt.[48]

As this political campaign gathered momentum, privately funded right-wing, "research" institutions outside the mainstream of German academic life, such as Alfred Schickel's "Contemporary History Research Center" in Ingolstadt, began to gain a new, more respectable audience through the columns of the *Frankfurter Allgemeine Zeitung*.[49] Marginal, isolated right-wing researchers similarly found themselves now invited to contribute to the newspaper's columns.[50] But what lent these calls for a new national consciousness based on a more positive view of the German past their real weight was the fact that serious university historians with major international reputations now began to add their voices as well. The philosophical historian Ernst Nolte, best known internationally for his book *Three Faces of Fascism,* joined in with an article published in the *Frankfurter Allgemeine Zeitung* on June 6, 1986, under the title "The Past That Will Not Pass Away."[51] With the passage of time, he said, most events tended to lose their urgency and became the object of quiet and scholarly study by historians. Not so the events of the Third Reich, which continued to hang over the German present like an executioner's sword. The Third Reich was, he said, constantly held up as a negative example of militarism, even though in the Federal Republic everyone now at least *claimed* to be a pacifist; of austerity, even though the Federal Republic was now a highly prosperous society; of male chauvinism, even though no one was now openly male supremacist; of great-power imperialism, even though the role of the Federal Republic in world politics was now only that of a medium-sized state; of state-inspired mass murder, even though West Germany now enshrined human rights in its legislation. Yet the memory of Nazism, Nolte complained, awakened the constant fear that the old Adam would break through the surface of West German society in all these respects.

Nolte implied that this prevented West Germans from identifying positively with the state in which they lived. He sought to remove this obstacle with a variety of arguments. It was time, he said, to recognize that the historical reality of Nazism was as complex as any other historical reality: time to put away the black and white and start painting in shades of gray. It was, he insisted, absurd to regard this as politically dangerous or as threatening to result in the Germans' identifying once again with the Third Reich. Hitler's scorched-earth policy of March 1945 as well as the wholly negative effects of Nazism on Germany's place in the world would be enough to prevent this from happening. Fascism was extremely unlikely to gain any significant support in Germany, however much the Germans succeeded in escaping the legacy of Nazism. It was deplorable, said Nolte, that the German obsession with the "Final Solution" diverted attention from urgent issues of the present such as abortion in Germany or "genocide" in Afghanistan.

At the same time, Michael Stürmer, professor of history at Erlangen University, frequent columnist for the *Frankfurter Allgemeine Zeitung*, and "historical adviser" to Chancellor Kohl, also began to write a series of articles calling for a new sense of national identity. He complained of a "loss of orientation" among the Germans. The absence of a positive historical consciousness meant a "search for identity" which, in Stürmer's view, could only be fulfilled by a new vision of Germany's past, by a historically based sense of national identity and patriotism.[52] Germany, he said, was "now once more a focal point in the global civil war waged against democracy by the Soviet Union."[53] Yet Germany was in his view ill-equipped to stand up to the "campaign of fear and hate carried into the Federal Republic from the East and welcomed within like a drug."[54] Those who undermined German national self-confidence by depriving the Germans of a positive consciousness of their history up to 1945 were, he implied, working in Moscow's interest. Adenauer, he wrote, had been wise not to try and bring the guilty collaborators and fellow travelers of Nazism to book. He implied that Adenauer's successors in the 1970s had been unwise to abandon this policy. Opinion polls, said Stürmer, showed that while 80 percent of Americans were proud of being Americans and some 50 percent of Britons were proud of being British, only 20 percent of Germans were proud of being Germans. Only by restoring their history to themselves could Germans recover their pride again, and thus become reliable allies in the fight against Communism.[55]

Stürmer's and Nolte's views were reinforced by a conference of conservative West German historians held in Berlin on October 6, 1986. The meeting was funded by the Hanns-Martin-Schleyer Foundation, named after the president of the Employers' Association kidnapped and murdered by far-left terrorists in 1977. The theme was "To Whom Does German History Belong?" and the speakers were agreed that it was time for the West Germans to reclaim German history for themselves. Andreas Hillgruber, professor of history at Cologne University, warned the participants that the Communist regime in East Germany was now busily recapturing a positive relationship to Germany's older historical traditions, and that there was a danger that it would appropriate the sense of German national identity for itself. This opened up the threat of reunification under terms set by the GDR, which Hillgruber, alluding to the state which had taken the lead in bringing about Italian unification in the nineteenth century, called "the German Piedmont." West Germany, he said, had to counter this threat by building its own positive relationship to the German past and German nationhood.[56]

Such views, and even more, perhaps, the detailed historical arguments that have been deployed to lend them intellectual substance, have aroused heated debate in West Germany.[57] Liberal and Social Democratic historians have mounted a determined defense of their achievements of the 1960s and 1970s. Leading weekly magazines have devoted whole series of articles to the debate; television stations have broadcast special programs on it; the correspondence columns of the daily press have been filled with angry letters, rebuttals, and counter-charges. For the first time since the "Fischer controversy," fought out in the early 1960s over Germany's responsibility for the outbreak of World War I, professional academic historians—as no less a person than the president of the German Historians' Association has complained—are refusing to shake hands with one another in public. As the debate has gone on, it has become progressively more personal and abusive, and progressively less scholarly. It is not surprising, therefore, that a distinguished American observer of the German historical scene has voiced the suspicion that it might merely be a "fluttering in the academic dovecotes," another example of the peculiarly contentious style of German academic life.[58] Should it be a cause for concern, one might ask, that those cantankerous and self-important German professors are at each others' throats yet again? Or are there wider issues involved that should be of concern not only to every thinking person in Germany but also to all those who are concerned about Germany's future—indeed, to everyone who cares about the historical record, about political morality, about justice and peace? Answering this question is not a simple business—not least because the controversy involves issues of contemporary politics and morality as much as, or possibly even more than, problems of historical method and understanding.[59] But major questions are indeed involved. A determined attempt is under way to persuade the world that it is time to stop blaming the Germans for the crimes of Nazism. The arguments raised demand detailed consideration. In the following chapters, therefore, we turn to the substantive points at issue. For what is going on is no mere denial of the German past—that would be too simple, and too easily disposed of by reference to the historical record. The campaign now being waged to reassert German national pride is far more subtle and sophisticated, as we shall now see.

CHAPTER TWO

"ASIATIC DEEDS"

I

The most determined attempts to get around the obstacle of Auschwitz have been made recently by West Berlin professor of history Ernst Nolte.[1] Born in 1923, he established his reputation at the age of forty with a book called *Three Faces of Fascism*, which investigated the ideologies of Mussolini's Fascists, Hitler's Nazis, and Charles Maurras's Action Française.[2] Nolte's book was one of a number of publications by historians and political scientists in the mid-1960s which placed fascism on the map as a serious object of study.[3] These works moved the focus of scholarly attention away from the concept of "totalitarianism," dominant in the 1950s, according to which Nazi Germany and Soviet Russia were two sides of the same coin. They turned it instead toward the comparative study of "fascism" in Europe and elsewhere. Fascism was now seen as a phenomenon fundamentally different from that of Soviet Communism. This was possible not least because, as Nolte's contribution showed, fascist ideology was more than the mere rhetoric as which it had often previously been discussed; on the contrary, it was important to take it seriously, as a set of ideas in its own right.

The destruction of Poland was primarily a German action. 1,700,000 German troops soon defeated the 600,000 Polish soldiers. German air attacks destroyed the centres of the main Polish cities. The Poles hoped to make a final stand in the Pripet Marshes, but the USSR advances destroyed all chance of further Polish resistance against either Germany or the USSR

THE GERMAN AND RUSSIAN INVASIONS OF POLAND 1939

LATVIA

Baltic Sea

Memel

LITHUANIA

Vilna

Minsk

"Polish corridor"

Danzig

EAST PRUSSIA

Suvalki

Augustov

Grodno

Bialystok

Poznan

Modlin

WARSAW

Brest–Litovsk

Pinsk

Pripet Marshes

Lodz

P O L A N D

Lublin

Lutsk

Rovno

GREATER

Sokal

GERMANY

Tarnov

Cracow

Yaroslav

Lvov

Przemysl

Stanislavov

SLOVAKIA

HUNGARY

RUMANIA

Dividing line between the German and USSR zones of occupation, agreed between Germany and the USSR in August 1939.

German advances commencing 1 September 1939.

Russian advances commencing 17 September 1939.

Annexed to the USSR October 1939.

Annexed to Germany.

Annexed to Lithuania.

0   100
Miles

Three Faces of Fascism gained its author an international reputation not least because its publication fell squarely into the context of this shift in scholarly understanding of Europe's history in the first half of the twentieth century. It was taken as an important piece of support for the idea that it was the conflict between fascism and Communism, and not the general, rather vaguely defined phenomenon of totalitarianism, that dominated Europe in this period of upheaval and war. These ideas were widely taken up in the following years by historians, sociologists, and political scientists in many countries.[4] Yet in many ways Nolte's work stood outside the mainstream of research into the history of fascism. The original German title, in literal translation, was "Fascism in Its Epoch," suggesting that fascism was a thing of the past. This perspective was not shared by most other writers on the subject. Nolte's main interest lay in fascism as an ideology, not in its social, economic, or political history. What he offered was a "phenomenology" of fascism, or in other words, an account, and an attempted classification, of its ideas.[5] This approach reflected the fact that Nolte had trained not as a historian but as a philosopher, and approached his subject from the viewpoint, and with the methods, of a historian of ideas.[6]

While this background proved useful in tackling ideology, it soon became evident that it could be something of a drawback when it came to writing more conventional forms of political history.[7] In his next book, *Germany and the Cold War,* published in 1974,[8] Nolte approached the question of postwar Germany in a way that seemed to at least one distinguished reviewer both myopically Germanocentric and, when it came to major points of interpretation, disturbingly vague and unsupported by hard evidence.[9] Peter Gay, indeed, considered the book "a massive and sophisticated apology for modern Germany."[10] Gay was neither the first nor the last critic to find that Nolte's "tortuous syntax, his evasive conditional phrasing, his irresponsible thought experiments, make it nearly impossible to penetrate to his own convictions." However, enough was obvious for Gay to accuse him of "comparative trivialization," in which Nolte "humanized" Nazi atrocities "by pointing, indignantly, at crimes committed by others." For instance, Nolte claimed that in the 1960s there was a "worldwide reproach that the United States was after all putting into practice, in Vietnam, nothing less than its basically even crueler version of Auschwitz.'' Gay felt impelled to remind him that "there is a world of difference between Nazi Germany's calculated policy of mass extermination and America's ill-conceived, persistent, often callous prosecution of a foreign war." In the same book, Nolte also speculated that Franklin D. Roosevelt might have sympathized with an anti-Semitic movement in the United States had he been confronted by a powerful Communist Party. As Gay says, "such speculations even transcend comparative trivialization; they are a way of draining real experience, real policies, in a word, real murders, of their terror."[11]

By the time Nolte's third book, *Marxism and the Industrial Revolution,* appeared in 1983,[12] he was arguing not merely that fascism was a response to Communism, but that Communism—indeed, Marxism—provided both the motive and the method for the fascist response. In a number of articles published in the late 1970s, he portrayed German Nazism as a "mirror-image" of Communism.[13] What this meant in concrete historical terms became clear in further essays, and in another substantial book, *The European Civil War,* published in 1987.[14] Nolte's central theses were conveniently encapsulated in an essay which appeared, like a number of his shorter publications, in the *Frankfurter Allgemeine Zeitung,* in 1986. This became the initial focus of the present controversy over Germans' attitudes to the past.[15] Here he began by arguing that the commonly accepted stress on the uniqueness of Hitler's "Final Solution" constituted a major, and unnecessary, obstacle to the emergence of West German national self-confidence. For Auschwitz, he argued, was not unique. A previous, comparable act of genocide, he claimed, had taken place in 1915, when the Turks had brutally murdered some one and a half million Armenians. A prominent early Nazi, Max Erwin von Scheubner-Richter, who was present in Armenia at the time, described this act, says Nolte, as "Asiatic" barbarism. Yet little more than a quarter of a century later, the Nazis were committing similar acts themselves. How had this come about?

Nolte's answer is that the Nazis' change of attitude resulted from the fact that between 1915 and 1933 the "Gulag Archipelago" was erected in Russia. Following the argument of

the Russian novelist Alexander Solzhenitsyn, Nolte says that the
Soviet system of death camps, mass deportations and shootings,
tortures, and the extermination of whole groups of people,
backed by public demands for the physical destruction of millions of innocent individuals who were regarded by the Soviet
regime as hostile to it, began already in Russia in the 1920s.
Everything which the Nazis subsequently did in this line themselves, with the sole exception of the technical procedure of
gassing, had already happened years before in the Soviet Union.
These considerations bring Nolte to his central thesis, which he
puts in the form of a series of rhetorical questions. "Did the
Nazis, did Hitler only commit an 'Asiatic' deed, perhaps, because they thought that they and those like them were potential
or real victims of an 'Asiatic' deed themselves? Was not the
Gulag Archipelago prior in history to Auschwitz? Wasn't 'class
murder' by the Bolsheviks the logical and real precondition of
'race murder' by the Nazis?"[16]

These ideas are developed further in *The European Civil
War*. Here it is also argued that Nazism was a copy of and a
reply to Soviet Communism. The essence of Nazism lay "neither in criminal tendencies nor in anti-Semitic obsessions as
such. The essence of National Socialism," according to Nolte,
was to be found "in its relation to Marxism and especially to
Communism in the form which this had taken on through the
Bolshevik victory in the Russian Revolution." These events had
to be seen against the background of the social exterminism of
the Bolsheviks. Both were enmeshed in the same causal nexus.
Both represented attempts to solve "problems which were connected with industrialization, by removing a large group of
people." The crimes of the Bolsheviks, however, took on such
dimensions in the 1920s that they called forth a defensive reaction on the part of the bourgeoisie. This took the form of Nazism, a variety of fascism. The reaction was strongest in
Germany because "the mighty shadow of events in Russia fell
more powerfully" on Germany than on any other European
country. Thus Hitler's anticommunism was, as Nolte puts it,
"understandable, and up to a certain point, indeed, justified."
The Nazis needed an ideology to defend Germany and the
bourgeoisie against the Communist threat. Anti-Semitism provided such a counterideology. It was thus essentially a product

of anticommunism, and Hitler's "Final Solution" was a copy of the Gulag Archipelago in everything except the detailed procedure of gassing. It was "as the attempt at the complete destruction of a universal race . . . the exact counterpart of the attempt at the complete destruction of a universal class, and thus the biologically transposed copy of the social original."[17]

Thus Nolte seeks to rehabilitate, or at least to excuse, the Germans, the Nazis, the bourgeoisie, and fascism in general by portraying Hitler's policies as a defensive reaction to the Soviet and Communist threat. Violence, he is saying, always comes first from the left. Nazism was basically a "justified reaction" to Communism; it simply overshot the mark. The right-wing paramilitaries who killed leading German Communists Karl Liebknecht and Rosa Luxemburg in 1919—Nolte refuses to use the word "murdered"—did so out of fear that the crimes of the Bolsheviks in Russia would be repeated in Germany if the Communists came to power. Similarly, Hitler was (Nolte implies) broadly justified in launching a coup d'état in 1923, in the so-called beer-hall putsch. Nolte compares the trial of Hitler for this failed attempt to seize power in Bavaria and overthrow the Weimar Republic by force with the simultaneous trial of a group of Communists for planning an uprising against the Republic the same year. The uprising was called off in the end, though it went ahead, probably owing to a breakdown in communications, in the northern German seaport of Hamburg. Nevertheless, the Communists were condemned to death by the courts, while Hitler and his accomplices were let off with a short prison sentence under very light conditions, conditions so easy that Hitler was able to use the period of enforced leisure to compose and dictate his personal memoir and political tract *Mein Kampf.* This has usually been seen by historians as evidence of the conservative bias of Weimar's judges, most of whom, appointed before the revolution, were deeply unsympathetic to the Republic's institutions. But, says Nolte,

One must go on to ask whether at any time in world history a beleagured system has dealt with its enemies and with those who wanted to help it, according to the same criteria; and whether one is not robbing the Communists of the honour which they may be permitted to claim, if one denies that the violent overthrow of the capitalist, or in other words the European-industrial system, must have been a far more serious and revolutionary event than the establishment of an anti-parliamentary dictator in order to repulse this attack.

In any case, he points out, the accused were not actually executed. So in the end the Communists were not treated much worse than the Nazis were.[18] Time and again, Nolte comes back to the idea that the Communist threat to Germany was not so different from that of the Nazis. Leading Communist Walter Ulbricht, for example, was anti-Semitic in Nolte's view because he wanted in 1932 "to drive out" the bourgeoisie, and most German Jews, says Nolte, were bourgeois. Left-wing writer Kurt Tucholsky, he points out, even suggested the bourgeoisie should be gassed. Nazi and Communist rhetoric, he argues, was very similar, although the Communists were perhaps more violent. The social basis of the two movements was similar, and they cooperated on more than one occasion. Both were fundamentally proletarian, and both identified the bourgeoisie as the enemy, only in different ways. In 1932–33, there was, says Nolte, a real danger of a Communist revolution in Germany. While the Nazis only wanted to remove German citizenship from a relatively small number of people—the Jews—the Communists wanted the "social destruction of the whole bourgeoisie" and owed allegiance to a state—the Soviet Union—which had "physically exterminated these classes." The Communists wanted to destroy the capitalist system; the Nazis only wanted to destroy the "Versailles system." Nazism was a kind of narrowed-down socialism: for the Nazis, Communism was both something to be feared and something to be imitated *(Schreckbild und Vorbild)*. In a lengthy comparative account of the two, Nolte brings out their similarities and suggests that they were in many ways two sides of the same coin. This argument culminates in the assertion that the extermination of the Jews was itself a biological copy of the social exterminism of the Bolsheviks.

At the same time, he says, the Nazis equated the Bolsheviks with the Jews and so transferred their fear of destruction onto the latter. Nolte suggests that Hitler's fear that the Jews would destroy him was given credence by Jewish leader Chaim Weizmann's declaration at the Zionist World Congress of 1939 that Jews all over the world would fight on Britain's side against Germany. This, says Nolte, might well have been justification enough for the Nazis to intern all German Jews as prisoners of war, rather in the same way that the Americans interned U.S. citizens of Japanese origin after Pearl Harbor. Indeed, Nolte suggests that Weizmann's declaration may even have been intended to bring about the internment of the German Jews as a way of discrediting the regime. The German attack on the Soviet Union in June 1941, according to Nolte, was in part "preventive"; it followed on "mental acts of war" against Germany by Stalin. And Hitler's mass murder of millions of Jews in the extermination camps was a reply to Soviet acts of genocide against Germans. "Auschwitz," he concludes, "was above all a reaction born out of the anxiety of the annihilating occurrences of the Russian Revolution." It was a "copy"—still more horrifying than the original, but a copy all the same.[19]

Nolte backs up his argument that murderous violence came first from the left by trying to draw parallels between the Nazis' attempted genocide of the Jews, and what he sees as a long tradition, going back as far as the Middle Ages, of calls by agrarian and other radicals for the elimination of landowners and other dominant groups. Exterminism, he says, did not begin with Hitler. Indeed, the twentieth century in his view displays many parallels to Auschwitz, from the genocide of the Armenians by the Turks in 1915, and genocide (*Völkermord*) in Vietnam in the 1960s and 1970s and in Afghanistan in the 1980s, to the murder of millions of Cambodians by the Pol Pot regime. As for the Germans, Nolte reminds his readers that "the moving documentary film *Shoah*, by a Jewish director, makes it seem probable that the SS units in the death camps were victims in their way too, and that on the other side there was virulent anti-Semitism among the Polish victims of National Socialism." Hitler himself, indeed, says Nolte, knew of the tortures inflicted upon their opponents by the Russian secret police shortly after the revolution, as a reference made by him in 1943 to the "rat-cage," a method of terrorizing opponents, also referred to subsequently in George Orwell's novel *1984*, would seem to suggest. That this method originally, according to Nolte, had been practised by the Chinese, further underlines the "Asiatic" character of the barbarism to which Hitler was reacting.[20]

Thus Nolte, in a number of publications ranging from brief newspaper articles to substantial historical tomes, seeks to provide the West Germans with an escape from Hitler's shadow, or at least, since he realizes this is too tall an order at the moment,[21] to unburden themselves of the oppressive weight of the alleged uniqueness and gratuity of Hitler's crimes. Only by freeing ourselves, he argues, from collectivist generalizations about "the" Germans, "the" Jews, "the" Russians, "the" petty bourgeoisie, and so on, can we reach a more differentiated, less mythologizing understanding of these events. Only in this way will we cease to regard every tactless remark of a local politician in the Federal Republic as evidence that the Germans have not changed since the Third Reich. It is time to stop talking about the guilt of "the" Germans, not least because this continues the same kind of thinking by which the Nazis convinced themselves of the guilt of "the" Jews.[22] In an essay published in *Aspects of the Third Reich,* a collection (as the title suggests) of rather arbitrarily chosen contributions edited by H. W. Koch and published in 1985, Nolte makes it clear that in his view "the annihilation of several million European Jews, many Slavs, the mentally insane, and Gypsies is without precedent in its motivation and execution." "The innermost core of the negative picture of the Third Reich," he goes on, "needs no revision." But at the same time he repeatedly suggests that it had so many parallels in other countries that it can be regarded as a normal twentieth-century barbarity.[23]

Of course, says Nolte in his own defense, if Israel had been annihilated by the PLO and its history written by the Palestinians, nobody would dare to portray the state's foundation as a response to European anti-Semitism. This speculation is evidently intended to suggest a direct parallel to the historiography of the Third Reich. It is surprising that a scholar of Nolte's experience could seriously believe that the history of Germany had been written only by those who conquered it in 1945 and not by the Germans themselves. There is not a shred of evidence to support this, if this is what he means. Still, his choice of this particular analogy, out of a whole host of other possible analogies, does raise the suspicion that he means to imply that the historiography of the Third Reich has been written *from the perspective* of the victors, under the inspiration of the surviving victims. This suspicion is strengthened in *The European Civil War,* where Nolte goes out of the way to say that "the literature on the 'Final Solution' comes to an overwhelming degree from Jewish authors," which has given it a simple "perpetrator-victim" pattern. In Nolte's view this underplays the "fact" (for which he provides no evidence at all) that more "Aryans" than Jews were killed at Auschwitz, and it suppresses evidence that Poles and Rumanians were anti-Semitic, that many Jews were Communists, and that many Jews resisted. Nolte suggests that much of the evidence about the "Final Solution" is questionable, because the basic rules of interviewing have not been observed, and statements are judged by political criteria, not objective ones. If Hitler had won, he says, non-German historians would probably not have been any more critical of Auschwitz than they are now of the Gulag; it is only, he implies, because Nazism was vanquished, and Communism survived, that there has been a difference in the severity with which their respective crimes have been condemned by world opinion. More generally, Nolte intends these historiographical strictures to illustrate the general point that historical myths can act as state ideologies. From the context he apparently wants to suggest that the idea that Germany was uniquely or even primarily responsible for its own destruction in 1945 and for the crimes of Nazism is a myth that has become a state ideology since 1945. This, he suggests, is having an unfortunate effect on contemporary political culture in the Federal Republic, and so it is time it was done away with.[24]

These and other views have been put forward by Nolte in a manner that is often obscure, sometimes confused, and occasionally downright contradictory. This fact has in turn allowed Nolte's defenders such as the Bremen historian Imanuel Geiss to argue that Nolte's statements appear to justify Nazism only if they are "taken in isolation" by a "hasty reader." After all, he says, Nolte repeatedly condemns Nazism and states explicitly his view that its crimes were unique. Geiss regards these condemnations and statements as the context within which Nolte's other arguments must be viewed. In a similar way, Helmut Müller declares that it would be "absurd," in view of such statements, to suggest that Nolte was even attempting to relativize Nazism, let alone justifying it.[25] But in reality writers are being taken in by Nolte's method. Nolte makes ritual obeisances to current moral orthodoxies, while devoting the larger part of his energies to developing, often by innuendo and suggestion, a series of arguments intended to subvert them and to put forward an alternative view.

It is a technique reminiscent of the great eighteenth-century rationalist historian Edward Gibbon's account of the rise of Christianity. Gibbon secured his rear, as it were, by stating at the outset that the "first cause" of the rise of Christianity was indeed Divine Providence; but Providence worked in mysterious ways, which it would be unbecoming of a mere mortal such as himself to inquire into further. The historian, he argued, had to be content with investigating the "secondary causes"; and thus he was able to go on to devote a whole chapter to a lengthy and devastating account that explained the rise of Christianity in terms of moral degeneracy, greed, ignorance, fanaticism, and other vices. All this cast an ironic light on the "first cause" he had initially cited in such a deceptive manner.

As a historian, Nolte is hardly comparable to Gibbon; but the inclusion in his work of isolated affirmations of the uniqueness of Auschwitz, condemnations of Nazism, and the like, which are then completely undermined by the numerous claims, hints, and suggestions to the opposite effect, does bear at least a superficial resemblance to Gibbon's technique. As a result, the critical reader is forced inevitably to discount some of Nolte's statements in the interest of presenting the main thrust of his views in a reasonably coherent manner. What is important, it seems clear, is to concentrate on what it is that he is saying that is really new. It is scarcely surprising these confusions have allowed Nolte's defenders to advance the claim that he has been misrepresented. But has he?

II

In the controversy which has raged around these arguments, Nolte has had his defenders.[26] But they have been few in number, and even his most ardent sympathizers have seldom followed him all the way. Joachim Fest, for example, the author of a major biography of Hitler and one of the editors of the *Frankfurter Allgemeine Zeitung,* the newspaper in which a number of Nolte's articles on this subject have appeared, has pointed out that Hitler was in Munich in 1918–19 at a time when successive revolutions in the city culminated in the "chaos and terror" which formed a "real background" to Hitler's "extermination complexes." Moreover, Hitler's anti-Semitic obsessions were confirmed by the fact that a number of the leading figures in the revolutionary regimes that ruled Munich at that time were Jews. But even Fest is forced to admit that Hitler's central ideas and purposes were all in place well before the Bolshevik revolution.[27] Hitler got his anti-Semitism in pre-1914 Vienna, not in post-1917 Munich. It was socialism, not Bolshevism, that he initially identified as "Jewish." His virulent hatred of socialism was a product of his experiences in Austria, where he came to believe that socialism was a "Jewish" conspiracy to alienate the German-speaking workers of Vienna from their true racial allegiance. Nowhere in his autobiographical political tract *Mein Kampf* or anywhere else is there a hint that Hitler's ideas or purposes were formed by his observation of the Bolshevik revolution or the Communist regime in Russia.[28]

The suggestion by Nolte that Hitler and his kind regarded mass extermination as "Asiatic" in 1915 is not really sustainable in the light of the evidence. Even on Nolte's own evidence, the word "Asiatic" was used not by Scheubner-Richter in 1915, but by his biographer, writing long after Scheubner-Richter's death, in 1938. Even if Scheubner-Richter *had* used the term "Asiatic" in 1915, for which Nolte has not presented any evidence, this in itself would not demonstrate that Hitler thought the same way, since the two had not even met at the time. In the absence of any other evidence pointing in the direction of Hitler's aversion to exterminism in 1915, Nolte's argument cannot be sustained on this point. Nolte is on much safer ground when he suggests that Hitler's anti-Semitism was strengthened by the experiences of defeat and revolution in 1918, and influenced by Alfred Rosenberg, the Baltic German who joined the Nazi Party in 1920 after fleeing Russia during the revolution. But Nolte greatly overemphasizes the degree to which this represented something decisively new in the development of Hitler's ideas. Hitler himself, in *Mein Kampf,* is quite unequivocal on the point. He became an anti-Semite well before 1914, and he does not seem to have regarded his prewar anti-Semitism as either weak or halfhearted.[29]

Hitler left a substantial body of speeches and writings, backed up by numerous records of his private opinions by intimates such as Goebbels, Speer, and Bormann. Nowhere in any of these writings is there the suggestion that Hitler's anti-Semitism was the product of even a pathological fear of Communism, let alone a justified one.[30] Certainly, he learned from his opponents, as well as reacting against them. But the passages in *Mein Kampf* which deal with this learning process refer to propaganda, not to violence, still less to exterminism, and they refer to the Social Democrats, not to the Russian Bolsheviks. Moreover, such was the irrationality of Hitler's beliefs that what he thought he saw in the methods of the socialists was as much the product of his own imagination as the result of objective observation.[31] The same can be said *a fortiori* of the beliefs of the paramilitaries who murdered the Communist leaders Karl Liebknecht and Rosa Luxemburg in Berlin early in 1919. The murderers' actions, and the brutal language accompanying their deed, suggest that it was not fear, but loathing and contempt, which motivated them. Nor is there any evidence, judging from what we know of their personalities and their previous careers, that Luxemburg and Liebknecht would have instituted a reign of terror in the unlikely event of their coming to power.[32] Even if, as Nolte says, the murderers knew that the Cheka had killed defenseless prisoners in Russia (a supposition for which he provides no evidence), this still says little about the intentions of the Communists in Germany. Communism has always varied from country to country, and the indications are that had a German Communist revolution succeeded, it would have been substantially different from the Russian one: Russian dominance over international Communism was by no means complete until the mid-1920s. And Nolte himself notes that Rosa Luxemburg criticized the "Red Terror" in Russia. Moreover, the so-called "Red Terror" in Munich in 1918–19 was to a large extent the creation of fascist propaganda; the few excesses which did occur in the heat of the revolutionary events paled into insignificance in comparison to the reign of murder and terror imposed by the paramilitaries when the revolution was finally put down. Nor did Kurt Tucholsky—a pacifist—call for gassing the bourgeoisie, an allegation Nolte can sustain only by taking an ironic remark of Tucholsky's out of its contemporary context.[33] Finally, Hitler did not launch his beer-hall putsch in 1923 in defense of capitalism. Nolte himself argues that there were strong anticapitalist elements in the Nazi Party both at this time and later on. He is confusing the political and the socioeconomic, too, and largely ignoring the fact that it was mainly the democratic political system that was under attack from the Nazis and the Communists in 1923. The point surely stands that conservative judges were undermining Weimar democracy—and the rule of law—through their leniency toward violence from the right.

What Hitler meant by the "rat-cage" when he said, privately, that at least some of the German officers captured at the battle of Stalingrad were likely to go over to the Russian side because they would be put into the "rat-cage" *(Rattenkäfig)* in Moscow, is not necessarily what Nolte claims it was. Hans-Ulrich Wehler has queried Nolte's suggestion that the "Chinese torture" described in Orwell's *1984* was described already in the anti-Bolshevik Russian author S. P. Melgunov's *The Red Terror in Russia* (published in London in 1925). The source on which Melgunov relied, an anti-Semitic tract published in 1920, says Wehler, described quite a different form of torture, not involving a cage at all. In any case, like so many of the products of the undergrowth of anti-Communist literature at the time, it cannot be regarded as reliable unless confirmed by another, independent source, of which none has so far come to light in this case. Nor is there any evidence of either method having been used by the Chinese. Orwell's image of the torture which finally broke the spirit of Winston Smith in *1984* was, according to his biographer, derived not from anti-Bolshevik literature, but from English horror stories.

These criticisms are not entirely fair. Nolte does show that Hitler was likely to have read the "rat-cage" story, because it appeared in the Nazi Party newspaper, the *Völkischer Beobachter,* in 1920, and that the "rat-cage" was a torture that may well have been that described in Orwell's *1984.* But he does not establish its connection with the Chinese Cheka units. Nor does Nolte provide enough evidence to show that the belief in, and fear of, this torture, was an important factor in Hitler's mind. Nolte does succeed more generally in demonstrating the murderous intentions and spirit of Bolshevism in the Civil War phase up to 1921. But he is less successful in showing that they continued on through all the subsequent phases of the regime's development. Even if Nolte is right about the "rat-cage" and other aspects of Bolshevik violence in the Civil War, it seems an extremely tenuous and flimsy inferential structure on which to base such a far-reaching hypothesis. To prove that the Nazis deliberately copied Stalin's methods because they were afraid they would be Stalin's victims demands a great deal of hard evidence, far more than Nolte presents. Moreover, it fails to account for Nazi actions such as the mass murder of the inmates of mental hospitals, who could hardly be regarded as part of a Communist threat. In this and many other ways, Nolte's arguments on this point do not match up with the evidence available.[34]

The evidential shakiness of Nolte's attempts to argue that the Nazis were reacting to real threats of violence when they instituted their policies of warfare, terror, and extermination, becomes even clearer when we turn to the case of Chaim Weizmann and his statement in 1939 that the Jews were bound to stand on the side of Britain in the war. Nolte, as we have seen, suggests, following the radical right-wing British journalist David Irving, that this justified Hitler's "internment" of the Jews in the same way as the Japanese attack on Pearl Harbor justified American internment of U.S. citizens of Japanese origin. In fact, few people today would defend the U.S. treatment of these people at the time, however hard one might try to understand it as an emotional reaction to the shock of the sudden Japanese act of war. Even if one did want to defend it, it should be remembered, however, that the Jews had not bombed German naval bases or attacked German troops in 1939. The Jews were not an internationally recognized national group, nor were the majority of Jewish citizens in Germany immigrants or the children of immigrants from another country, let alone a group which was at war with the Germans. Most of them came from families which had lived in Germany for centuries, and considered themselves fully German. Most important of all, Weizmann was only offering the British government the support of the Jews in *Palestine,* as the context of the letter makes clear. He was writing to Neville Chamberlain, in fact, to assure him that the Jewish Agency in Palestine would back military measures taken by the British Mandate "in this hour of supreme crisis"; he was in no way referring to Jews in Germany or anywhere outside Palestine.

In any case, Jews worldwide were not a nationality in 1939, although Nolte treats them throughout his work as such. The Zionist World Congress could not in any way speak at that time for Jews worldwide even had it wanted to; indeed, very many German Jews rejected the idea of Zionism. The congress was a pressure group, but it had no international recognition as the representative of the Jewish community in the sense, say, that the Japanese government was internationally recognized as the representative of the Japanese. There was no conceivable justification for a German internment of German citizens of Jewish origin in 1939. Moreover, "internment" is far too mild a word for the harsh, brutal, and eventually murderous discrimination meted out to Jews by the Nazis at the time. Such acts of violence and oppression had reached their height in prewar Germany the year before, in the pogroms of the so-called "Night of Broken Glass" on November 9, 1938. On orders from Goebbels, local Nazis all over Germany arrested more than 20,000 Jews, maltreating and abusing them, and killing an undetermined number, probably around a hundred. Jewish property, shops, houses, and businesses were damaged and destroyed, and synagogues in virtually every German town were set on fire. Germany was not at war with anyone at the time.[35]

The victims of 1938 would have been surprised to learn that in comparison to the Soviet Union under Stalin, the Nazi regime, according to Nolte, "must be termed practically a liberal idyll in which the rule of law obtained." Because Hitler criticized German judges for what he saw as their leniency during the war, Nolte argues that the rule of law continued to be strong at least until 1942 in Germany. He accepts Nazi lawyers' leader Hans Frank's description of himself as a "protagonist of security under the law and the independence of the judiciary." Evidence such as this is highly unpersuasive, however. The rule of law was in fact undermined from the very start of the Third Reich, and judges provided an increasingly threadbare fig leaf for rapidly growing arbitrariness in criminal and civil law.[36] As many of those who survived these events, along with millions of other Jews from all over Europe, went into the gas chambers of Auschwitz a few short years afterward, they would have been even more astonished to learn that a respected historian, less than half a century later, would describe their executioners as victims too, in their way. Although it is evidently shared by men such as U.S. President Ronald Reagan and Sir Alfred Sherman, one-time adviser to British Prime Minister Margaret Thatcher,[37] this view, even though it might seem to spring from the breadths and depths of a universal human sympathy, cannot be sustained either on legal, or on moral, or on historical grounds. A murderer is a murderer, however persuasive the mitigating circumstances of the act. There is in any case not much evidence of mitigating circumstances in this instance. As the expert witnesses in the Auschwitz trials demonstrated in great detail a quarter of a century ago, no one became an executioner in an extermination camp without having taken moral decisions at a number of possible escape points along the way. Not only was it possible to avoid joining the SS, or, once in, to avoid being posted to an extermination camp, or, once there, to avoid having to commit acts of murder and brutality, it was also possible to extricate oneself from these situations or even use them to try and help the victims. Difficult though such choices were, a small number of Germans did indeed take them, and not always at the cost of their own lives.[38]

Nazi anti-Semitism was gratuitous: it was not provoked by anything, it was not a response to anything. It was born out of a political fantasy, in which the Jews, without a shred of justification, were held responsible for all that the Nazis believed was wrong with the modern world. Of course, the Nazis, seen in broad perspective, were exploiting in a demagogic fashion an array of problems, from mass unemployment and business failure in the Depression to widespread public anxiety about new forms of art and new social phenomena such as sexual freedom and women's emancipation, which were part and parcel of the "crisis of modernity" in the Weimar Republic.[39] These problems included the rise of a strong Communist movement which was not led by Jews, but which was undoubtedly seen as a social and political threat by many of the Nazis, although there is little evidence that they considered this was actually murderous. Problems such as these would not have been there without industrialization. It is equally true that Marxism, and later, Communism, also addressed itself to problems attendant upon the growth of industry. But to say this is rather like saying that both Nazism and Bolshevism were radical political movements, or that both of them established dictatorial regimes: the level of generalization involved is so broad that it does very little to link the two movements, except by suggestion. On a more detailed level, the comparison fails to convince. The social basis of Nazism was much more diverse, with a high proportion of middle- and lower-middle-class elements, than that of Communism, which in Germany was by the early 1930s the party of the working-class unemployed. Nolte cannot explain why Stalinism stabilized itself successfully, while Nazism did not. And he ignores altogether the fact that Hitler's fight against "Marxism" was directed as much against the Social Democrats as against the Communists, and through them, against the Weimar democracy that the Social Democrats had been so instrumental in creating.

Nazi propaganda claimed that there was real danger of a Communist revolution in Germany in 1932–33: the Reichstag fire was proclaimed as conclusive evidence for this view. But the fire was started by a single disturbed individual, and there is really very little hard factual evidence to support Nolte's assertion that Communism was threatening to take over Germany. The Communists, on the contrary, were weak in political terms, won only half as many votes as the Nazis in November 1932, were hampered by mass unemployment and poverty, and were faced with far stronger violence from the right. And it is quite wrong to suppose that the bourgeoisie in Russia had been physically exterminated, or that—despite the sarcastic rhetorical exaggerations of a publicist such as Tucholsky—they were threatening the same in Germany. On the other hand, the Nazis did far more than merely threaten to destroy "the Versailles system." Nazi anti-Semitism in all its virulence was there, in essence, in Hitler's mind, long before the Bolsheviks came to power, and it was already wreaking its terrible violence and injustice upon the Jewish population before the outbreak of the Second World War.

III

Nolte's argument that Nazism was a defensive reaction to the Communist threat finds its way into his account of the origins of the Second World War as well. Hitler's aim, he says, was to ally himself to the "Western world," and he saw himself as fighting for Western individualism, for the rule of civilized people over barbarians, a view which Nolte describes as "the exaggeration of an insight which was basically right in its essence." Nazi Germany, he says, was right to feel threatened by the USSR. Had there been a violent civil war in Germany, the USSR would have pushed its frontiers forward to the Elbe. It was the Germans who, on June 22, 1941, accused the Soviet Union of marching troops up to the border ready to invade. Thus, Hitler "understood the invasion of the Soviet Union as a preventive war." The Russians had frequently threatened to carry Communism westward. These threats "must be seen," says Nolte, "as mental acts of war, and one may even ask whether a completely isolated and heavily armed country did not constitute a dangerous threat to its neighbors on these grounds alone." Stalin was, in Nolte's view, convinced that the decisive struggle between Communism and capitalism was imminent, though not necessarily in 1941 and not necessarily in the form of a war against Germany. Nevertheless, when Hitler launched it, it was in his understanding a renewed episode in the "European civil war" which had been started by the Bolsheviks in 1917.[40]

A substantial number of German historians have recently been arguing along similar lines. One of these is Klaus Hildebrand, professor of history at Bonn University and author of two well-known and very useful textbooks, *The Foreign Policy of the Third Reich* (1973) and *The Third Reich* (1984), as well as of a massive monograph on Nazi policies on the colonial question. Hildebrand came close to Nolte's position in an article published in the flagship journal of the German historical profession, the *Historische Zeitschrift,* early in 1987. Here he draws so many parallels between the foreign policies of Hitler's Germany and Stalin's Russia that it becomes virtually impossible in the end to distinguish between the two. Hildebrand regards it as an open question whether Stalin's postwar territorial aggrandizement, and his establishment of an effective Soviet empire including Poland, Czechoslovakia, Hungary, Rumania, and East Germany, was a reaction to the experiences of the war or represented the culmination of long-term plans. Hitler's Germany and Stalin's Russia, he says, pursued war-aims programs which were autonomous and which in the long run could not avoid coming into conflict with one another. While Stalin held his troops ready to spring, Hitler attempted the "flight forward" *(Flucht nach vorn)*—an untranslatable German term which means that instead of fleeing a danger by retreating from it, the threatened person or state goes in desperation to meet it head-on. "Independently," Hildebrand concludes, "the National Socialist program of conquest met the equally far-reaching war-aims program which Stalin had drawn up in 1940 at the latest."[41]

If the suggestion here still falls short of arguing that Nazi Germany invaded the Soviet Union in 1941 in order to forestall a Soviet invasion of Germany, it nonetheless points in that direction. Others have not been so cautious. Between August 1986 and February 1987 the *Frankfurter Allgemeine Zeitung* carried a series of articles debating the theory that Stalin intended to invade Germany in 1942 or even in the summer of 1941. Hitler struck first, it was argued, and so "gave Stalin the opportunity to present the war, without reference to its complicated prehistory, as a war to defend Russia, as a great patriotic war." It was therefore a "war of the dictators" in which both sides were acting on more or less equal terms. Certainly, the end result of the debate was presented by the newspaper as inconclusive. No one could really know, it was claimed, until the Soviet archives were opened. But this did not prevent others from going further. The military historian Joachim Hoffmann, for example—a staff member of the respected Military History Research Office in Freiburg—argued explicitly that Hitler took the last chance available to him of forestalling a Soviet invasion when he launched his attack on Russia in the summer of 1941. Already in that year, he argued, Stalin's intentions had been made clear in a speech, delivered on May 5, in which he had said that "the era of a policy of peace on the part of the Soviet Union is in any case over, and expansion westward by armed force is now necessary." To back this up, Russian troops began practicing offensives on the western Soviet borders. Hoffmann, who had also developed his thesis in volume 4 of the Research Office's official history of Germany and the Second World War, was supported by another historian, Bernd Stegemann, as well as by a series of academic, semiacademic, and political commentators, including Viktor Suvorov, a Soviet officer who recently defected to the West and also claimed that the Russians intended to attack Nazi Germany in 1941.[42]

These claims, however, have not been taken very seriously by most professional historians. Even Hildebrand still describes the Nazi invasion as an *Überfall,* a word to which the determined supporters of the preventive-war thesis take strong exception because by stating that Hitler "fell upon" Russia, it underlines the autonomy of his policy and its lack of dependence on alleged Soviet war plans. A leading conservative specialist in this area, Andreas Hillgruber, has roundly condemned the preventive-war theory.[43] Indeed, the general tenor of the multiauthored history of World War II in which Hoffmann's contribution appeared was so critical of the German Army's role on the eastern front that the Research Office became the object of vociferous attacks from the right. The absurd result was that Hoffmann's account of the invasion of Russia was printed between the same book covers as a diametrically opposed account by one of his colleagues. The conservative critics of the Research Office managed to persuade the Bonn government to install a three-man committee, consisting of conservative historians Klaus Hildebrand, Michael Stürmer, and Thomas Nipperdey, under the chairmanship of an octogenarian retired general, to vet its publications. The general attitude of the committee can be gauged by the fact that they turned down the first publication that came into their hands, a massive, thoroughly researched but deeply critical biography of Gustav Noske, the "bloodhound of the revolution," and the man ultimately responsible, as the Weimar Republic's first Army minister, for the murder of Liebknecht and Luxemburg. The book eventually appeared, but with a foreword by the Research Office's new director (a retired Army major), which distanced it as far as possible from the book's contents without actually going so far as to remove its imprimatur. What the case demonstrated was on the one hand, therefore, the degree to which politics and scholarship are becoming entangled in the conservative intellectual atmosphere in West Germany, and the pressures to which historians in government-sponsored, official historical institutions are being subjected. But on the other hand, it showed the resilience of serious scholarship. Hoffmann remains an outsider, and the preventive-war thesis remains unaccepted by serious historical research.[44]

The reasons for its failure to win mainstream support should not detain us long. The evidence presented by the supporters of the preventive-war thesis is weak. The views of Viktor Suvorov, as outlined in his article on the subject, rest on speculation and hearsay. Stalin's speech of May 5, 1941, exists in at least four different secondhand versions, but no reliable firsthand documentation has been found, so that little or no weight can be placed on the passage quoted. The Russian border maneuvers in 1941 were defensive and are no proof of an intention to invade Germany. On the other hand, a good deal more is in fact known about Soviet foreign policy and plans at this time than either Hildebrand or the *Frankfurter Allgemeine Zeitung* would appear to be aware of. Specialists on Soviet history seem agreed that the USSR had been gravely weakened by the successive purges unleashed by Stalin during the 1930s. Something like two-thirds of the higher-ranking officers of the Soviet Army had been killed or otherwise removed from office, including three out of five marshals, sixty out of sixty-seven commanding generals, all eight senior admirals, and vast numbers of other senior military personnel. Moreover, the purges affected a substantial part of the management of the munitions, transport, communications, vehicle, and other industries, as well as removing large numbers of skilled workers from these and other areas. Not surprisingly, the British government and its military advisers regarded the Red Army as hopelessly demoralized in 1939. Stalin was well aware in 1941 that it was in no condition to launch an attack on Germany; and the experience of the first months of the war was to prove the point in the most dramatic fashion, as thousands of square miles of Soviet territory and millions of Soviet troops fell to the German invader.[45]

Just as important, however, was the fact that Hitler and his generals were also aware of Russian weakness at this time. They did not expect any serious opposition from the Russians, still less a general offensive. Through 1940 and well into 1941, the Nazis were thus able to concentrate the overwhelming mass of their troops in the West for the invasion and subjugation of France, Belgium, Holland, Denmark, and Norway. In all the records of Hitler's military conferences and discussions, there is not the slightest hint that he feared a Russian attack. For the Nazis, the Russians were Slavic *Untermenschen*, subhumans, from whom bestial ferocity might be expected, but no serious, organized resistance. As early as 1926, in *Mein Kampf*, Hitler declared that Soviet Russia was on the verge of collapse. It was, he thought, run by Jews, and Jews were incapable of anything but destruction. Hitler had not changed his mind by 1941. It did not suit the purposes of Nazi propaganda, still less the need to motivate the troops, to advertise the Nazis' and the German Army's knowledge of the weakness of the Red Army. To convince the troops of the need to fight, their commanders asked in 1941, during the early months of the invasion, "What would have happened had these Asiatic Mongol hordes succeeded in pouring into Europe, and particularly into Germany, laying the country waste, plundering, murdering, raping?" On the eve of the invasion, another order of the day described its purpose as the eradication of Bolshevism, "the deadly enemy of National Socialism." But, with the well-known cynicism of the Nazi propaganda machine (which was operating very well in the German Army by this time), all this was very far from the actual assessment of the Red Army's strength arrived at by Hitler and the leading German generals in private. Hitler thought that it would take no more than four months to defeat Russia. His generals were contemptuous of Soviet military strength. The recently published Goebbels diaries show that the inner leadership of the Nazi regime thought the Soviet Union would keep out of the war as long as possible, until all sides were exhausted, and then use the opportunity to extend its power. In 1941, however, the Nazi leaders, according to Goebbels, had no fear of Russian military action at all.[46]

CHAPTER THREE

BULWARK AGAINST BOLSHEVISM?

I

While some West German conservatives were trying to boost national self-confidence by rewriting the history of the origins of World War II, others were concentrating their attention on the end of the war. The debate was opened at a serious level of discussion by Andreas Hillgruber. Hillgruber, born in 1925, is a leading specialist in twentieth-century European, and especially German, diplomatic and military history. He has published a major work on Hitler's strategy in the conduct of war in 1940–41, a massive scholarly edition of the war "diary" of the German Army High Command, a textbook on German history since 1945, and a study of the war aims and strategy of the combatant nations in the Second World War.[1] In 1982, he was the subject of an article in the leading American specialist journal *Central European History,* which showered lavish praise on him for his contribution to the field.[2] Like Nolte, in other words, Hillgruber is an internationally known and respected historian. In 1986, he published a short book entitled *Two Kinds of Downfall (Zweierlei Untergang).*[3] The book, just over a hundred pages long, brings together two essays, one on the expulsion of

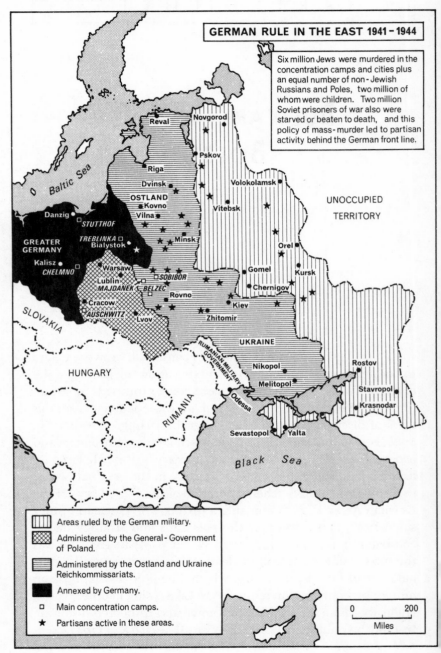

GERMAN RULE IN THE EAST 1941-1944

Six million Jews were murdered in the concentration camps and cities plus an equal number of non-Jewish Russians and Poles, two million of whom were children. Two million Soviet prisoners of war also were starved or beaten to death, and this policy of mass-murder led to partisan activity behind the German front line.

Baltic Sea

Reval
Novgorod
Pskov
Riga
Dvinsk
Volokolamsk
OSTLAND
Kovno
Vitebsk
Danzig ☐ STUTTHOF
Vilna
GREATER GERMANY
TREBLINKA ☐
Bialystok
Minsk
Orel
Kalisz ☐
CHELMNO
Warsaw
Gomel
Kursk
Lublin ☐ SOBIBOR
MAJDANEK ☐ ☐ BELZEC
Chernigov
Cracow
Rovno
AUSCHWITZ
Lvov
Kiev
SLOVAKIA
Zhitomir

UNOCCUPIED TERRITORY

UKRAINE

HUNGARY

RUMANIAN MILITARY GOVERNMENT

Nikopol
Rostov

Melitopol
Stavropol

Odessa
Krasnodar

RUMANIA

Sevastopol
Yalta

Black Sea

	Areas ruled by the German military.
	Administered by the General-Government of Poland.
	Administered by the Ostland and Ukraine Reichskommissariats.
■	Annexed by Germany.
☐	Main concentration camps.
★	Partisans active in these areas.

0   200
Miles

the Germans from East-Central Europe at the end of the Second World War, and the other (rather shorter) on the Nazi genocide of Europe's Jews. "Both catastrophes," Hillgruber remarks, "belong together." The mass murder of the Jews, he says, was a consequence of the radical racism of Hitler's Germany. The expulsion of the Germans and the destruction of the German Reich were not merely responses to the Nazis' crimes—which in any case were not fully known during the war—but also, more importantly, corresponded to the long-term aims of the Allied powers. Taking the two events together makes it clear, according to Hillgruber, that the war involved not just a Jewish catastrophe and a German catastrophe but rather a catastrophe for the whole of Europe, especially its center. He argues that the events of the war have hitherto been seen in far too simple and monocausal a way as consequences of Hitler's expansionism and its racist foundations. The destruction of Germany also had independent roots in the long-held aims of the Allies.[4]

Hillgruber turns his attention first to the end of the German Reich in 1945. He notes that it has been argued that the mass extermination of Jews at Auschwitz and other camps in the East could have been ended much sooner if the German troops had yielded to the onslaught of the Soviet Army faster than they did; indeed, the Christian Democratic politician Norbert Blüm has contended that this is exactly what they should have done. Hillgruber does not directly criticize this argument, but he suggests that the areas earlier occupied temporarily by the Russians revealed a picture of the rape and murder of women and children that made it only too clear what the German population could expect if the Army gave in. Thus they fought on to protect the population from a Soviet "orgy of revenge." A Soviet victory would have been no "liberation," argues Hillgruber, except for the surviving victims of the concentration camps. Even the Western Allies aimed at far more than the mere removal of National Socialism from German soil. They had long since agreed that the Red Army should be allowed to occupy a large part of Central Europe. Here, as the German armies withdrew, the soldiers of the Red Army committed countless murders and rapes and enforced the mass deportation of hundreds of thousands of Germans into the interior of the

USSR as well as westward. These excesses reflected the barbarism of Soviet ideas of war under Stalin, rather than a desire for revenge on the Germans. Defending the Prussian East against such barbarism called forth great heroism from the German armies and the civilian population, who were not helped by the fanaticism and cowardice of some local Nazi leaders. But despite their heroism, the end of the war was followed by the flight and expulsion of the Germans from these areas. In the course of these mass deportations and expulsions, he says, over 2 million Germans lost their lives, although the Potsdam Conference between the Allied powers had demanded on August 2, 1945, that this policy should be carried out humanely.[5]

How did these events relate to the war aims of the combatant nations? Did they result from long-term plans, or were they the outcome of short-term developments—of the course of the war itself? Hillgruber discusses four conceptions of the future of Central and Eastern Europe. He first points out that Hitler's plans for a postwar European settlement included not only the mass murder of the Jews but also the expulsion of more than 30 million Slavs from East-Central Europe into Siberia to make way for German settlers. The old Prussian ruling class, he says, did not share this radical, racist vision. Their aims were a good deal more modest, even though they included the incorporation of Austria and the Sudetenland into a Greater Germany, the recovery of the territories lost at Versailles, and the reduction of Poland and Czechoslovakia to German client states. These plans were essentially those of the mainly aristocratic groups within the Army who tried to kill Hitler in July 1944. But the plot failed, putting an end to this option. Both German conceptions of a postwar settlement took as their fundamental premise the creation of a Europe led—or dominated—by Germany as its center. However, the Western Allies saw the presence of a strong Germany in Central Europe as the root cause of both world wars, and they therefore sought its permanent subjection. Influenced by exiled Polish nationalists, they agreed to achieve this by creating an enlarged Poland stretching as far west as the Oder-Neisse Line. Central Europe's security would be strengthened by an alliance between Poland, Czechoslovakia, Hungary, and perhaps Austria. German disarmament and the expulsion of the potentially destabilizing German population from Poland and Czechoslovakia were thought of as further necessary measures toward this end. The eastern areas of the German Reich were to be removed and more ethnic Germans expelled as a consequence. Russia was to be appeased by the transfer of territory on the eastern edge of the new Central Europe.[6]

The last thing Stalin wanted, however, was the establishment of a strong, nationalist, anti-Soviet Poland led by a right-wing government similar to the one which had ruled the country before the war. The Russo-Polish conflict of the early 1920s was warning enough of the consequences. Thus, Hillgruber notes, the Soviet Union largely accepted the boundary changes and directed its attention to what it saw as the more important task: that of making the *cordon sanitaire* against the Germans into a protective girdle for itself by installing Communist regimes in all of Eastern Europe, especially in the new, enlarged Poland. The Western Allies were obsessed with a crude image of Prussian militarism and anxious to continue smooth cooperation with the Russians. They also overestimated the potential power of an enlarged Poland. So they ignored the possibility of this Russian action and carried on supporting the boundary changes that would destroy the German East. Thus, according to Hillgruber, every city, every village overrun by Soviet troops on the eastern front was "lost forever for Germany and for its German inhabitants," even though this was by no means clear to the Germans at the time. The German Army on the eastern front was a last protection "for a centuries-old area of German settlement, for the home of millions of Germans who lived in a core land of the German Empire—namely, in eastern Prussia, in the provinces of East Prussia, West Prussia, Silesia, East Brandenburg, and Pomerania." And it was the inhabitants' last hope for preservation from the terrible fate that awaited them at the hands of the Red Army. Hillgruber insists that the German role in Eastern Europe had been at least in part civilizing and Christianizing. He does concede that during the nineteenth century conflict became more and more prevalent between the Germans and the indigenous populations, and under the Nazis the Germans became identified with the criminal policies of the

Third Reich. But the impression he leaves, not least by the language he uses, is that this was on balance outweighed by the legacy of the previous centuries.[7]

Like Nolte, Hillgruber sees a connection between the Nazi "Final Solution" and other twentieth-century horrors:

> The mass expulsion of the Germans from a quarter of the territory of the 1937 Reich was a provisional end station on the journey that had begun with the spread of the idea of a rationalization of territory according to national allegiance and that had led to the nationality struggles on the European periphery during the First World War. These struggles were followed by the first genocide—that of the Armenians in Turkey—and by the mass expulsions of Greeks from Asia Minor. The extermination and resettlement practices of Hitler and Stalin in their respective "spheres of influence" in the period of their partnership in 1939–40 had continued such "exchanges of populations," and mass murder then reached an extreme degree in Hitler's "Eastern War" from June 1941 onward; first the Jews in Poland and in the entire East were to be exterminated, then those in the whole of German-occupied Continental Europe. The idea of mass resettlement in East-Central Europe won ever more support—first in Great Britain and then in the United States, in a complete departure from their humanitarian traditions—as victory became more certain and as the aim of the destruction of Prussia as the allegedly permanent hard core of the German Reich became more and more clearly an actual war aim.[8]

The hard core of Prussianism, in turn, was seen to be in the eastern provinces, and their removal was to be the means of destroying Prussianism's historical influence. Thus the mythical idea that German expansionism was the result of traditional Prussian militarism—enunciated by British Foreign Office mandarin Sir Eyre Crowe in his famous memorandum of January 1, 1907, and shared fully by Prime Minister Winston Churchill—resulted in the expulsion of the Germans from the alleged Prussian core territory, the Prussian East. Hillgruber contends that Europe's chance to be a world power had depended on German leadership. This vision was clear enough in the 1920s and 1930s, as Chamberlain had recognized, but it was lost because of Hitler's racial ideology and his ambition to dominate totally the whole of Europe. The threat of domination could only be countered by Russian and American intervention and by the division of Germany—and with that, the division of Europe itself. Thus the gradual growth of German nationhood since 1871 was stopped, and wholly new social formations emerged in western and central Germany. The question of whether the destroyed center of Europe can be reconstructed, Hillgruber concludes, remains open.[9]

II

Hillgruber's book is written with all the authority of a leading, internationally respected specialist in the field. Much of what he has to say amounts to a summing up of recent research, some of it his own. It is for these reasons, perhaps, that many contributors to the ensuing controversy—among them, historians Martin Broszat, Gordon A. Craig, Imanuel Geiss, Hans Mommsen, Heinrich August Winkler, and Eberhard Jäckel—have objected to Hillgruber's and Nolte's being lumped together, have largely exonerated the former, and have concentrated their fire on the latter. Similarly, at least one contributor to the debate from the other side, Klaus Hildebrand, had preferred to direct his rhetorical shafts against critics of Hillgruber and has largely left Nolte to fend for himself.[10] But those who reject the view that Nolte's and Hillgruber's arguments point in similar directions do so only by overlooking the fact that both authors, in their different ways, attempt to relativize the Nazi policy of genocide toward the Jews.

While Nolte's arguments are relatively obvious, Hillgruber's are more complex and can only be teased out by a close analysis of the text, which is perhaps why they initially featured so little in the ensuing debate. Both Nolte and Hillgruber set Auschwitz in a broader twentieth-century context. Both of them concede its singularity in some degree: Nolte sees it in the method of extermination used, while Hillgruber sees it in its extremism. It has been argued by West German historian Hagen Schulze that to compare Auschwitz with the actions of Pol Pot or the liquidation of the kulaks is not to equate them.[11] But comparison involves weighing the differences and similarities and reaching a cool, sober balance at the end. Nolte is concerned merely to obscure the differences. As we have seen, he regards Auschwitz

as both a copy of and a reply to the Gulag Archipelago. Hillgruber, as we might expect, is more subtle and less direct. His
intention in the long passage quoted above seems to be, first, to
relativize Auschwitz by setting it in the context of genocide—
Stalin's "extermination practices" in 1939–40 and the massacres
of the Armenians by the Turks in 1915. Hillgruber's use of the
terms "extermination" and "genocide" here really does place
him in the same camp as Nolte on the issue.[12]

Hillgruber takes a second step by situating all these policies of genocide and extermination in the context of the mass
resettlement of European populations. Hitler's "Final Solution"
represented an extreme version of such policies, but the clear
implication of the passage is that it was not qualitatively different from them. This view allows Hillgruber to portray the expulsion of ethnic Germans from East-Central Europe after the
war as another facet of the same political tradition that led to
Auschwitz—even to the extent of being based on a political
fantasy (the myth of Prussia). He also protects himself from the
accusation of being overcritical of the Western Alliance by
representing the expulsion as a temporary aberration in the
normally humanitarian practices of Britain and the United
States. The language that Hillgruber uses regarding the Red
Army's conduct in the invaded territories derives much of its
strength from this contextualization and stands in marked contrast to the neutral way in which he describes the "Final Solution" in the second part of the book. Thus the destruction of
Prussia and the German Reich really does appear in Hillgruber's book as comparable to the destruction of the European
Jews. This impression of comparability is achieved precisely by
portraying them both as consequences of a third factor—the
growing practice of population resettlement and extermination—and by implicitly downplaying any direct links between
them. The political consequences of this argument are un-
spoken except in the concluding sentence of the first essay,
where Hillgruber describes the question of the reconstruction
of Central Europe, presumably meaning the reunification of
East and West Germany and the lost eastern territories, as still
open. But clearly he means to suggest that a European settlement based on such crimes cannot be defensible. The silent
implication of these arguments, therefore, would seem to be

that it is time the question of German reunification was put on the political agenda once more.

These views are echoed by powerful voices on the right of the West German political spectrum. The parliamentary majority leader of the Christian Democrats, Alfred Dregger, for instance, was already saying similar things in 1985. Writing on April 20 to fifty-three U.S. senators who had requested President Ronald Reagan to cancel his visit to Bitburg, Dregger described their request as an insult to his brother and others who had died on the eastern front fighting against Communism. He told them that he himself had fought to defend Silesia against the Russians. Dregger's view, enlarged upon in another speech, delivered in 1986, is that the German troops on the eastern front were soldiers like any others, doing their duty for their country. The responsibility for the crimes of the Third Reich lay with Hitler and the Nazi leadership. Most German soldiers, he said, knew little or nothing of the crimes of National Socialism. Thus although the military opposition which culminated in the unsuccessful bomb plot of July 1944 was carried out by people who "in view of the situation behaved honorably, were conscious of their responsibility, and were patriotic in the best sense," those who decided to carry on fighting to the bitter end also behaved honorably. "This is particularly the case," he added, "for the soldiers of the German Army in the East, and for the German Navy, which had to cover the flight of millions of Germans in the East from the Red Army in the last months of the war."[13]

All this reflects, among other things, a widely held view of the German Army's conduct during the war, which saw it as broadly conforming to the normal rules of combat. In the 1950s, as the surviving German generals came to write their memoirs, they insisted that the war had been fought on their part according to the best German military traditions. Patriotism and a sense of duty had been the motives; Nazi ideology had always been kept at bay. Whatever "excesses" there were did not exceed those committed by Allied troops and were no more than could be expected in a long and hard-fought conflict. The crimes of Nazism were committed by the SS. One general described the battles fought by his command, the Twelfth Infantry Division, as "always fairly conducted, though tough and bitter. Its name," he added "its coat of arms, and its weapons remained unsullied till the very last day, as even the enemy has conceded." And indeed a leading British military historian, B. H. Liddell Hart, even claimed that "the German Army in the field on the whole observed the rules of war better than it did in 1914–18." That many senior military men objected to those Nazi excesses of which they were aware, and that some of them eventually took the step of trying to remove Hitler altogether, was widely seen as further proof of the Army's honorable conduct during the war.[14]

These views are in many respects also endorsed by Ernst Nolte, who cites with some sympathy an official in Hitler's Foreign Ministry who said that the war was being fought in defense of Western values and in order to liberate the oppressed peoples of the USSR. Hitler was a "European citizen," who in essence represented the European middle class in its struggle against the attempt of Bolshevism to destroy it. He suggests that what made this basically justifiable aim of liberation impossible to sustain was Hitler's "total egocentrism" in wanting to go on to exterminate the Slavs and the Jews. Nevertheless, in Nolte's view the nature of the eastern campaign as an episode in the "European Civil War" between Communism and fascism, begun by the Bolsheviks in 1917, made at least some aspects of its harshness justifiable. German brutality in the East was conditioned by memories of Soviet brutality in 1917–21. In this sense, Nolte defends the German command to execute all political commissars in the Red Army upon capture—the notorious *Kommissarbefehl*. "Insofar as this command is to be seen in the context of the war between two ideologies, it was thus not 'criminal' but consistent." In any case, he adds, the command was mostly disregarded, and was rescinded in 1942. Moreover, "the war against Poland began with a tendency to genocide on the Polish side, namely the so-called 'Bromberg Bloody Sunday,' the gunning-down of some thousands of citizens of German origin by furious Poles. Whether the German minority would have survived," he adds, "if the war had lasted longer than three months, must appear doubtful." So in this sense too, he implies, German harshness toward the occupied populations was justifiable.

But it is rather sophistical to suggest that the German Army was justified in executing all captured Soviet political commis-

sars merely because of a general belief in the brutality of Bolshevik revolutionaries two decades earlier. Nor is the putative
existence of a twenty-year ideological "war" any justification
either, for in the end the notion of an ideological war is a
metaphor, a construct put upon the political struggles of the
twenties and thirties by the historian, by Nolte. Moreover, it is
a substantial exaggeration to claim that the Poles were bent on
exterminating the Germans in their territory in September
1939. What seems to have happened, according to the most
thorough and critical investigations (as usual, not cited by Nolte)
is that some four thousand to six thousand ethnic Germans in
Poland met their death in the German invasion of 1939, a number of them by German aircraft on bombing or strafing mis-
sions, others at the hands of panicky Polish troops—enraged in
many cases, it seems, by the employment of some of the ethnic
Germans as fifth-columnists for purposes of subversion and sab-
otage by the German Army (against the advice of the German
Foreign Office). The events at Bromberg occurred on September 3, after the outbreak of war, as Polish troops claimed to have
been fired on by local ethnic Germans. Many innocent ethnic
Germans suffered appallingly in the process; but these sufferings, inflicted in a very short space of time, in no way compared
with the prolonged and murderous savagery meted out to the
Poles by the occupying Germans in the following years.[15]

In making his points, Nolte is recognizing that Germany did
indeed employ great brutality on the eastern front. This is an
insight which has only gradually become accepted as a result of
research carried out in Germany and abroad, and based on still
barely explored documentation in the German Military Archives at Freiburg, in the captured Nazi documents, and elsewhere. In accepting the German generals' account of their
conformity to normal standards of military conduct, American
and British writers in the postwar years were to a large extent
reflecting the experiences of Allied troops on the western front
and in North Africa. They pointed to the fact that only 4 percent
of British and American troops captured by the Germans died in
captivity, and contrasted this with the brutal treatment meted
out by the Japanese to Allied prisoners of war, of whom over a
quarter—27 percent—died in captivity. Massacres in German-
occupied Western Europe, such as the destruction of the French

village of Oradour and its inhabitants by German armed forces, gained their notoriety precisely because of their rarity. Yet conditions on the eastern front were completely different. Fifty-eight percent of Soviet prisoners of war taken by the Germans died in captivity—some 3,300,000 out of 5,700,000 all told. And in German-occupied East-Central and Eastern Europe there was not one Oradour but thousands. According to Soviet figures, the Germans destroyed some 1,710 towns and 70,000 villages, along with most of their inhabitants. Altogether the Soviet Union lost 13,000,000 soldiers and 7,000,000 civilians killed by the Germans during the Second World War, or 40 percent of all deaths caused by the conflict.

These appalling figures reflect the fact that, in contrast to the campaigns on the western front, the German invasion of the Soviet Union, as Hillgruber admits, was from the beginning an ideologically motivated war of total subjugation and extermination. Almost from the very beginning, long before the outbreak of the Second World War, as we have seen, Hitler and the Nazis saw the creation of so-called "living space" *(Lebensraum)* for Germans in the East as a central aim of their policy. Those who inhabited these areas were dismissed as Slav "subhumans"; the Russians were declared to be under the leadership of evil Communist fanatics, whom the Nazis, in defiance of all the facts, thought were mostly Jewish. Thus contempt for the Slavs was joined with hatred of Communists and Jews into a potent ideological mixture. This was used by the Nazis to justify a series of orders sent via the German High Command to the Army immediately before the invasion of Russia in 1941. The Army was told to allow free rein to the SS death squads *(Einsatzgruppen)* sent into their areas under the command of Reinhard Heydrich to begin the extermination of the Jews. It was told to shoot all political commissars in the Red Army immediately on capture. It was empowered to execute all guerillas and partisans and those civilians thought to be helping them, and to take collective reprisals against whole communities if no individual culprits could be found in the aftermath of partisan actions. Finally, the official "Guidelines for the Conduct of the Troops in Russia" ordered the Army to eliminate all resistance (even passive resistance) and to take ruthless measures against "Bolshevik agitators, guerillas, saboteurs and Jews."[16]

A number of different influences combined, as historian Omer Bartov has shown, to dispose the Army on the eastern front, at all levels, from the commanding generals to the common soldier, to take full advantage of these orders, which were subsequently condemned as "criminal orders" by the Nuremberg Trials after the end of the war. The troops were exposed to massive indoctrination through films, radio programs, lectures, newspapers, books, and leaflets. This was carried out not only by "National Socialist Leadership Officers" appointed for the purpose, but also, right from the start, by the junior officers. Unlike many of the senior commanders, who were often aristocratic and who provided most of the leaders of the opposition in 1944, these men were mainly middle-class and were young enough to have been exposed for most of their adolescent and adult years to the Nazi indoctrination which was such a central part of the education system from 1933 onward. About a third of them were members of the Nazi Party. As victory turned to defeat, and the Army began its long withdrawal in the face of the Soviet onslaught, Nazi ideology became ever more important, as the troops sought for a set of beliefs which would motivate them to carry on the struggle.[17] Conditions were extremely harsh. Casualties were heavy from the beginning of the campaign, amounting in the end to as much as three times the number of troops who originally took part in the invasion. The troops had to march vast distances on foot, to live off the land, and to survive the extreme conditions of the Russian winter with totally inadequate clothing and shelter. Fatigue, illness, exhaustion, and desperation increased still further the degree of brutalization.

Thus the Army commanders at the front increasingly used Nazi terminology in their everyday orders. The Jews were described as "vermin" in information issued to the troops during the invasion of Poland in October 1939, and the soldiers were told from the start that the Russians were "Jewish-Bolshevik subhumans" or "Mongol hordes." By 1945, indeed, the troops were being supplied with battle slogans calling for resistance against the "Asian flood" and the "red beast." The junior officers were given a special responsibility for instilling such beliefs into their troops. Given this situation, therefore, it is hardly surprising that the conduct of the German Army on the eastern front was brutal in the extreme. The West German historian Christian Streit has shown, for example, how the German soldier from the outset refused to regard his counterpart in the Red Army as an ordinary fellow soldier, to be treated according to the normal rules of war. Russians taken prisoner behind the lines—and there were many thousands of these, as a result of the Germans' success in encircling and cutting off Russian units—were shot as "partisans," whether or not they were in regular units. The rest were marched off on foot, after having been stripped of their winter clothes and boots, deliberately deprived of adequate food rations, and often decimated by massacres, sometimes against the orders of the Army command. Those who survived to reach the prisoner-of-war camps continued to be treated as "subhumans" and were effectively condemned to death by starvation and neglect.[18]

Not only did the German troops in the East behave, on the whole, with extreme brutality and barbarism toward the Red Army, they also laid waste whole areas of the territory they occupied and massacred or otherwise caused the deaths of millions of innocent civilians as a matter of policy. Living off the land meant plunder and theft of livestock and food supplies to such an extent that the inhabitants had nothing left. Harvests were destroyed, and agriculture collapsed. The German Army forcibly evacuated large areas of territory behind the front, either shooting the civilian population because of so-called "partisan" operations or leaving them without adequate food supplies. Civilians found "wandering about" were shot; houses suspected of sheltering partisans were burned down, together with the people inside them; people thought to be "tolerating partisans" were publicly hanged. When the German Army began to retreat after the battle of Stalingrad, it embarked upon a "scorched-earth" policy in which the areas it evacuated were systematically destroyed, the villages burned, the livestock killed, and the machinery wrecked. The people were driven out in the direction of the advancing Red Army into the "desert zone," where many of them died.[19]

All this makes it difficult to sustain the idea that the German Army in the East was fighting to defend German culture and civilization against Communist barbarity in 1944–45. Still less does it support the idea that the German troops were normal soldiers engaged in conventional military conflict and largely free from the taint of Nazism. It was not the Soviet Army which adhered to a fundamentally barbarous concept of war, but the German Army. As the Soviet troops advanced, it was inevitable under the circumstances that they should be motivated by feelings of hatred and revenge against the enemy which had inflicted such terrible destruction on their land and on the other areas of Eastern Europe through which they passed. Moreover, many ethnic German civilians in these areas had willingly taken part in atrocities against other ethnic groups during the conflict. The crimes committed by German troops in the East were well known long before the full extent of the mass extermination of European Jews became clear. Secret police reports indicate widespread guilt feelings within the German civilian population inside the Reich even before 1945, including an oft-repeated popular belief that it was only to be expected that the Russians would commit atrocities in view of what the Germans themselves had previously done in Russia.[20]

None of this of course excuses the conduct of the Soviet troops, the mass rape of German women, the looting and plundering, the deportation and lengthy imprisonment in Russia of many German troops, or the unauthorized killing of many German civilians. But it has to be said that the conduct of the Red Army in Germany was by no means as barbarous as that of the German Army in Russia. The Russians did not deliberately lay waste whole towns and villages in Germany, nor did they systematically exterminate whole communities during their occupation of German territory. Out of an estimated 3,155,000 German prisoners of war taken by the Russians, just over a third, it has been claimed, died in captivity, but these figures, while far better than those quoted above for Russian troops in German hands, have been disputed by recent Soviet scholarship, which claims they are much exaggerated. Moreover, with a substantial part of their territory under enemy occupation, and their own military position in disarray, the Russians were scarcely able to look after their own troops in the early and middle stages of the war, let alone care adequately for captured Germans, while most Russian prisoners of war died in German captivity during the years of the Third Reich's greatest power and success. Finally, while the rape of German women

was a common accompaniment of the Red Army's takeover of
German towns and villages, rape was also, despite denials of
German officers in their subsequent memoirs, widespread during the German occupation of Western Russia. Here too there
was a sharp contrast with the western front. In France, for
example, the rape of French women by German troops was
described as such in courts-martial and subject to disciplinary
action; on the eastern front, such cases were described as "frat-
ernization" or "racial offenses" or even "collaboration with partisans." They were not, in other words, described as "moral
offenses," and were not severely punished. In the context of the
mass killings of Russian men, women, and children by German
troops, such offenses were bound to be considered relatively
trivial.[21]

It is hard to see how anyone aware of these facts could wish
to "identify" with the German troops on the eastern front
during the final phases of the war. Moreover, the implication
of this argument is that present-day Soviet citizens should
identify with the Red Army troops who overran the eastern
German territories in 1944–45 and committed so many crimes
against ethnic Germans. This would surely not be acceptable
to Hillgruber. And the contrast with the western front makes
identification by a present-day West German with the German Army of 1944 even more difficult. The conduct of German troops in the West was generally far better; yet no one
has suggested that present-day Germans should identify with
these troops, for the very good reason that they were not
fighting against Communism but against the Western democracies. Denying them the grace of posthumous identification
would somehow seem to suggest that they were less heroic,
less honorable than their counterparts on the eastern front because they had the misfortune to be fighting against a different enemy. The fact is that all the German troops were
fighting for the same cause. They were not fighting to pre-
serve Europe from Communism. Almost to the end, they believed they were fighting for Hitler and fighting for Germany.
Even as late as January 1945, opinion polls carried out among
German prisoners of war showed that the great majority still
retained their faith in Hitler.[22]

III

According to Hillgruber, the majority of German troops, at least in the East, were, in carrying on fighting until the bitter end instead of joining the opposition and ending the war in July 1944, acting out of a more realistic sense of moral responsibility than that shown by their colleagues who took part in the resistance. Hillgruber draws a distinction between the ethical stand of the plotters, born out of inner conviction, and that taken by the local party, state, and military leadership in the East, which, he says, was born out of the responsibility of the individual in a given situation. He expresses sympathy for German Army commanders on the eastern front who failed to support the plot. He is surely correct in casting doubt upon the realism of the 1944 conspirators. Their vision of a conservative Greater Germany, leading Europe but not dominating or enslaving it, was, as Hillgruber, despite his sympathy for it, concedes, completely unrealistic by this time.[23] The most likely outcome, had Stauffenberg's bomb succeeded in killing Hitler, and had the Army succeeded in taking command of the situation, would have been confusion and chaos. The more fanatical Nazis and SS men would have resisted, and a rapid worsening of Germany's military situation would have led to surrender to the Allies some months before it finally occurred. Belief in Hitler was an important factor in maintaining morale among the troops by this stage; his removal from the scene would have seriously weakened the will to fight. Even though their wider aims were doomed to failure, the plotters' immediate purpose, that of assassinating Hitler, was still well worth achieving. The plotters were conscious of their historic mission of demonstrating to the world that "another Germany" existed besides the Germany of the Third Reich. They sought to show that some Germans were prepared to oppose Nazi criminality even at the cost of their own lives. Even more important, however, was the fact that had they succeeded, they might well have halted the extermination of the European Jews. Although the great majority of German military leaders were heavily implicated in the murder of the Jews, the minority who organized or carried out the Bomb Plot were in some cases deeply opposed to the extermination of the Jews on moral grounds. Their action could be said to have reflected a sense of responsibility for the lives of those Jews who were yet to enter the gas chambers. This was in no way morally or ethically inferior to the other Army commanders' responsibility to the German populations in the East.[24]

Of course, it might be objected that each nation's primary responsibility is for the lives of its own citizens. Even if this point is conceded, however, it remains the case that the prolongation of the war from July 1944 to April 1945 brought with it the deaths of millions of German soldiers and civilians as well. Their lives might have been saved had the war ended sooner. Moreover, the Nazis wreaked a terrible revenge for the Bomb Plot, not only on those who had planned it and carried it out, but also on ever-wider circles of those aristocratic, Christian, and other groups whom they considered sympathetic to it. And as it became clear that the war was being lost, they set about eliminating non-Nazis whom they thought likely to take a leading role in postwar Germany. All these people too might have been spared by an earlier end to the Nazi regime. If the choice is for present-day West Germans to identify with the soldiers on the eastern front or the conspirators of July 1944, all these considerations point categorically in favor of the latter.[25]

Yet the choice as it is posed here is too restrictive. It implies that the German resistance to Hitler began and ended with the July conspirators. This does a grave disservice to the far more numerous Communist and Social Democratic resistance groups whose members actively opposed the Nazis from the very beginning, often paying for it with their lives. They may not have been in a position to topple the regime, but they did all they could to keep alive the spirit of opposition to it. In this their behavior contrasted sharply with that of the men of July 1944, most of whom had begun by collaborating with the regime and generally approving of what it was doing. The ideals of most of the conspirators were far from democratic; they believed, on the whole, in an authoritarian political system for Germany and in German hegemony over the rest of Europe. Only gradually did they come to see that Hitler, while he certainly shared these beliefs, also went far beyond them. When they finally moved against him, it was much too late. None of this should be taken as belittling their tremendous courage, or as an attempt to minimize the importance of their gesture. But it certainly should be taken to mean that there are grave problems in the way of an identification with these men on the part of West German democrats today. Federal President Richard von Weizsäcker was right to say in his address to the West German people on May 8, 1985, that it is important to honor the memory of *all* those who sacrificed their lives in the resistance: the civil, military, and religious resistance, the resistance in the trade unions and the working class, and the resistance of the Communists.[26]

CHAPTER FOUR

AUSCHWITZ AND ELSEWHERE

I

No one in the present debate is seriously denying either the virulence of Nazi anti-Semitism or the horrors of its eventual realization. Yet views differ considerably on the question of how it came about. Nolte, as we have seen, regards it as a response to Bolshevism. Hillgruber is more precise. In the second part of his book, he turns to the "historical location of the annihilation of the Jews" and attempts to trace back the roots of Hitler's "Final Solution" as far as he can. Its long-term origins, he says, lay in the tradition of anti-Semitism that had haunted Europe since Christian medieval times, then in the fluctuating currents of hostility accompanying the emancipation of the Jews in the nineteenth century. These culminated in the rise of a strong wave of anti-Semitism in the German Empire founded by Bismarck and in the last decades of the Habsburg monarchy. Before the First World War, however, anti-Semitism was beginning to decline in Germany. There was, to be sure, a new, more virulent kind of racial, as opposed to religious, anti-Semitism, but it was restricted to very limited areas of German society up to 1914. It was, says Hillgruber, far

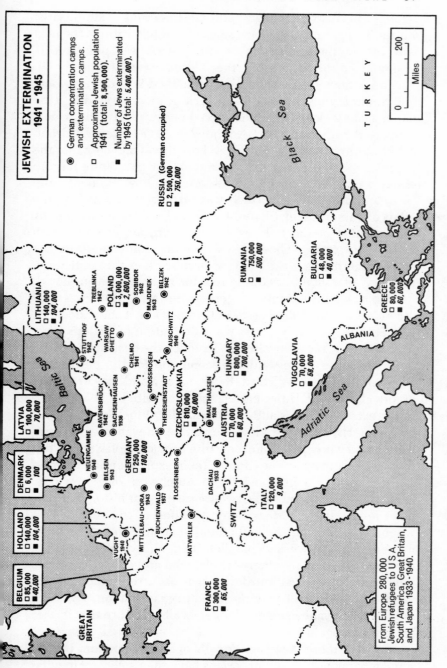

JEWISH EXTERMINATION
1941 - 1945

◉ German concentration camps
and extermination camps.

□ Approximate Jewish population
1941 (total: 8,500,000).

■ Number of Jews exterminated
by 1945 (total: 5,400,000).

0   200
Miles

TURKEY

Black Sea

RUSSIA (German occupied)
□ 2,500,000
■ 750,000

RUMANIA
□ 750,000
■ 500,000

BULGARIA
□ 48,000
■ 40,000

GREECE
□ 80,000
■ 60,000

ALBANIA

Adriatic Sea

YUGOSLAVIA
□ 70,000
■ 58,000

HUNGARY
□ 800,000
■ 700,000

LITHUANIA
□ 140,000
■ 104,000

TREBLINKA
1942

POLAND
□ 3,000,000
■ 2,600,000

SOBIBOR
1942

BELZEK
1942

MAJDANEK
1943

AUSCHWITZ
1940

STUTTHOF
1942

WARSAW
GHETTO

CHELMO
1941

GROSSROSEN

THERESIENSTADT

CZECHOSLOVAKIA
□ 810,000
■ 60,000

MAUTHAUSEN
1938

AUSTRIA
□ 70,000
■ 60,000

RAVENSBRÜCK
1942

SACHSENHAUSEN
1936

NEUENGAMME
1940

BELSEN
1943

GERMANY
□ 250,000
■ 180,000

MITTELBAU-DORA
1943

BUCHENWALD
1937

FLOSSENBERG

DACHAU
1933

SWITZ.

ITALY
□ 120,000
■ 9,000

NATWEILER

VUGHT
1940

FRANCE
□ 300,000
■ 65,000

LATVIA
□ 100,000
■ 70,000

DENMARK
□ 6,000
■ 100

HOLLAND
□ 140,000
■ 104,000

BELGIUM
□ 85,000
■ 40,000

Baltic Sea

GREAT
BRITAIN

From Europe 280,000
Jewish refugees to U.S.A.,
South America, Great Britain,
and Japan 1933 -1940.

stronger in Austria-Hungary, and most marked of all in tsarist Russia. The progress from one stage of anti-Semitism to the next was by no means inevitable. Auschwitz was not preprogrammed in the history of either Germany or Europe.[1]

A new stage was reached during the First World War, when, Hillgruber argues, anti-Semitism became incorporated into the nationalist ideology of the short-lived but extremist and widely supported Fatherland Party founded in 1917 by retired Grand Admiral Alfred von Tirpitz. From here it was taken up into the program of the reorganized, expanded far right. White Russian émigrés and Austrian influences brought new elements into German anti-Semitism, which was further radicalized by the influx of numerous Jewish refugees from Eastern Europe and by the equation of the Bolshevik threat with an alleged Jewish world conspiracy. These developments culminated in the emergence of the Nazi Party. Hillgruber says that anti-Semitism played a vital integrating role for the Nazis, even though its importance in winning voters to the Nazi cause was only secondary. From 1933 anti-Semitism became a state ideology. The Second World War saw the culmination of Hitler's long-held idea of a "racial revolution" in which the destruction of the Jews was to be the essential precondition for the permanent establishment of the Third Reich as a world power. Here, argues Hillgruber, Hitler parted company with his fellow Nazis in the extremity of his anti-Semitism. The "Final Solution" was his alone. His extremist views depended on war for their realization and were quite different from previous anti-Semitic traditions in Germany. They found their expression in the mass murder of over 5 million Jews in Auschwitz and elsewhere, bringing a violent end to the two-thousand-year history of European Jewry. If the historical constellation of the year 1941— when Hitler thought he had a unique chance to put his plans into action—was without parallel, then, Hillgruber concludes, the fact that so many otherwise civilized and educated people took part in the mass murder, that it occurred under the advanced conditions of twentieth-century civilization, gives it a universal relevance and challenges us all to ensure that it does not happen again.[2]

Not all of these views are equally open to objection. Understandably enough, many historians have seen a certain inevitability about the rise of anti-Semitism in Germany. They have regarded hatred of the Jews as an integral component of the modern German national character.[3] But this is a dangerous view to take. If we are to uncover the roots of racism and anti-Semitism and to understand why they flourished more in some countries and in some conditions than in others, then we have to be very careful in our judgment of the true extent and virulence of anti-Semitism at any given place and time. If we blur distinctions in this area, we run the risk of robbing ourselves of the ability to judge the degree of danger which racism poses in our own society, and so to take an appropriate level of action against it. Drawing distinctions here, difficult though it is, should in no way be taken to imply a tolerance or a trivialization of lesser forms of racism and anti-Semitism. The behavior of rowdy Germans who threw Jewish citizens out of Hamburg's coffeehouses in the anti-Semitic disturbances of the 1830s remains utterly repulsive and objectionable.[4] But it is important to note that the victims of these acts of violence were Jewish by virtue of their religion, not just by ethnic identity, and that they were manhandled and beaten up, but not tortured or murdered.[5]

Nevertheless, Hillgruber's account does substantially underestimate the degree and importance of anti-Semitism in Germany before the First World War. In the 1880s and early 1890s, racist anti-Semitism pushed out Christian anti-Semitism, and eugenic and social-Darwinist elements inserted themselves into anti-Semitic ideology. A number of small parties and organizations emerged whose central aim was to remove ethnic Jews from their supposed positions of influence in German society. After enjoying a brief electoral success and gaining a handful of seats in the German parliament, these groups suddenly declined and by 1914 had all but vanished from the scene. But this did not reflect a general decline of racist anti-Semitism: on the contrary, what had happened was that the mainstream political parties, above all the Conservatives and the Catholic Center Party, feeling themselves threatened by this new development, had responded by incorporating racist anti-Semitism into their own ideologies. Moreover, anti-Semitism was given powerful official backing through its undoubted presence at Court, where Kaiser Wilhelm II and his friends commonly indulged in virulent anti-Semitic prejudice, language, and behavior. Thus racist anti-Semitism moved from the backwaters of the political scene into the mainstream. It became respectable, and it became widespread, though some political parties, notably the Social Democrats, on the left, remained more or less immune.[6] The radicalization of the German right which accompanied the growing realization of defeat during the First World War did indeed mark a further step in the spread of racial anti-Semitism, culminating in the emergence and growth of the Nazi Party. But this had little to do with the influence of White Russian émigrés. Nor did Hitler bring any startling new components of anti-Semitic ideology with him from Austria. Of course, additional touches were added here and there, but Russian and Austrian influences had already been present in German anti-Semitism before the First World War, as in the notorious propaganda forgery, the so-called *Protocols of the Elders of Zion*. Moreover, it is important not to exaggerate the impact of Jewish refugees from Eastern Europe during the Weimar years. Their numbers were relatively insignificant compared to those of Jews already resident in Germany. Nazi anti-Semitism was in any case directed primarily at the mass of largely assimilated Jews within Germany itself, not against a handful of immigrants. Finally, although the Bolshevik "threat" was indeed equated with an alleged Jewish world conspiracy during the Weimar era, this was nothing particularly new, since the ascription of socialism to "Jewish" influences was a central feature of anti-Semitic propaganda in Germany before the First World War. It is important, therefore, to restate the well-known fact that the major causes of the spread and radicalization in Germany of racist anti-Semitism lay within Germany itself; they cannot be attributed to Austrians, Russians, or Jewish immigrants from the East.[7]

To be sure, the Nazis did not find anti-Semitism to be a major vote-winner at the time of their greatest electoral success between 1930 and 1933. Often, indeed, they played it down in order not to put voters off.[8] Far more important was their promise, in word and deed, to destroy the hated Weimar Republic, end the misery of the Depression, and crush the Social Democrats and Communists. Of course, for anyone who thought about these things, the Nazis' anti-Semitism was obvious enough, and those who voted for them had no excuse for pretending that it did not matter. But it does not seem to have been the main reason why the Nazis won such popularity in the last elections of the Weimar period. It would be quite wrong to see the mass of German electors clamoring for the opportunity to unleash their anti-Semitic hatred on the German Jews. The political respectability which anti-Semitism had attained in Germany rendered it acceptable to the 37 percent of the voters who supported the Nazis at the moment of their greatest triumph at the polls in July 1932. But when the Nazis tried to stir up public hostility toward the Jews, in the boycott they instituted as soon as they came to power in 1933, they met with only a limited response. And the mass violence of the pogroms of November 1938 aroused such public dismay and disquiet that it was not repeated: on the contrary, the Nazis went to some lengths to keep the realities of the "Final Solution" hidden from the mass of the German people, although anyone who wanted to find out could doubtless have done so. "The road to Auschwitz," therefore, in the memorable phrase of historian Ian Kershaw, "was built by hate, but paved with indifference."[9]

Hillgruber's attempts to pin the responsibility for the "Final Solution" on Hitler alone and to portray him as isolated within the Nazi leadership on this issue have led to charges that he intends to exculpate the German people. Nevertheless, no serious reading of Hillgruber's text could possibly support the claim that he maintains that Hitler pushed through his policy of extermination "against the will" of his lieutenants. On the contrary, Hillgruber delineates the levels of responsibility quite precisely, ranging from Hitler through his immediate subordinates to the "much greater number of people" who carried out the forced deportations; he also considers the mass of the German people as culpable in their indifference.[10] West German philosopher Jürgen Habermas has criticized Hillgruber's book for its subtitle, *The Destruction of the German Reich and the End of European Jewry.* This implies, says Habermas, a contrast between a violent process forced on the German Reich against its active opposition, with an almost spontaneous process of termination neither actively willed by the Nazis nor actively resisted by the Jews. Gordon A. Craig has pointed out that, in contrast to the title (where the word "end" is used), Hillgruber always uses the terms "murder" or "destruction" in the text of the lecture. However, as other commentators have noted, the neutral phrasing of the second part of the book does contrast strongly with the often passionate, committed, and argumentative style of the first part, so Habermas, although perhaps using an unfair example, has put his finger on a real difference between the two texts.[11]

To Hillgruber, Auschwitz seems to appear as something remote and distant; in his account of the eastern front at the end of the war, there is a real sense of personal involvement. This sense of distance is not fortuitous. Throughout his account of anti-Semitism, Hillgruber seems concerned to emphasize its lack of deep roots among the German people. The distinction he draws between Hitler and the other Nazi leaders helps to underline this point. Yet in the end it is unconvincing. Many of Hitler's immediate subordinates yielded little to the "führer" in the fanaticism of their anti-Semitic convictions. Men such as Goebbels, Streicher, and Himmler were utterly convinced of the rightness of the "Final Solution," and the language they used in public and private can leave no doubt in the mind of the reader about the depths of their hatred for the Jews. When Hillgruber describes the motives of Hitler's lieutenants in this question as "apolitical," he may be thinking, perhaps, of men such as Albert Speer, Hitler's wartime minister of munitions. Both at the Nuremberg Trials, and subsequently in his memoirs, Speer painted a skillful portrait of himself as an apolitical technocrat, seduced by the possibilities of modern technology into complicity with crimes, such as Auschwitz, which he knew nothing about. But historian Manfred Schmidt, in a recent book, has relentlessly exposed the manipulations and falsifications undertaken by Speer in order to persuade posterity that he was not a Nazi from ideological conviction. Speer certainly knew all about Auschwitz. And even if he was less a fanatic than a technocrat, this still makes no difference to the fact that the great majority of Hitler's henchmen, from his immediate entourage through the local Nazi *Gauleiters* in the provinces to the senior men in the SS, were anti-Semites from conviction, not "apolitical" instruments of one man's will.[12]

II

The question of whether the "Final Solution" was the product of Hitler's will alone, or the outcome of broader historical processes, has been debated by historians for much longer than the present controversy. It has been bedeviled by several major problems of evidence. Hitler's regime was not an orderly, bureaucratic administration, nor was Hitler an orderly, bureaucratic ruler. Decisions at the top were often made in a casual, ad hoc way by word of mouth, in a so-called "führer command"; only subsequently were they incorporated into the more conventional administrative machinery of implementation. Hitler's reluctance to make firm decisions on matters of domestic policy was well known. Often he left it to his subordinates to fight out policy between themselves, and only under some pressure did he then endorse the one or the other. Written evidence of policy decisions at the highest level is a lot less easy to come by than it is for the implementation of such policies further down the line. Moreover, the Nazis' propaganda, as we have already seen in the case of the Red Army in 1941, and to a more limited extent in the case of anti-Semitism during the elections of 1930 through 1932, was sometimes at variance with their personal beliefs and intentions. Finally, the language they used cannot always be taken at face value. At the level of public rhetoric, for example, it may have served the purpose of intimidating opponents by incorporating frightening but unspecific threats, while at the level of administration it was frequently designed to conceal the true nature of what was going on.[13]

During the 1960s and 1970s, some of the more conservative German historians, including Andreas Hillgruber and Klaus Hildebrand tended to place most stress on the individual responsibility of Hitler and to portray the events of the Third Reich in terms of the unfolding of Hitler's will. The war, the invasion of Russia, and the extermination of the Jews, happened above all because he intended these things to happen. Nazism was a radical, extremist ideology, and its major elements were implemented by Hitler with a ruthless determination that transformed virtually all other Germans into moral automata. Thus Nazism could more properly be termed "Hitlerism"; it was a unique phenomenon, the product of one man's ability to manipulate beliefs and forces present in interwar Germany and turn them to his own purposes. Over the last two decades, however, some West German historians, broadly associated with the Social Democrats and the liberals, have mounted a determined attack on this view. While it does not relieve the Germans from the burden of guilt for the crimes of Nazism, it does, they believe, minimize the responsibility of the established German elites for the rise and eventual triumph of the Nazis, and it underestimates the extent to which Nazism represented the culmination of long-term developments in German history.[14]

There can be little doubt that this recent work has broadly succeeded in establishing the central role of the Army, the business elite, the senior civil service and the German aristocracy in the early years of the Third Reich, and in underlining the extent to which many of their aims and beliefs coincided with those of the Nazis.[15] German conservatives too wanted a Greater Germany, dominating Europe and ruled by an authoritarian dictatorship; even as late as 1944, as we have seen, the conservative opposition to Hitler was still firmly wedded to these ideas.[16] But as the attitudes of the opposition also showed, a number of German conservatives did not approve of the barbarities of Hitler's "Final Solution" or the crimes committed during the war in Russia; and a comparison of the eastern front from 1941 to 1943 with the eastern front a quarter of a century earlier, in 1914–18, indicates that the Germans did not attempt to exterminate the population of the occupied territories in the earlier war; indeed, it seems that Russian prisoners of war in 1914–17 actually preferred to stay in German hands rather than escape back to the chaos and misery of their own lines. Nor, for all the strength of their anti-Semitic prejudices, did German or Austrian Army commanders encourage or countenance atrocities against the Jews in Poland and other areas under their control during the First World War.[17] The problem therefore arises of how to explain the willingness of the bulk of the German elites to take part in the extermination policies of the Second World War.

The answer given by historians of a broadly Social Democratic persuasion, such as Hans Mommsen, professor of history at the Ruhr University in Bochum, is that the Third Reich underwent a process of cumulative radicalization. As the various satraps of the Nazi regime fought for power among themselves, the all-important approval of Hitler could best be gained by presenting him with the most National Socialist, that is to say, the most radical policy toward the matter in hand. When in 1941 the Nazis were faced with the administrative problem of looking after millions of Jews in the occupied areas of Eastern Europe, they dealt with it first by sending in the SS murder squads, then by setting up the gas chambers. Finally, this policy, once it had been established, was then extended by the same process of radicalization to the Jews in the other parts of occupied Europe. Thus the actual unfolding of Nazi genocide was the product of ad hoc decisions following on the invasion of Russia, not just the implementation of a long-held intention in the mind of Adolf Hitler. In order to back this argument, Mommsen has to suggest that Nazi rhetoric before 1941 revealed no clear aim of exterminating the Jews. Thus for example when Hitler declared, in a notorious speech delivered on January 30, 1939, that if a world war came, this would lead to the total destruction *(Vernichtung)* of the Jewish race, Mommsen argues that this meant not physical extermination but merely their removal from the economy.[18]

It is important to consider the implications of this argument very carefully. Mommsen is one of the most eloquent and determined critics of Nolte's attempt to relieve the Germans of the burden of the past. In his view, pinning the blame on Hitler and reducing everyone else to the status of terrorized instruments of his will lets the Germans off far too lightly. By portraying Nazi genocide as the outcome of a cumulative and unplanned process of collective decision-making, Mommsen seeks to pose the awkward question of how it was that so many Germans could participate in such an active way not just in committing such a crime, but actually in originating it. But while recognizing all this, it is surely the case that the argument has now been carried a little too far. Important though it certainly is to avoid the perils of hindsight and to refrain from reading into every hostile reference to the Jews on the part of German politicians and writers before 1941 the intention to exterminate them, it still seems very unlikely that when Hitler talked of the *Vernich-*

tung of the Jews in 1939 he meant anything other than what common sense dictates he meant, namely their physical destruction. As British historian John P. Fox has commented, before coming to a judgment such as Mommsen's, one "really ought to examine the film of Hitler's speech, and in particular the split second when Hitler strikes upon that word, and relate all this to the leitmotiv which had dominated his political thinking and language throughout." Moreover, Hitler repeatedly referred to this speech during the war, after the "Final Solution" got under way. It is clear enough, therefore, what he himself meant by the word.[19]

The arguments advanced by Mommsen, despite their intentions, have also been accused of containing an element of exculpation. Historians who put forward such views have been accused by their conservative critics of absolving Hitler from blame and of trivializing the enormity of his crimes. And certainly when German historians claim that Hitler's anti-Semitic utterances were not evidence of "any firm intention to translate the metaphor of extermination into reality," this does have the appearance of excessive caution. But this is still a world away from the assertion of right-wing British writer David Irving that Hitler was unaware of the extermination of the Jews while it was taking place. As the responsible leader of Nazi Germany, he certainly was aware of it and put all his authority behind it. No serious historian in fact denies this; the argument is simply about whether he intended it all along and seized the opportunity when it came, or whether his action was a response to the particular circumstances of the late summer and autumn of 1941. The degree of exculpation implied by the latter position would seem, in view of the enormity of the crime involved, relatively small. More serious, perhaps, is the consideration that less moral blame would attach to so many Germans for voting for or failing seriously to oppose Hitler during the years 1930–32 and thus providing the basis for his seizure of power the following year if there had been no real intention on his part at that time to exterminate the Jews. Yet German voters could see with their own eyes the violence and murder, the militarism and terrorism exercised daily in the streets by the Nazis in 1930, 1931, and 1932, and it is still difficult to accept that they could merely have discounted all this when giving their vote to Hitler.[20]

With all due accounting for the benefit of hindsight and after all due allowances have been made for the haphazard, chaotic, and often unpredictable nature of Hitler's rule, it does in the end stretch credulity to believe that the will to exterminate the Jews was absent from Nazism before the late summer of 1941. We have already seen, for example, how the "criminal orders" issued to the German Army on the eve of the invasion of Russia in June 1941 included the command that Jews, along with "partisans" and "Bolshevik agitators," should be shot. In matters of foreign policy and military strategy, Hitler was more decisive and interventionist than in home affairs, which seldom really captured his imagination. The creation of "living space" in the East was one of his central aims, and numerous studies have demonstrated that the idea became inextricably intertwined with the disposal through murder of the Jews who lived there. Hitler and his fellow Nazis saw the Jews from the very beginning as subhuman "parasites" who were conspiring, above all through Communist and socialist politics, to undermine the Teutonic race. If they could be eliminated, German, Soviet, and European Communism would collapse, since the mass followers of the "Jewish-Bolshevik" creed would be left leaderless.[21]

The Nazis conceived of the "Jewish threat" in biological terms; it was "Jewish blood" that was threatening, and from the Nuremberg Laws of 1935, which forbade intermarriage between Jews and "Aryan" non-Jews in Germany and required everyone, man, woman and child, to show proof of their ancestry and descent, there could be no doubt that when the Nazis spoke of destroying the Jews, they meant this in a comprehensive, biologically defined way. The entire Jewish "stock" or "race" was to be removed, so that no chance would remain that Jewish "blood" could "contaminate" the "Aryan master race" in the future. Of course, this ideological imperative only set the context and the agenda for the "Final Solution"; it did not determine when, or how, it would be carried out. But there should surely be no doubt as to the fact that a murderous ideological anti-Semitism provided the driving force behind the progressive radicalization of Nazi policies toward the Jews.

There is plenty of evidence of Hitler's strong and continuous ideological pressure for a radical anti-Jewish policy. The opportunity may have occurred first of all in the summer of 1941, but the motive was there long before.

Nazi exterminism may be seen, therefore, not simply as the product of Hitler's individual will, but as the predictable outcome of a broader, biologistic ideology, shared by many leading Nazis and radical anti-Semites between the wars, and not a few before 1914 as well. Yet the Nazis' belief that society and history were shaped primarily by forces of race and heredity, by "blood and soil," went far beyond the elimination of the Jews from the human race in its implications and effects, for the Jews were not the only victims of Nazi oppression. Recent years have seen a growing amount of work devoted to recovering the history of the "forgotten victims of Nazism," slave laborers, inmates of innumerable small local branches *(Aussenlager)* of the major concentration camps, Gypsies, Soviet POWs, the mentally ill, the disabled, the retarded, so-called "antisocial elements" *(Asoziale)*, vagrants, beggars, prostitutes, homosexuals. These people too were arrested, tortured, imprisoned, and killed. In the case of the biologically, rather than merely politically, defined, such as the Gypsies or the mentally retarded or ill, massive extermination programs were launched. The "euthanasia" action against the inmates of mental hospitals preceded the extermination of the Jews by almost two years. By recovering the history of these groups, left-wing historians in the Federal Republic have succeeded in bringing home the crimes of Nazism to Germans in a way which they find it easy to grasp, since some of these groups—unlike the Jews—are present in today's Germany in large numbers and are part of Germans' everyday experience.[22]

The concentration on the "forgotten victims" of Nazism, however, has made left-wing historians in Germany increasingly reluctant to accept the uniqueness of Auschwitz. The Jews, in this view, were only one category of victims among many, even if they were the most numerous. Jews, Gypsies, the "antisocial," the mentally ill, Soviet prisoners of war, and the other groups were all comparable because they were all victims of racism. Concentration on the uniqueness of the Nazi extermination of the Jews has diverted attention too long from the

Nazis' many other victims. Racism as a phenomenon was neither directed by the Nazis exclusively against the Jews, nor did
it die with the end of the Third Reich.

Nazism, argues Detlev
Peukert, for example, was an attempt to solve the problems of
modernity by terror, and to dispose of the "social ballast" of
modern industrial society by extermination—a point of view
not dissimilar to that taken by Nolte, as Peukert himself ac-
knowledges.[23]

However, these arguments have some serious flaws. It is difficult to see how regarding the Nazi extermination of the Jews
as a unique phenomenon *necessarily* involves the neglect of
other victims of Nazism, even if it may have done so in practice.
Nor does it seem plausible to suggest that the Nazis simply
regarded the Jews as "social ballast." After all, these were not
people who were being supported by the state, like the mentally ill, or not engaged in regular jobs, like the Gypsies, or not
making children for the labor force and the Army, like the
homosexuals; on the contrary, the removal of Jews from the
economy and the diversion of resources to pay for their extermination was economically counterproductive by any rational
criteria. It is even less plausible to argue that the Jews were only
exterminated because of the burden on the state created by the
acquisition of a large extra Jewish population after the invasion
of Russia. There had already been a major increase in the Jewish
population by the annexation of western Poland in 1939. The
Jews of Western Europe, who were also exterminated, were in
general neither poor nor a burden on the Nazi state.

Finally, it seems to be stretching the concept of racism too
far when it is used to cover "eugenic" policies toward the allegedly hereditarily diseased or toward homosexuals. The
Nazis' policies toward these groups were obviously part of the
general mixture of biological determinism and anti-Semitism
which characterized Nazi ideology, but their rationale was in
many ways different. It was not these people's racial identity
that marked them out for elimination, but their supposed biological inferiority, irrespective of race. Nazi policies toward the
Gypsies were more clearly racist, but here too an element of
economic calculation was involved, since the Gypsies, just like
"Aryan" vagrants and tramps (who were also eventually taken
into the Nazi camps and murdered), refused to be enlisted in

the Nazi labor force and were thereby thought to be sabotaging the preparation and prosecution of the war, and in general to be failing to make their contribution to the Nazi regime. And the Nazis certainly did not regard the Gypsies as the prime movers in a world conspiracy to subvert the German race, as they did the Jews.

III

For all the horrors inflicted on the many different kinds of people who fell victims to German National Socialism, the fate of the Jews still stands out above the rest. Here was a category of people, who in many cases regarded themselves, and were widely so regarded by others, as an integral part of the communities in which they lived. Most German Jews between the wars were assimilated into German society and were no different from other Germans in most respects. The Nazis first of all defined them as a category, then subjected them to increasing violence and discrimination. They removed them from the rest of German society by a mounting tide of laws and restrictions, and finally deported and murdered those who failed in the meantime to make good their escape. Upon invading and subjugating other European nations, from France, the Low Countries, Denmark, and Norway in the West, to Poland, Czechoslovakia, Greece, Yugoslavia, the Soviet Union, and other states in the East, they proceeded to follow the same policies there. No other group of people in Europe was subjected to this treatment. Those whom the Nazis regarded as racially or genetically inferior, as "social ballast," as a liability on the state, such as Gypsies, the handicapped, or Russian prisoners of war, were killed in very large numbers as an act of policy. But the murder of the Jews has so far been seen as a crime of different dimensions altogether.

It is this fact that Ernst Nolte, among others, has recently tried to get around, in the effort to encourage a more positive, less guilty attitude to the German past in the Federal Republic. Nolte adopts five different lines of approach. First, as we have already seen, he has argued that other, comparable acts of genocide have been committed by other peoples in the twentieth century, from the Americans in Vietnam to the Turks in Armenia. In his most recent book, he goes further and suggests that German acts of genocide and barbarism were a direct response to similar, prior acts on the Allied side. The strategic bombing offensive against German cities, he says, was a war of extermination waged by the English against the German people. It was not a response to German bombing. And "the conduct of war by the Soviet Union was characterized by genocide to an even greater degree than that of England was." In this context, he mentions Stalin's deportation of the Crimean Germans; he also, as we have seen, refers to Polish attacks on ethnic Germans in 1939. So it was no longer, in this version, a limited threat to the German bourgeoisie that prompted Nazi anti-Semitism, but a general threat to exterminate the German race.[24]

Second, Nolte also argues that Nazi exterminism was a copy of previous genocidal policies adopted by other nations. A variant of this idea, as we have seen, can be found in the attempt by Hillgruber to locate Auschwitz in the context of twentieth-century forced population transfers. But Nolte goes further. In some places, he says that the Nazis transposed Soviet social exterminism into racial terms. Elsewhere, he speculates: "Were the Jews in the end, as far as Hitler was concerned, merely a particularly prominent part of the intelligentsia, and did this not prompt the question of whether German intellectuals under Hitler would in the end suffer a similar fate to that of the Russian intelligentsia under Lenin?" Nolte quotes in this context a press conference at which Hitler, the day after the pogrom of November 9, 1938, speculated that he might one day exterminate the intellectual classes in Germany if they no longer proved to be of use. Many prominent intellectuals, Nolte notes, were Jewish; so the extermination of the Jews, he implies, might be seen as an aspect of Hitler's anti-intellectualism and a copy of Soviet policies in this respect.[25]

Third, Nolte suggests that the majority of the German people were unaware of what was going on in Auschwitz. In his view, it was Hitler, personally, who converted a basically justifiable war against Communism on behalf of Western industrial civilization into a war of racial destruction. The German people were, as this distinction implies, engaged mainly in fighting the former war. Thus he emphasizes Hitler's personal responsibility. "Anyone who takes *Hitler* seriously" (my italics), Nolte says, "cannot deny the exterminatory actions of Auschwitz and Treblinka, nor the gas chambers." Authors like the American specialist on the destruction of the European Jews Raul Hilberg, who argue that thousands, even millions, of Germans, from the administrators in Eichmann's office to the railway timetable clerks and train drivers who ran the transportation of Jews to Auschwitz, knew what was happening, are in Nolte's view ignorant of the extent to which the extreme division of labor in modern societies isolates people from the consequences of what they are doing. And Nolte cites examples of senior Nazis and German generals who denied ever having known about the gas chambers.[26]

Fourth, Nolte implies that German policies toward the Jews were to a certain extent justified. We have already seen how he uses Weizmann's 1939 declaration to suggest the idea of the "civil internment" of Jews by the Nazis. In *The European Civil War,* he argues that the Jews could be seen as a belligerent group after the pogrom of November 1938. He goes on from this to hint that the German Army and the SS death squads engaged in mass executions of Jews on the eastern front from 1941 because many partisans were Jews. It would, he says, have been possible to exterminate the Belgians during the occupation of their country by Germany during the First World War, from 1914 to 1918, because they supported partisan and guerilla attacks on the occupying forces, "in order to achieve preventive security against acts committed in contravention of the law of nations." Thus, he implies, the extermination of an entire people is a possible policy if an occupying army wants to destroy the basis of illegal resistance in the occupied population. So "the actions of the death squads" were in Nolte's view "the most radical and comprehensive example of a preventive attack on the enemy, which went far beyond all concrete demands of the immediate conduct of war." Once again, therefore, he seems to suggest, the policy of exterminating the Jews was justifiable in principle, but carried out to an excessive degree. Auschwitz was an exaggerated form of the preventive suppression of partisans.[27]

Fifth, however, Nolte also goes some way toward entertaining the view that the "Final Solution" never happened at all. Hitherto, this argument—that there was no Nazi policy of exterminating the Jews, that Auschwitz is a fantasy invented by Jews for their own ends, that 6 million Jews did not die—has been confined to far-right, neofascist circles whose work has not been taken seriously by scholars. Nolte says it should be taken seriously. The motives of those who put forward these arguments, he says, are "often honorable." These people are often non-German; some of them are former inmates of concentration camps; and so, he implies, they possess a certain degree of detachment. Some of their arguments, he says, are "not obviously without foundation." Thus the Wannsee Conference, at which, it has hitherto been accepted, the implementation of the "Final Solution" was discussed, might in fact never have happened; certainly, the records for its existence are, he argues, of dubious authenticity. It is in this context that Nolte adds that most of the authors who have written on the "Final Solution" are Jewish. The context inevitably, and surely not unintentionally, thus arouses the impression that the bulk of the scholarly literature on Auschwitz is biased because of its (allegedly) Jewish origin.[28]

Nolte may be justified in saying that these historians' political views are irrelevant to the validity or otherwise of the arguments they put forward. The reason why authors who deny the reality of the Nazi genocide of nearly 6 million Jews are not taken seriously by professional historians is, however, not because these authors are right-wing radicals, but because they ignore such an overwhelming mass of evidence to the contrary that they cannot be accepted as possessing the ability to reach a reasoned assessment of the past. Their right-wing radical political motives, in other words, overcome all barriers of evidence, truth, and rationality. Applying conventional criteria of the critical assessment of the available documentation makes not only the existence of the "Final Solution" but also the reality of the Wannsee Conference indisputable. Serious research on these subjects has been carried out not just by Jewish scholars but also by scholars of many different nationalities, religions, and political persuasions; all of their work has been subject to the same criteria of critical judgment in the usual processes of assessment and debate in the international scholarly community.

When we subject Nolte's own arguments to the same criteria, it quickly becomes clear that his hypotheses are unpersuasive. First, they are internally contradictory, involving simultaneously justifying an event, suggesting it had evil parallels elsewhere, and hinting that it never happened. Throughout his book, Nolte presents fascism and Nazism as fundamentally justifiable responses to Communism, movements which aimed to defend the bourgeoisie and its achievements. But on the other hand, in arguing for a parallel with Communism, he also suggests that Nazism was in many ways anticapitalist and antibourgeois. These arguments are so contradictory that it is in the end difficult to take either of them very seriously. Second, his views rest on an implausible interpretation of the evidence. We have already seen, for example, that Weizmann was not speaking for Jews in general in 1939. To repeat: Jews during the period 1939–45 were not a nationality, did not act in unison, had no internationally recognized representation, and cannot therefore be regarded as a belligerent group.

Third, Nolte's hypotheses rest on inferential structures of reasoning which are frequently unsupported by evidence. Thus, for example, Nolte fails to cite any documentation in support of his view that Auschwitz and the previous activities of the death squads were a form of counterinsurgency action. Fourth, much of Nolte's evidence is anecdotal or unreliable. Stories of General Guderian denying knowledge of the gas chambers in March 1945, or uncorroborated quotations from memoirs of participants written after the event, are not solid or comprehensive enough as evidence to sustain Nolte's far-reaching conclusions. Fifth, Nolte is contradicted by a great mass of other evidence which he completely fails to address. Thus we saw in chapter 3 how Jews were added as a *separate* category for extermination to partisans and guerillas on the eastern front, and how the very term "partisan" became arbitrary and meaningless in the context of the primary Nazi thrust to extinguish whole populations. Similarly, not all Jews were intellectuals, and many Jewish intellectuals had left Germany by November 1938, so that most German intellectuals by that time, if not before, were certainly not Jewish. There is in any case no evidence that Hitler connected the two in the speech quoted by Nolte, nor that Lenin exterminated the Russian intelligensia either, though Stalin certainly went a long way toward doing so.

As we have seen throughout, many of Nolte's arguments are speculative, theoretical, or even cast in the form of rhetorical questions. Even those who, like the Bremen historian Imanuel Geiss, think that he has been unfairly criticized and his views widely distorted, have had to concede that Nolte rests some of his assertions on an extremely thin basis of evidence. Not infrequently, Nolte simply bypasses generally accepted procedures of historical verification and argumentation altogether. His references and bibliography show an ignorance of—or disregard for—the relevant scholarly literature that is frequently surprising. Thus, for example, it is not enough for Nolte simply to deny that many Germans knew about the extermination program by referring to the extent of the division of labor in a modern industrial society. The evidence accumulated by Hilberg, Laqueur and others has to be confronted directly.[29] A broad generalization such as Nolte makes remains merely hypothetical unless it is tested against the concrete evidence. What he says about the division of labor may be true as a general sociological principle, but the fact remains that even in a society with such advanced bureaucratic structures as Nazi Germany, railway timetable clerks and other officials had to make a positive effort to avoid the recognition that the consignments they were dealing with were cargoes of human beings, transported in degrading and inhuman conditions to places where they would be put to death. Nolte's view that the German invasion of the Soviet Union was undertaken in defense of Western civilization is even more speculative. Certainly, the vast majority of senior civil and especially military officials seem to have had a definition of Western civilization very far removed from any which might be broadly acceptable today.

Finally, Nolte's attempts to establish the comparability of Auschwitz rest in part upon an extension of the concept of "genocide" to actions which cannot plausibly justify being described in this way. However much one might wish to criticize the Allied strategic-bombing offensive against German cities, it cannot be termed genocidal because there was no intention to exterminate the entire German people. Dresden was bombed after Coventry, not the other way around, and it is implausible to suggest that the latter was a response to the former; on the

contrary, there was indeed an element of retaliation and revenge in the strategic bombing offensive, which is precisely one
of the grounds on which it has so often been criticized. There
is no evidence to support Nolte's speculation that ethnic Germans in Poland would have been entirely exterminated had the
Nazis not completed their invasion quickly. Neither the Poles
nor the Russians had any intention of exterminating the German people as a whole. At this point, it is useful to recall the
conclusion of German historian and Hitler specialist Eberhard
Jäckel that "the Nazi murder of the Jews was unique because
never before has a state decided and announced, on the authority of its responsible leader, that it intended to kill in its entirety,
as far as possible, a particular group of human beings, including
its old people, women, children, and infants, and then put this
decision into action with every possible instrument of power
available to the state."[30]

The attempts undertaken by Nolte, Hillgruber, Fest, and
other neoconservative historians to get around this fact are all
ultimately unconvincing. It requires a considerable degree of
myopia to regard the policies of the USA in Vietnam in the
1960s and early 1970s, or the occupation of Afghanistan by the
USSR in the 1980s, as "genocide." However much one may
deplore the conduct of the occupying armies, there is no evidence of any deliberate policy of exterminating the inhabitants
of the countries in question. The terrible massacres of the Armenians by the Turks in 1915 were more deliberate, on a wider
scale, and concentrated into a far shorter time, than the destruction of human life in Vietnam and Afghanistan, and they
were not carried out as part of a military campaign, although
they did occur in wartime. But these atrocities were committed
as part of a brutal policy of expulsion and resettlement; they did
not constitute an attempt to exterminate a whole people. Similar things may be said of the forcible removal of Greeks from
Asia Minor during the 1920s, although this has not, in contrast
to the events of 1915, generally been regarded as genocide.[31]

The Pol Pot regime in Cambodia witnessed the horrific spec-
tacle of a nation's rulers turning upon their own people, in a
manner comparable to that of the Ugandan dictator Idi Amin
a few years previously. The victims, whose numbers exceeded
a million, were killed, however, not on racial grounds but as

part of a deliberate policy of terror to subdue opposition and revenge against those thought to have collaborated with the American enemy during the previous hostilities. Moreover, the barbarities inflicted on the Cambodian people by the Pol Pot regime were to a considerable extent the result of a brutalizing process that had accompanied a terrible war, during which vast quantities of bombs were dropped on the country, destroying a large part of the moral and physical basis of Cambodian society in the process.[32] This in no way excuses the murderous policies of the Khmer Rouge. But it does show up, once more, the contrast with the Nazi genocide of the Jews, which, as we have seen, was a gratuitous act carried out by a prosperous, advanced industrial nation at the height of its power.

Similar distinctions can be made between Auschwitz and the Gulag. There can be no doubt of the severity of the repression begun by Lenin and continued and extended by Stalin. In the course of the 1930s, for example, Stalin pushed through a collectivization of Russian agriculture in the course of which some of the peasantry were held to be exploiting the rest and were accordingly dispossessed, so that the collectivization scheme could be presented as a social revolution in which exploitation was abolished and the mass of the Russian peasantry came into their own. At least, this was the theory. In practice, things were very different. The aims of collectivization—the final subjugation of the countryside to Bolshevik rule and its conversion to a source of food to support the forced industrialization which Stalin was pushing through at the same time—were achieved with ruthless brutality.

It is not true to say, as some of Nolte's critics have done, that only those who opposed collectivization were deported or killed, and all peasants had to do to survive was to agree to give up their private farms. Local police and party officials were often issued with "quotas" of kulaks to be dealt with that were unrelated to the real numbers of kulaks or opponents of collectivization. Definitions of kulaks varied widely. Many peasants had no choice as to whether they survived or not. Large numbers slaughtered their livestock and destroyed their crops rather than surrender them to the state. Widespread famine and starvation accompanied the chaos of collectivization and was compounded by the massive and arbitrary terror meted out by the regime and its servants. The arbitrariness of Stalin's terror contrasted starkly with the absolute predictability of Nazi terror, which was directed demonstrably at identifiable groups within the population, above all the Jews. Finally, claims advanced that Stalin's reign of terror was responsible for a greater number of deaths than Hitler's have to be treated with extreme skepticism, in view of the fact that they are generally made with the motive of suggesting that the Soviet Union was—perhaps still is—more murderous and thus more reprehensible than Nazi Germany.

Stalin's purges of the 1930s were one of the twentieth century's greatest crimes. It is indeed only now, at the end of the 1980s, that the Soviet Union is beginning to come to terms with them. Nevertheless, the distinctions between these events and those of the Third Reich, some of which Nolte himself concedes, were not without significance. When Communist spokesmen announced their intention to "exterminate the bourgeoisie as a class" or "liquidate the kulaks," they were not stating that they would physically eliminate every man, woman, and child of bourgeois or "big-peasant" origin, no matter what their opinions were or how they conducted themselves. Bolshevik and Stalinist mass murder was carried out as an instrument of terror, subjugation, and social reconstruction; Nazi mass murder was an end in itself. Nor did Stalin seek out kulaks to exterminate in those parts of Europe which fell under his control, as Hitler did with the Jews, despite repressions and atrocities carried out on a considerable scale in occupied Poland and the Baltic States. The Communist use of the term "destruction" or "liquidation" was, as Nolte realizes, not biological but political in its essence. The consequences of this fact for Stalin's reign of terror were not trivial, but they do set it apart from the genocide practiced by the Nazis. As Charles Maier has observed, "No Soviet citizen had to expect that deportation or death must be so inevitable by virtue of ethnic origins" as it was for the Jews in Nazi-dominated Europe. There was no Soviet Treblinka, built to murder people on their arrival.[34] Finally, there is no evidence that the Soviet Union under Stalin planned to launch a war of conquest against the West, nor that it intended the mass murder of the Western bourgeoisie. Serious historical scholarship overwhelmingly accepts that Stalin's suspicious and narrow mind looked upon the West in primarily defensive terms. There is very little reason to suppose that Soviet intentions toward the West of Europe even remotely resembled German intentions toward the East.

Engaging in a comparative study of barbarities along these lines is a difficult and in some ways a distasteful business. As Joachim Fest has remarked, from the most basic point of view, it made little difference to those at the receiving end of the mass murder whether they faced death because they belonged to a racial group or a social class. Similarly, it did not alter the guilt of those individuals who carried out these appalling crimes whether they did so in the name of an ideology like socialism, with a grand humanitarian tradition, however much it may have been perverted by Stalin, or in the name of a "worldview" like fascism, which was evil from the very beginning. But the historian cannot be content with the most basic point of view. Distinctions have to be made, because otherwise we risk sacrificing a rational understanding of these problems on the altar of moral disapprobation. As soon as one makes distinctions, one runs the risk of being accused of playing down or trivializing the one or the other phenomenon under discussion. It is important to reiterate, therefore, that to describe the Nazi genocide of the Jews as a unique crime in human history in no way excuses or condones the many other terrible collective crimes that have disfigured the face of the twentieth century, and for which parallels and precedents can also be found in the more distant past. Nor does it imply that such a crime may not recur in a similar form in the future, elsewhere. Secular historians can surely make this point without in any way placing themselves on the ground of religious writers who suggest that the Nazi "Final Solution" was an event of almost sacred significance, explainable only in terms of the relation of the Jewish people to God—a "Holocaust," in fact. The fact that an event was unique does not mean that it cannot be rationally explained.[35]

Nor is it necessarily wrong to stress the exceptional nature of Nazism's crimes on a narrower front, in comparison to the policies and traditions of other advanced European societies such as Britain or France. Hillgruber, indeed, singles out for special mention the fact that the extermination of the Jews took place under the conditions of a highly developed modern civilization, and that those who took part in it included many well-educated and otherwise cultivated individuals. Joachim Fest regards this line of argument as a regression into the old Nazi distinction between "superior peoples" and "peoples on a more primitive level," or, by implication, the "master race" and the "subhuman." But it is surely not Nazi or even racist to recognize that Germany is in Europe, and shares in Europe's historical experience of the Enlightenment, the growth of constitutionalism and democracy, and the establishment of a general respect for fundamental human rights. So a comparison with other European countries at the same stage of economic, social, and political development is more appropriate than, say, a comparison with the Mongol Empire under Genghis Khan, or Cambodia under Pol Pot. No one seems to have tried to compare Germany with Japan in the present debate, for example, because it is clear that Japanese brutality during the Pacific war, in China, Korea, and the Philippines, was not part of a planned attempt to exterminate whole peoples although it caused the deaths of millions in the most horrifying circumstances. More to the point, there seemed to be an "absence in the Japanese social system of a generalized code of ethical behavior," as one historian has put it. Those more limited traditions which prevailed in the Army dictated that a defeated enemy who failed to take the honorable course of committing suicide was not worthy of respect as a human being. And, more generally, racism, imperialist ambition, and the brutalizing effects of a long period of bitter war all combined to destroy whatever weak restraints on military barbarism might have remained.[36]

It does seem the case, as historian Omer Bartov has pointed out, that a refusal to regard opponents in a war as human beings, convictions of racial superiority, and ideological fanaticism (whether of a political or a religious nature) are all factors which have tended throughout human history to encourage brutality, massacre, and lack of ethical restraint in warfare. But the Nazi war in the East, and the connected phenomenon of the Nazi policy of genocide toward the Jews, was different. Not even the Thirty Years' War, from 1618 to 1648, in which large numbers of people in Central Europe were slaughtered for no other reason than that they belonged to the wrong religious denomination, had the same features of deliberate genocide, or was fought with the aim of enslaving millions of people and killing in its entirety a whole racial group.[37] As Charles Maier remarks, "Nowhere else but in German-occupied Europe from 1941 to 1945 was there an apparatus so single-mindedly established to carry out mass murder as a process in its own right."[38] To point this out is not to say that the relevance of Nazism is limited, or to take Nazism out of history, or to render it immune to rational explanation. Just because it has only happened once does not mean it will not happen somewhere, sometime in the decades or centuries to come. The act of historical comparison does not involve an equation of two or more events, or a blurring of distinctions between them; on the contrary, it means isolating what they have in common in order to find out how they differ. This applies to Auschwitz and the Gulag as much as it applies to anything else. Only by engaging in this exercise with rigor and dispassion can we guard against their repetition in the future.

CHAPTER FIVE

RESHAPING CENTRAL EUROPE

I

Unless we bear constantly in mind the horrors visited
not only upon the Jews but also on the entire resident population of occupied Eastern Europe by the Germans during the
first half of the 1940s, it is impossible to understand the events
which followed on the end of the war in this area. Already as
the German armies retreated, millions of ethnic Germans in
this region fled their homes before the advancing Red Army. As
the Russian troops arrived, they carried out many acts of brutality, rape, and murder against those Germans who were unfortunate enough to fall into their hands. Nor was this by any means
the end of these people's sufferings. As the boundaries of East-
Central Europe were redrawn at the Potsdam Conference in
the summer of 1945, the victorious Allies decided upon a far-
reaching compulsory transfer of ethnic Germans to the West.
In fact, the expulsions had already begun. They were accompanied, particularly in the early months of 1945, by numerous
atrocities. They continued through 1946. By 1950, some 11
million Germans had been driven from the eastern territories.
In the process, the official West German account of the expul-

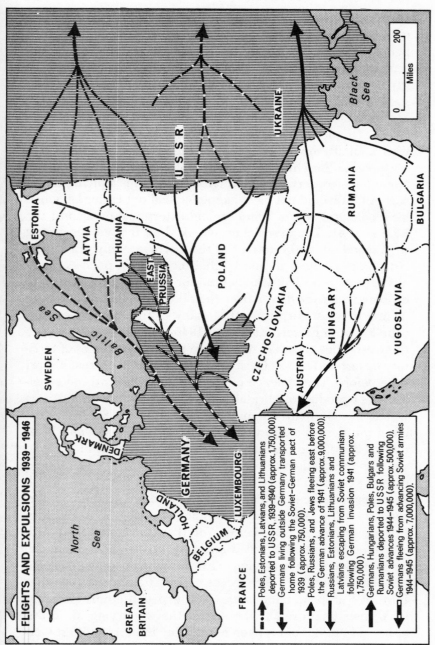

FLIGHTS AND EXPULSIONS 1939–1946

Poles, Estonians, Latvians, and Lithuanians
deported to USSR, 1939–1940 (approx.1,750,000).

Germans living outside Germany transported
home following the Soviet–German pact of
1939 (approx.750,000).

Poles, Russians, and Jews fleeing east before
the German advance of 1941 (approx.9,000,000).

Russians, Estonians, Lithuanians and
Latvians escaping from Soviet communism
following German invasion 1941 (approx.
1,750,000).

Germans, Hungarians, Poles, Bulgars and
Rumanians deported to USSR following
Soviet advances 1944–1945 (approx.500,000).

Germans fleeing from advancing Soviet armies
1944–1945 (approx. 7,000,000).

sions, published in 1969, estimates that more than 610,000 Germans were killed by Romanian troops, Polish militia, Czech people's guards and Yugoslavian partisans. A further 2.2 million remained unaccounted for, although the official account explicitly warns that it would be wrong, given the chaotic circumstances of the time, to count all of these among the dead.[1]

This was not, as Nolte puts it, a policy that "is to be categorized . . . under the concept of genocide."[2] It was not, in other words, an attempt to exterminate the German people. It was not another Auschwitz, although Nolte is by no means alone among neo-conservative German historians in implying that it was. And it would not have happened had not Hitler launched his ideological war of conquest and extermination against the East in 1941. The destruction wreaked on these areas during the "scorched-earth" retreat of the German Army during the last phases of the war, and by their occupation policies previously, rendered them wholly unfit for sustaining the masses of civilians who were driven from their homes by the resettlement policy. It is not surprising that many of the ethnic Germans expelled from Eastern Europe in 1945–46 died on their way to the west, since they had to traverse hundreds of miles of territory devastated by the German Army during its retreat a short time before. The violence of the Red Army toward the expellees was a product of a brutalizing of ethnic relations in this area which the Germans themselves had initiated. Similarly, the often murderous and brutal behavior of the Czechs and Poles toward the ethnic Germans within their territories in 1945–46 was also the product of years of suffering, hardship, terror, and death at German hands. None of this excuses the crimes which accompanied the expulsions. But it does help put them in perspective. The expulsion of ethnic Germans from Eastern Europe at the end of World War II was accomplished with appalling harshness. But it was not equatable with Auschwitz. The Russians were not trying to exterminate the entire German population, nor were the Czechs or the Yugoslavs or the other Eastern European nationalities who expelled ethnic Germans from their territories at the end of the war trying to do this either. There has often been a tendency in postwar West Germany to write about the expulsions either in isolation from the barbaric policies of the previous German occupation of Eastern

Europe, or in terms that suggest that they were a crime as great as the Nazis' "Final Solution." Neither position, it should be clear from the preceding chapters in this book, is tenable.

Moreover, it is often forgotten that the process of forced removal and resettlement of ethnic Germans from Eastern Europe was begun by the Nazis themselves. Hitler's aim was to bring all Germans within the boundaries of the Reich, and the process began as soon as the Nazis marched into Poland in September 1939. Over three-quarters of a million ethnic Germans were removed from their homes (including many from Soviet-occupied territories as well) and put into camps, where they were subjected to examination and interrogation by SS officials. Those who were deemed to be "racially unfit," or were opponents of Nazism, or disliked by the SS for some other reason, were handed over to the Gestapo to be killed. Thousands remained in the camps for months on end, living often in quite harsh conditions, while the SS decided whether to send them to the old Reich or the East. And through this action, of course, numerous villages and other areas of German settlement were emptied, destroyed, or turned over to the Poles (who were forcibly deported under far more brutal and murderous conditions, and in far greater numbers). The Nazi definition of what constituted a "German" or a "Slav" area of settlement for the purposes of this action was, as can be imagined, arbitrary and elastic.[3]

As far as the postwar resettlement is concerned, it is surely clear that the wholly unacceptable means by which the expulsions were effected can and must be distinguished from the end sought by the expulsions themselves. Here Hillgruber's account is contradicted by recent research both in its detail and in its overall thrust. The emphasis which he puts on the alleged desire of the Western Allies, under the influence of the Polish government-in-exile in London, to weaken Germany by creating an "enlarged Poland," seems particularly misplaced. The Allies certainly agreed in principle to move the western boundary of Poland further west as early as 1943, although its precise position remained to be determined. But this step was taken not least in order to compensate the Poles for the prospective loss of much of their eastern territory to the Soviet Union. It was also agreed, at the first Allied war conference, held in Teheran at the end of November 1943, that the Russo-Polish border would be moved westward to run along the so-called "Curzon Line." The eastern territories which Poland thus lost had changed hands a number of times over the previous decades. They had been part of the Russian Empire since the partition of Poland in the eighteenth century. They had been reconquered by the Polish army in the war with Russia in 1920–21; less than twenty years later, in 1939, they fell into Russian hands once more, as Poland was divided between Stalin and Hitler under the terms of the Nazi-Soviet Pact. The Curzon Line thus formed the western boundary of the Soviet Union between 1939 and 1941. Ironically, Hitler's Germany, by agreeing to this line of demarcation, had in effect provided the precondition for the westward shift of Poland after the war.

It was clear as early as 1941 that Stalin was unlikely to give up the territory east of the Curzon Line. A resurrected Poland would therefore require territorial compensation from Germany in the west. Britain and the United States were simply recognizing this fact, and bowing to the *fait accompli* of the occupation of the territory in question by the Red Army in the later stages of the war, when they agreed to the boundary changes. And they did so not under the influence of the exiled Polish government in London, but against its impassioned opposition. The Polish exiles were determined not to abandon the territory their predecessors had conquered in the war of 1920–21. In addition, they were also reluctant to countenance a western boundary of their country running along the Oder-Neisse Line, since they thought this would wreck any chance of reestablishing good relations with a reconstructed Germany after the war. By 1944, it was clear to the Western Allies, moreover, that the Soviet Union was intent on giving power to its own puppet Polish government in Lublin. Bypassing the London exile government even more clearly than before, the Allies now tried to use a provisional approval of the new boundaries as a bargaining counter to persuade the Russians to reconstruct the Lublin government on a broader basis.[4]

That all of this would involve a transfer of as many as 7 million ethnic Germans from Eastern Europe to the West was clear to the British as early as 1941, though a realization of this consequence of the boundary changes was not the same as an actual decision to expel the Germans until the boundary changes themselves had been agreed. The Allies wanted naturally enough to create a postwar settlement that would last. It was out of the question that Poland should disappear from the map again, as it had done in the eighteenth century—Polish national feeling was too strong. The new Polish state had been created at the end of the First World War by taking back much of the territory annexed by Russia, Austria, and Germany in the original partitions. But a substantial area—East Prussia—remained in German hands, cut off from the rest of Prussia and Germany by the "corridor" which gave the Poles access to the Baltic Sea. Once the westward shift of Poland after the Second World War had been agreed to, it was fairly clear that the bulk of East Prussia would have to go to Poland. As a consequence, the Americans agreed in 1943 that the German population of this territory would have to leave.[5]

What made the Western Allies believe that expulsions were necessary was not least the history of German minorities in Eastern Europe between the wars. The many millions of ethnic Germans who found themselves living in newly created states such as Poland and Czechoslovakia at the end of the First World War were never fully reconciled to this situation. They remained reluctant citizens of the new states throughout the interwar years. Certainly, the majority nationalities, Poles and Czechs, did little to help reconcile their German fellow citizens to the new state of affairs. But even in the peaceful years of the Weimar Republic, neither the German government nor the ethnic Germans in the Polish state gave up working for a territorial revision that would restore these "lost" areas to Germany. It is impossible to say what the outcome of this would have been in the long run. Hitler's advent to power in Germany in 1933 altered the situation at one blow. Publicly committed to the aim of gathering all Germans together into a single Reich, Hitler immediately set about manipulating the resentments of ethnic Germans under Czech and Polish rule in order to destabilize these two states and provide an excuse for invading them. In addition, increasing numbers of Sudeten Germans became enthusiasts for Konrad Henlein's homegrown version of the Nazi Party after 1933. By 1935 Henlein was supported by over two-thirds of Sudeten German voters. By 1937 he was working full-time for Hitler. The bitter memory of the role played by the Sudeten Germans in these years—in first destabilizing Czechoslovakia and then, via the Munich Agreement in 1938, in provoking the country's dismemberment—was a major factor in the violent hatred displayed by the Czechs to the German population in their midst at the end of the war.[6]

The Allies' consciousness of the disruptive potential of minorities such as the Sudeten Germans, as revealed in the interwar years, was one of the principal reasons behind the decision to expel such German minorities from the resurrected small states of Eastern Europe in 1945. For the areas in question were not simply "German." One can sympathize with Hillgruber's passionate commitment to the view that they constituted a "centuries-old area of German settlement," since he himself was born and grew up in East Prussia (and indeed fought briefly on the eastern front toward the end of the war). But he knows as well as anyone that the situation was far more complex than this. The German presence in areas like Upper Silesia was to some extent the result of forced Germanization beginning in the Bismarckian period. Even after this, the Germans were only one among a number of ethnic groups in these parts of East-Central and Eastern Europe. Insofar as they lived within the German Empire before 1918, the other ethnic groups were, as Hillgruber concedes, already being subjected to increasing discrimination and oppression by their German rulers.[7] Indeed, it was the sheer complexity of ethnic divisions in this part of Europe that rendered ethnic rivalries and conflicts so intractable. The experience of the previous half century, and above all the experience of the German destabilization, invasion, and occupation of Eastern and East-Central Europe between 1938 and 1945 provided powerful arguments for the compulsory removal of ethnic Germans from these areas. What this experience should also have done, of course, was to have persuaded the Allies that such population transfers could not be accomplished peacefully and humanely without a great deal more planning, a great deal more official supervision, and above all a great deal more time than was actually provided.

While these plans were being discussed, other ideas were also being floated for a division of Germany itself after the war. But these were not, as Hillgruber claims, firm Allied policies.

Many possible options were being mooted at this time, including the notorious "Morgenthau Plan" for the deindustrialization of postwar Germany. Neither the Morgenthau Plan nor the idea of dividing Germany was ever officially adopted, although it was agreed that Prussia should be broken up into smaller units within a united Germany. It was the Cold War that brought about the division of Germany; the future development of two German states was far from inevitable in 1945. In any case, the European settlement of 1945 cannot stand or fall by the way in which it was brought about. With all due reservation, it must ultimately be judged by its long-term effects. The European boundaries drawn at the conferences of Potsdam and Yalta have now lasted over twice as long as those drawn at Versailles and Trianon in 1919. The political stability achieved by the settlement of 1945 has proved more durable than the arrangements reached by almost any comparable European settlement of modern times, including those brought about by the Congress of Vienna in 1815 or the Congress of Berlin in 1878. Forty years of uninterrupted peace add up to an unanswerable defense of the arrangements reached in 1945. Armed conflict in Europe over the previous century had been generated mainly by nationalist passions and ethnic rivalries. The transfer of populations and the division of Europe into two blocs, each with a different social system and each dominated by an outside superpower, has, by one of history's savage ironies, brought this century of conflict to an end.

Hillgruber, as we have seen, suggests that it would have been a good thing if Europe, led by Germany, had established itself as a world power in the interwar years. Nolte, too, suggests that "if Europe was to succeed in establishing itself as a world power on an equal footing [with, presumably, the United States and the USSR], then Germany had to be the core of the new 'United States.' " A militarily weak Germany in the 1930s would have fallen prey to her neighbors and so destroyed this possibility.[8] But neither of these speculations seems very realistic. Even the present-day European Community, with its drive toward European integration and its plethora of supranational institutions which had no parallel in Neville Chamberlain's day, is seldom able to speak with a single voice on international problems of major importance. Nor is it at all clear that the world would be a better place if Europe had become a world power along the lines Hillgruber and Nolte suggest. In any case, since the first half of the twentieth century proved that Europe was unable to order its own affairs peacefully and was liable to involve the rest of the world in murderous conflict, it was probably no bad thing that the continent was brought under outside control in 1945. Some may argue that the price paid by those who now live under Soviet hegemony has been particularly high. Yet inhabitants of many countries in Eastern Europe knew little personal freedom or respect for human rights even when they were wholly self-governing, and there is little evidence that they would have become more liberal after 1945.

Finally, the postwar settlement in Europe effectively removed the continent from the field of conflict between the two superpowers. Of course, there were moments of tension, most notably over Berlin, during the airlift in 1948 and then over the building of the wall in 1961. But on the whole, it would be reasonable to say that the division of Europe into two camps, cemented by the transfer of population, has eliminated most potential sources of serious clashes between the United States and the USSR in the region. If there had been millions of discontented Germans under Russian, Polish, or Czech rule, or if the Soviet regime, still reeling from the terrible experiences of the German invasion, had been confronted with massive and bloody national conflicts in postwar East-Central Europe, conflicts from which the Western Allies would have found it very difficult to stand aside, ethnic and political instability in postwar Europe might easily have provided the tinderbox with which to ignite a fresh world conflict, this time with all the destructive potential available to it in the nuclear age. In Europe in the second half of the twentieth century, it is not just fear of nuclear weapons that has prevented the reemergence of the terrible conflicts which tore the continent apart in the first half. A major factor has been a resolution of some of the fundamental causes of those conflicts, ethnic and social, by the division of Europe into two halves by social system and the defusing of ethnic antagonisms through the mass transfer of populations. It is in recognition of the benefits of stability that neither side has made a serious attempt to impose its own values and norms upon the other.

II

Although the final collapse of the empire created by Bismarck clearly happened at the end of the Second World War with the zonal division of Germany and the westward shift of Russia and Poland, the boundaries established in 1871 had in fact been revised in a number of stages. To begin with, less than half a century later, after Germany's defeat in World War I, Alsace-Lorraine was returned to the French and substantial parts of Prussia were lost to the Poles. Much more significant, however, were the steps taken by Hitler in 1938, with the *Anschluss* of Austria and the annexation of the Sudetenland. This marked the definitive abandonment of the Bismarckian *kleindeutsch* solution of the German question through a "little Germany" without Austria or Bohemia and a reversion to the earlier *grossdeutsch* idea favored by German liberals in the years leading up to the 1848 Revolution. Indeed, it was only Allied pressure that had prevented German-speaking Austria from merging with Germany following the collapse of the Habsburg empire in 1918–19. The Bismarckian version of German unification thus lasted all of sixty-seven years. More and more, it appears not as the culmination of German history but as a mere episode in it. Nineteen eighty-eight marked the fiftieth anniversary of its demise.

Even leaving aside the dramatic boundary changes of 1938, it is impossible to get around the fact that the dismemberment of Germany in 1945 would not have occurred had the Nazis not launched an ultimately unsuccessful ideological war of conquest and extermination against the rest of Europe, and particularly the East, shortly before. As German historian Heinrich August Winkler points out, the Reich of 1871 was ultimately destroyed by the Germans themselves. "In view of the role that Germany played in the origins of the two world wars," he cautions, "Europe cannot and the Germans should not desire a new German Reich, a sovereign nation-state, any longer." Germany, as another German historian has put it, is now a "postnational society." The Austrians, who were formally part of Germany for centuries before Bismarck threw them out in 1866, and were part of it again from 1938 to 1945, possessed no strong national consciousness of their own before the Second World War. Since then, however, they have come to think of themselves as very different from the West Germans. The same may be said, though far less emphatically, of the developing national consciousness of the East Germans. German national consciousness no longer exists even in the sense in which it did, within limits, between 1871 and 1945.[9] There is no fundamental reason why a linguistic or cultural group such as the Germans should need to be united under a single state, any more than that the same principle should be applied to other linguistic or cultural groups, such as the English-speaking nations. To argue for reunification in the name of freedom for the people who live under Communism in the GDR is to risk serious international conflict and upheaval, even in the altered political climate of the late 1980s. Moreover, for its most vociferous advocates inside West Germany, reunification means, not the extension of Western freedom to the East, but the resurgence of an old-style German nationalism whose commitment to freedom and democracy is extremely doubtful.[10]

More than one contributor to the debate has remarked that as far as the Germans' relationship to their own past is concerned, it is ultimately irrelevant whether Auschwitz was unique or not.[11] West Berlin historian Hagen Schulze asks, "Does the special responsibility of the Germans for the misdeeds that were committed in their name depend on their singularity? Are the mass murders any less reprehensible, is the Germans' obligation to draw lessons from the misdeeds of the National Socialist era any smaller, if comparable misdeeds have been committed elsewhere and at other times?"[12] Yet in view of the Germans' position and reputation in the world, the uniqueness or otherwise of Auschwitz surely does make a difference. For if the Germans did not commit a crime that stood out from all others in its horror, then they have no more to be ashamed of than any other nation, and so it becomes possible for them to tread the international stage unburdened by a historical responsibility without parallel anywhere else in the world. If the relativization of Auschwitz succeeds, an important obstacle to a resurgence of German nationalism and to the campaign for German reunification is thereby removed.

Not only Nolte but many other historians as well also clearly think it is important for West Germans to identify more positively with their national past. Hagen Schulze, for example, has declared that national identity is far more powerful than an identity based on loyalty to the Federal German constitution. Schulze combines a clear desire for a takeover of East Germany by West Germany ("a reunification under free, Western auspices") with an equally clear recognition of its impossibility in the foreseeable future and a warning that it must be part of a European scheme of unity, echoing Hillgruber's linking of German power with European power. He warns that if historians do not play their part in molding that identity, then other, more dangerous groups will. Schulze identifies a "danger from the right" among the Greens and the "classical left," which he alleges have taken up virtually all the traditional themes of German conservatism. But he never says what these themes actually are. The Greens have, it is true, argued for reunification on the basis of disarmament and neutrality, but this is a long way from the reunification demands of the radical right, which regards a reunited Germany's right to independent armaments as axiomatic. Even if some of their themes, such as the protection of the natural environment, carry echoes from the *völkisch* past, there can surely be no doubt about their commitment to democracy and human rights, as their relentless uncovering of political corruption and their determined opposition to intrusive state information-gathering in West Germany has shown.[13]

If historians are busy trying to manufacture a national identity, it is not because there is a need to prevent anyone else from doing so. Why they are engaging in this business has been put most clearly by Michael Stürmer. In his contribution to the Römerberg Colloquia—an annual series of debates held in Frankfurt, which in 1986 dealt with "the past that will not pass away" and which formed the original stimulus for Nolte's essay of the same title—Stürmer complained of the Germans' "obsession with their guilt," their lack of national identity, their inability to decide where they stood in time and space. The 1960s in particular saw the destruction of any remaining sense of cultural identity—a result, he implies, of overemphasizing the importance of the Third Reich in German history. It is time, argues Stürmer, to give history a meaning—*Sinnstiftung* is the word he uses—on the basis of which the Germans can build a genuine sense of nationhood: "We cannot live by making our own past . . . into a permanent source of endless guilt feelings."[14]

Stürmer hinted how this might be achieved when he referred during the Römerberg Colloquia to "the deadly idiocies of the victors of 1918" and suggested a significant parallel to the peace settlement of 1945. Hitler, he asserted, came to power because Germany had lost its sense of orientation and had no defenses against the crisis of modernity. Stürmer suggests that the Weimar Republic was destroyed by the heavy burden of guilt laid on it by the Treaty of Versailles, clearly implying that the same is, or could be, happening to the Federal Republic. His use of the phrase "as Stalin's men sat in judgment in Nuremberg" seems to suggest that German guilt after 1945 was the product of a Communist plot.[15] He has also attempted to downplay German responsibility for the outbreak of the First World War by returning to the old notion of geopolitical determinism—the notion that Germany's position in the center of Europe caused it to become embroiled in major international armed conflicts.[16] Stürmer's emphasis on geopolitical explanations of German history is worth a little closer consideration, not least because it is shared by a number of other neoconservative German historians. Hagen Schulze, for example has declared that "Germany's fate is geography . . . the logic of geography, the position of Germany [on the map] remains a decisive explanation of its internal constitution."[17] Klaus Hildebrand too has placed a similar emphasis on what he sees as the political imperatives of "the country in the middle."[18] Like Schulze, Stürmer has argued that Germany's location in the center of Europe meant that it was threatened on two fronts (namely by France and by Russia). This in turn made it necessary for reasons of national security for the country to be governed by an authoritarian system, under Bismarck and, later, Wilhelm II; and conversely, it rendered the durability of a democratic polity under Weimar extremely problematical.[19]

According to Schulze, the democratization that had already begun to take place before 1914 was the prime factor in undermining Germany's stability in the international system and so in unleashing the First World War. Schulze has also defended the paramilitary Freikorps of the early Weimar Republic, the murderers of Karl Liebknecht and Rosa Luxemburg, as essential guarantors of political stability, and has placed a large part of the blame for the Republic's demise on left-wing intellectuals and Communists.[20] Stürmer has argued along similar lines.[21] These views represent a recrudescence of traditional conservative beliefs going back to the early years of the Weimar Republic. Germany, in this interpretation was "encircled" by her enemies before 1914; the Treaty of Versailles, the Communists, and in general the replacement of authoritarian stability by an excess of democracy combined to destroy Weimar.[22] Such views are quite widely held on the political right. Alfred Dregger, for example, claimed in 1986 that Versailles and reparations delivered Weimar into Hitler's hands.[23] And at the annual convention of the association of German expellees from Silesia in 1985, attended by Helmut Kohl, journalist Timothy Garton Ash reported that "a provincial Christian Democratic leader is hissed and booed when he suggests that the division of Germany was the result of a war *Hitler* began. A brave Young Liberal who suggests in a public discussion that the Versailles Treaty was also the result of a war Germany began is met with hoots of derisive laughter. What, *Germany* began the First World War? Preposterous suggestion!"[24]

It is this kind of thing, surely, that Peter Pulzer, professor of government at Oxford University, means when he warns that "it is with fire that some of the West German conservative historians and their political allies are playing." The danger is, as Pulzer says, not national sentiment in itself, but "a national sentiment that arouses unfulfillable expectations."[25] For insofar as the revival of nationalism in West Germany is linked with the demand for reunification, as it undoubtedly is, for example, in the editorial columns of the *Frankfurter Allgemeine Zeitung*, it is indeed indulging in dangerous political fantasies.[26] Better contacts and easier times for East Germans can only come if East German statehood is accepted. An "Austrian solution"—reunification on the basis of neutrality and disarmament—would still leave open the question of guarantees to the 17 million East Germans that those things many of them evidently believe in, such as an extensive welfare state and social security, would not be taken away from them by a government brought to power by a majority of electors among the 60 million West Germans and determined to dismantle these things. The degree of autonomy that would have to be allowed the territory of the GDR would be such as to create a decentralized, nonunitary national state with a very weak center along the lines of the old German Confederation set up by the Vienna Congress in 1815. One wonders whether it would really be worth the trouble.

III

Mention of the German Confederation reminds us that the present debate implicitly involves questions relating to the interpretation of the nineteenth as well as the twentieth century. In some ways it is the old continuity debate in a new guise. There has been a veritable explosion of good historical research on modern German history since the 1960s. We now know a great deal more about it than we did when the views represented by Stürmer and Schulze, and to some extent Hildebrand and Hillgruber, were more widely current. Virtually all the historians who have looked closely at the origins of World War I have come to the conclusion, often on the basis of impressive archival research, that there was no question of Germany being "encircled" by aggressive foes as a consequence of its geographical position after 1870. Germany itself, above all by starting a massive arms race through the construction of an enormous navy, and then by repeated, aggressive interventions in European, North African, and other world trouble spots, brought about a coalition of the powers which rightly felt threatened by this new policy after the turn of the century— Britain, France, and Russia. Germany was in no sense forced to tread this path as a result of her geographical situation; the experience of the previous thirty years made that abundantly clear.[27]

Nor was it inevitable that the German government should respond to growing internal discontent, expressed above all in the increasing popularity of the Social Democrats, who became the largest party in the German parliament in 1912, by playing the nationalist card. There were voices within the government that favored defusing the campaign for democratization through timely reforms such as the extension of voting rights in Prussia. More important still, the pressures inside Germany for

an aggressive foreign policy were by no means simply the creation of an anxious ruling class: the strident and vociferous
radical nationalism of the prewar years drew much of its
strength from an independent dynamic of self-mobilization
from below. Here some significant social groups, notably the
petty bourgeoisie, engaged in an increasingly desperate search
for survival by stirring radical ideologies, anti-Semitism, extreme nationalism, hostility to modern economic structures,
and demands for political authoritarianism into a potent mix
that was to be brewed up again after the war, to much greater
effect, by the Nazis. Finally, the evidence for supposing that the
German government launched the First World War primarily
in order to escape from internal pressures for more democracy
is extremely thin.[28]

For all these reasons, therefore, it is impossible to accept the
view that the First World War came about for the geopolitical
reasons suggested by Stürmer. There can be no doubt that
Germany bore primary responsibility for the outbreak of the
war. Within a month, the German government had drawn up
an ambitious plan of annexation and conquest. German war
aims were far-reaching, and greatly exceeded those of other
combatant nations in their scope. They included territorial
gains and financial reparations that far outweighed those imposed by the Allies after the German defeat, in the Treaty of
Versailles. Whatever terms had been concluded in 1919, it is
very unlikely that nationalists and conservatives in Germany,
having backed a strongly annexationist program during the war
(and in many cases before it too) would have found them acceptable. The treaty did, to be sure, contain many dubious
provisions. Instead of taking the wind out of the nationalists'
sails, it merely succeeded in giving them further reasons for
discontent. Yet as the criticisms voiced of the treaty by the
Liberals, the Social Democrats, and the Catholic Center
Party—the so-called "Weimar coalition"—showed, opposition
to the treaty did not have to mean opposition to democracy.
Nor was the treaty the sole or even the main cause of Weimar's
demise: a far greater role was played by the Depression of 1929
to 1933, which owed little to the effects of Versailles and was
only marginally influenced by the impact of reparations.[29]

It was not the Communists who brought about the Republic's

collapse: after all, they never succeeded in winning more than 17 percent of the vote. Nor was it Weimar's left-wing intellectuals, many of whom did more to try to strengthen Weimar democracy than to undermine it. The destruction of the Weimar Republic, as numerous scholarly studies have shown, was in the first place the work of the Nazi Party, which gained 37 percent of the vote in 1932, more than any other party had done in the whole history of the Republic, and of the conservative groups which tolerated it or collaborated with it in its establishment of the dictatorship in the first six months of 1933, namely the Army, the industrialists, the large landowners, the senior civil service and other elites who wanted the end of democracy and were not too particular as to how it came about. There is still, of course, considerable controversy about the degree of responsibility borne by each of these groups, but the research of the last two decades leaves little room for doubt that, seen in broad perspective, it was the alliance of the Nazis and the elites that destroyed Weimar, not the activities of Communists and left-wing intellectuals or the Treaty of Versailles.[30]

Seen from this point of view, a more authoritarian, less democratic form of government in Germany after 1919 would only have benefited the nationalists, who wanted to reembark on a course of military expansionism, because the checks imposed on their activities by the Social Democrats and other democratic forces would have been largely removed. What Germany needed in 1919 was a more determined attempt by the Social Democrats to establish democracy. Their failure to bring the Army under firm civilian control was to prove a fatal mistake, while their encouragement of the murderous activities of the paramilitary Freikorps did nothing to stabilize the Republic. Instead, the Freikorps seriously undermined the Republic by attempting a coup in 1920 and then by channeling their activities into the assassination of leading republican politicians by far-right death squads. And the Social Democrats' use of the Freikorps, instead of a workers' militia, to deal with Communist uprisings and revolutionary activities at the beginning of the Republic led to numerous excesses against Communist politicians and their supporters. These stored up bitter resentments for the future and contributed not a little to the division of the labor movement which was to weaken its resistance to Nazism later on.[31]

As we have seen, the advent of Nazism to power led within a few years to the launching of a second major war by Germany against Britain, France, and Russia, this time in pursuit of a program of conquest and domination that was, above all in the East, far more radical and extreme than its counterpart in the First World War. The crimes committed by the Nazis in the process surely demanded a reassertion by the international community of the principle that wars, when they occur, must be conducted according to generally accepted rules designed to maintain as far as possible under the circumstances the basic principles of human decency, and that, however they are fought, wars should not be launched without reasonable justification. It was for these reasons, therefore, that Britain, France, the United States, and Russia decided to try those responsible for these crimes, both at Nuremberg and in lesser trials elsewhere. It may be possible to criticize these procedures on legalistic grounds,[32] but in view of what had happened over the previous few years, it was both necessary and justifiable to bring the culprits to trial and to condemn the crimes they had committed. It was not just "Stalin's men" who sat in judgment at Nuremberg, but the representatives of all the major wartime Allies; in a wider sense, it was humanity.

The experience of the previous half century had shown another thing too. Twice within the space of a few decades, Germany had unleashed global conflict on humankind. Terrible suffering and destruction had been the result. Was it not reasonable, therefore, to take steps this time to ensure that it would not happen again? The decision to reduce German power, to give the eastern territories to Poland and the Soviet Union, to deport the Germans from East-Central Europe, and to divide the Germany that remained was defensible in the light of this experience. It was not carried out in pursuit of a fantasy. Sir Eyre Crowe's famous memorandum of January 1907, in which he made clear to his colleagues the danger to world peace that Germany was then coming to pose, was neither the reflection of a myth nor did it mark the creation of one. The dismemberment of Germany and the transfer of populations did not simply reflect a long-held desire on the part of the British to destroy Prussia. It could be justified, as we have seen, in many ways. Nevertheless, the role of the old elites, of militarism and authoritarianism, in German history from 1870 to 1945, clearly demands closer scrutiny. The Prussian influence on Germany has been widely interpreted by historians as an influence pulling the country away from "Western" values of freedom and democracy toward an "Eastern" model of the strong state. In the final chapter, therefore, we turn to the question of Germany and its relations with the West, and ask, in conclusion, whether the present debate gives us cause for anxiety for the future on this account.

CHAPTER SIX

GERMANY AND
THE WEST

I

Reviving the idea of a reunited Germany dominating
Central Europe is not the only way in which, as Peter Pulzer
has pointed out, the new historical conservatism in West Germany is playing with fire. Dangerous too in his view is its assertion of "a patriotism that seeks to suppress genuine pluralism of
opinion and interests." Michael Stürmer and Hagen Schulze
apparently believe that Germany can only be a stable, peaceful
power, as it was under Bismarck, on the basis of an authoritarian
political system allied to a strong and unified national consciousness. If the logic of geopolitics holds good, then the same must
be true today. Stürmer argues repeatedly that too much pluralism of values and interests, unchecked by a unifying national
consensus, destabilized Wilhelmine Germany and helped overthrow the Weimar Republic once it got into economic difficulties. Thus for today he seeks nothing less than the creation of
a substitute religion, a nationalist faith held by all, which will
lend calculability to West Germany's foreign policy by providing its citizens with a new sense of identity held together by
patriotism, and resting on a unitary, undisputed, and positive

consciousness of German history unsullied by negative guilt feelings about the German past.[1]

It was perhaps above all on this point that Stürmer drew the fire of Jürgen Habermas, in a newspaper article published in 1986. As the first person to place Nolte, Hillgruber, and Stürmer in the same context and to sound the alarm about their collective contribution to the revision of German history, Habermas has good claim to be considered the originator of the whole debate. Habermas, who teaches at Frankfurt University, is probably Germany's best-known contemporary philosopher, but he is equally at home in the fields of history and sociology. This breadth of interest—and influence—reflects his indebtedness to the "Frankfurt School" of Marxist social scientists, whose most prominent member was probably Herbert Marcuse. The Marxism of the Frankfurt School was anything but politically activist, despite Marcuse's involvement in the radical movements of the 1960s, and it had long since become detached from any real identification with Communism. Indeed, Habermas considered the thrust of the neoconservative historians' program, toward a "reconstruction of the destroyed center of Europe" in a Germany unified by an undisputed national consciousness, as a call to abandon the "unreserved opening of the Federal Republic to the political culture of the West . . . the great intellectual achievement of our postwar period."

Yet what Habermas meant by "the West" was not the same as what was meant by those whom he criticized. While Stürmer considered "the West" to mean NATO, Habermas viewed "the West" in terms of the liberal and democratic political tradition established by the eighteenth-century Enlightenment. Like most liberal and Social Democratic German intellectuals of his generation, Habermas considered that the history of Germany before 1945 had taken a "separate path" from that of the West (by which was meant Britain, France, and the United States). German intellectuals and academics in the late nineteenth and early twentieth centuries tended to reject values such as pluralism and democracy, and regarded the "German way" of thinking, with its emphasis given to nationalism and authoritarianism, as superior. This situation was particularly evident in the West German historical profession, which, as Habermas pointed out, had been all but hermetically sealed against alternative points of view until long after the Second World War.[2]

It is worth digressing for a moment, to explore briefly the development of West German historical scholarship since 1945, in order to make clear precisely what are the developments against which Stürmer is reacting. Up to the early 1960s, the old school of historians trained in the Weimar Republic continued to dominate the academic scene in the Federal Republic. Politically and methodologically conservative, they perpetuated the tradition of German historicism, with its claim to understand the past on its own terms, its concentration on high politics and diplomacy, and its allegiance to a fundamentally nationalist viewpoint. They absolved Germany from any special blame for the outbreak of the First World War, saw the Third Reich as an aberration from the sound traditions of German history, and in many ways their views were similar to those which Stürmer now expresses. Then Hamburg historian Fritz Fischer broke ranks by presenting a meticulously documented account of Germany's far-reaching plans for European hegemony and world power between 1914 and 1918 and a challenging thesis of a continuity between Imperial Germany and the Third Reich. A heated controversy ensued. Fischer was accused of besmirching Germany's good name. A government grant enabling him to lecture in America was withdrawn. Prominent conservative historians refused to shake hands with him in public. All the methods which had previously guaranteed unanimity in the historical profession were brought into action.

But this time things were different. The political and intellectual scene in West Germany was now too open for such a discussion to be strangled at birth. Contact with American historians and the international scholarly community made isolation impossible. The debate continued unabated over several years in the 1960s, when it was fought out not only in books, learned journals, and academic conferences, but also in the mass media. Finally, the dust began to settle. It became clear that Fischer's work had inspired a wholesale revision of German historiography undertaken by a generation of younger historians. Historicism was out, social science was in. Germany was assigned the lion's share of responsibility for the outbreak of war in 1914. The Third Reich appeared not as the negation of German nationalist historical traditions but as their culmination. The blame was laid squarely at the feet of the Prussian aristocracy, with its antidemocratic, militaristic ideology and its ever-growing willingness to employ radical methods to ward off the democratizing consequences of the industrial age. By the early 1970s, historians were speaking of a "change of paradigm" in German historical scholarship which had succeeded in establishing the intellectual dominance of a "new orthodoxy" that was in many respects highly critical of the German past.[3]

Central to this view is an acceptance of the singularity of German history. It is argued that, uniquely among modern nations, Germany experienced industrialization without going through a bourgeois revolution. Thus economic might was subordinated to political reaction. The middle classes were bribed into political quiescence through the lure of "feudalization"—titles, honors, and other trappings of the aristocracy. The proletariat was denied full participation in the political process. The petty bourgeoisie was mobilized against democracy by the demagogy of the ruling elite. This unique path to modernity eventually culminated in the unique phenomenon of National Socialism, whose crimes were without parallel in human history. Only with the destruction in quick succession of the Prussian aristocracy and of the Third Reich itself could Germany finally achieve a normal modernity. The price paid was total military defeat and (as it increasingly seemed) permanent political dismemberment. It is time, in this view, to come to terms with the German past—time to admit and ruthlessly to expose its shortcomings, time to make a fresh start. The continued success of a pluralist, Western-style democracy in the Federal Republic demands, it is argued, that the Germans free themselves from the burden of the German past. Nineteen forty-five was zero hour. The rest belonged to history.[4]

Thus two diametrically opposed routes to overcoming the German past have been presented. Conservatives like Stürmer emphasize the modernity of Nazism, its lack of roots in German history, its complete dependence on the demonic genius of Hitler, and its affinities with Stalinism as a "totalitarian" creed. The way to prevent it from happening again, they suggest, is to return to the sounder traditions of the German past, to Christian morality, to the old Prussian virtues of honor, rectitude, disinterested service to the state by its servants, and obedience to its dictates by its subjects. Liberal and Social Democrat historians like Hans-Ulrich Wehler emphasize the traditional aspects of Nazism, its harking back to a pseudomedieval past, its inheritance of the Prussian legacy of militarism and authoritarianism, and its roots in the disaffection of agrarian and aristocratic elites and peasants and "preindustrial" artisans from the modern world. The way to prevent it from happening again, they suggest, is to embrace fully the achievements of modernity: to return from the "special path" by which Germany had failed to emulate the West's conjunction of economic industrialization, social openness, and political democratization in the nineteenth century, to a world of "Western" values of modern life in which these things had long since been joined.

Yet it may be appropriate for an outsider to the debate to suggest that other positions are also possible. We have already seen, for example, how Hitler's own beliefs and aims can neither be plausibly left out of account in trying to explain the course of anti-Semitism in the "Third Reich," nor on the other hand can they be made convincingly responsible for the entire timing and sequence of the terrible events which those beliefs and aims so fatefully encouraged. On a larger historical time scale, it seems equally reasonable to argue that Nazism was neither wholly a product of the modern age, nor wholly a vehicle for pre- and antimodern ideologies and social classes. Too much emphasis has been placed on "preindustrial traditions" in the explanations offered by liberal and Social Democratic historians for the rise of Nazism. A comparison with other industrializing countries in the nineteenth century suggests that it is very difficult to maintain that industrialization failed to bring democracy with it only in the German case. France, for instance, underwent authoritarian episodes both after its successful revolution (under Napoleon I) and at the height of the industrialization process (under Napoleon III), while Britain industrialized only under conditions of a very limited franchise and, from the 1790s to the 1820s, with draconian laws against political radicalism that far outdid any of the restrictions imposed on the Social Democrats in Imperial Germany in the late nineteenth century.

To make these points does not mean abandoning the location

of Nazism's roots in the German past. Bismarckian Germany has been seen either as a stable, well-run state which should have been a model for later regimes, or as an authoritarian, semifeudal dictatorship which preserved many of the features of Prusso-German traditionalism so that they could survive and eventually come to fruition in the Third Reich. Yet if we argue that both pictures overestimate its stability and its inability to reform itself and suggest that both Bismarckian and Wilhelmine Germany were dynamic, rapidly developing societies with a considerable capacity for change, this is not to deny that among the changes that took place in that era were some that were later, though by no means inevitably, to lead to Nazism. The rise of racial anti-Semitism and radical nationalism at this time might be a case in point. Pre-1914 Germany saw many progressive developments, such as the beginnings of welfarism or the rise of a feminist movement and the first adumbrations of women's emancipation, which, whatever their limitations, and whatever the direction they eventually took, make it impossible to regard the era merely as one of conservative stagnation. The beginnings of the "crisis of modernity" which was to engulf Weimar were already there before the First World War.

To point this out is not to prescribe a solution involving the rejection of modernity and a return to some imaginary past stability. It is, rather, to say that historical problems such as the preservation of democracy in the Weimar Republic must be addressed in their real historical context. In this case, the context was a modernization that nobody, least of all the historian, could wish away. The task of avoiding the collapse into barbarism could only be undertaken on the basis of an acceptance of democracy and welfare and a rejection of militarism and national aggrandizement. It was Weimar's tragedy that, in the end, circumstances conspired to prevent this task from being successfully accomplished.[5] Yet historians like Stürmer are less interested in trying to understand Weimar's collapse than in using it for their own political purposes in the present day. And their opponents react against the new conservatism with a vehemence that is similarly the product not least of contemporary political commitment.

Thus from the very start, the debate has been locked into two opposing interpretations. Each side has become increasingly entrenched in its own position, and the possibilities of a more nuanced view, in which a synthesis of the most persuasive features of each could be achieved as the basis for moving research forward, has been rendered all but impossible. Such is the political sensitivity of the issues in question, such is the moral charge with which each attempt to stake out a position on these matters has become loaded, that even the slightest move to criticize the one or the other, to mediate between them, or to go beyond them, has met with violent polemics, accusations of trivialization, moral denunciation, and allegations of trying to undermine the West German political system. Thus the bitterness and rancor with which the controversy has been waged. Scholarly decency and civilized standards of academic debate have been among the most obvious losers in the present debate. As a historian of the younger generation, Detlev Peukert, has remarked, the cultivation of civilized controversy is necessary in every academic discipline if progress in understanding is to be achieved. This means, however, the ability to give and take and above all to modify one's position in the light of new arguments or new facts. To an outsider, the standards of historical controversy in West Germany have long seemed rather low in this respect. There can be little doubt that in the present debate they have plumbed new depths.[6]

That is not to say, of course, that all this is the product of some innate predisposition to quarrelsomeness in the West German academic profession.[7] British historians, for example, can look back on a no less combative tradition, stretching from the great controversies waged in the Victorian era between J. H. Round and E. A. Freeman over the meaning of the Norman Conquest, through the perennial all-out fight that seems to constitute the historiography of the English Civil War, to the notorious rows of the 1950s and 1960s between Eric Hobsbawm and R. M. Hartwell on the standard of living during the industrial revolution, or between A. J. P. Taylor and Hugh R. Trevor-Roper over the origins of the Second World War. Similarly, French historians have an even longer tradition of arguing with one another, sometimes with considerable bitterness and rancor, about the origins, meaning, and consequences of the great French Revolution of 1789. *Odium scholasticum* is not a German monopoly. It has, indeed, frequently manifested itself in the United

States—recently, for instance, in the debate on the role of heavy industrial and agrarian interests in the coming of the Third Reich sparked by David Abraham's controversial *Collapse of the Weimar Republic.*[8] To declare that one's opponents have been manipulating quotations, are lumping together people and arguments that do not belong together, are accusing one of saying things one has not said, are filled with ill will, are ignorant outsiders, or do not deserve to be treated as colleagues at all—these methods of argument seem to be the stock-in-trade of scholarly debate once it reaches a certain stage of animation. Nevertheless, the degree of rhetorical aggression compatible with respect for one's colleagues and the maintenance of reasonable human relations within the historical profession now seems to have been exceeded in West Germany. The actual purpose of it all seems to have been largely submerged under an accumulation of personal animosities.[9]

II

Making these points should cause us to reflect on the implications of the present debate for the future study of modern German history. In many ways, the discussion we have been following in this book, despite—or perhaps in part because of—the passions it has aroused, has very little to offer anyone with a serious, scholarly interest in the German past. It brings no new facts to light; it embodies no new research; it makes no new contribution to historical understanding; it poses no new questions that might stimulate future work. It is quite different from the Fischer controversy, which was fought out by traditional scholarly methods, for all the violence of its rhetoric, and brought a mass of new documentation to light, as well as facilitating the employment of a variety of new methods in the study of the German past. So it is scarcely surprising that some commentators on the present discussion have wanted to stop the whole affair and get historians back to writing real history.[10] But the debate is much more than a diversion. It has obvious implications for the way in which history is written. What seems to be going on, as Martin Broszat has commented, is an attempt to revive the old Prussian tradition of historicism, which assigned to history the function of supporting the political status quo. Like a substitute religion, it served the interest of the state by confining itself to an affirmative chronicling of the state's past.[11] History seems to be understood by this tradition in a metaphysical sense as the past in itself, not as the past critically reconstructed by historians—hence, one might note, Hillgruber's assumption that the historian "identifies" with a particular past actor or actors (in his case, the German Army fighting on the eastern front in 1944–45) and his failure to understand that these actors are in part constructed by the interpretations that he himself advances. Yet historians cannot simply content themselves with taking on what they imagine to be the viewpoint of the past itself; they must also adopt their own viewpoints, independently and self-consciously, with benefit of hindsight. The diplomatic historian Paul Kennedy observed some years ago that nationalist historiography was on the wane in the West. Politically speaking, the tradition of German historicism resulted in generations of German historians becoming the willing tools of German great-power ambitions, up to and including those of Hitler. Surely, this should serve as a warning to those who would seek a revival of this tradition in the present.[12]

At a less political, more scholarly level, many of the new nationalist West German historians also seem to share a common belief in political history of the most traditional kind, whereby the study of the past once more becomes the study of kings and battles, chancellors and cabinets, and history is again seen as being made not by broad, general forces but by great (or not so great) men such as Hitler or Stresemann, Bismarck or Brüning. Such, at any rate, is the message of Hagen Schulze's *Weimar* and of Michael Stürmer's recent brief biography of Bismarck.[13] Social and economic history is condemned as irrelevant or simply ignored altogether. It is entirely characteristic, for example, that Hillgruber suggests that the task of explaining how otherwise civilized German people could take part in the crimes of the Nazis belongs not to historians but to psychologists and anthropologists.[14] An approach to the past that dismisses social and economic factors may help deliver a new nationalist ideology, but it cannot deliver good history. It is what one critic has called "an attempt to turn the clock back to 1955, when the

West German historical scene had not yet been cluttered with social history" and when historical scholarship moved "within the relatively familiar and comfortable parameters of party politics and the constitution."[15] Such a narrowing of focus represents a real impoverishment of historical understanding, and it is not surprising that, in arguing against the neoconservatives, some of West Germany's leading historians of the Weimar and Nazi periods have explicitly defended social-historical approaches to Germany's recent past.

These proponents of social history include Martin Broszat, who elsewhere has also argued for what he calls a "historicization" of National Socialism. This fact should alert us to the need to avoid confusing the neoconservative "historicism" with the call for "historicization." The latter involves a rational approach to Nazism rather than a simple reliance on moral condemnation. Nazism and its effects cannot be made real to people who, like most of today's West Germans, were born long after the event, if they are presented in crude terms of heroes and villains. The nature of the moral choices people had to make can only be accurately judged by taking into account the full complexities of the situations in which they found themselves. Not everything that happened under Hitler was equally evil; not everyone who resisted was equally good. German society shows many continuous developments cutting across the period 1933–45, with deeper roots in the past and with consequences stretching beyond the collapse of the Third Reich into the present.[16] This approach has yielded many important new insights into the nature of Nazism. Far from blurring moral distinctions, as some have claimed, it makes them more precise. This is surely a gain rather than a loss for historical understanding.[17]

The growth of such a broader, more nuanced approach to the history of the Third Reich is a world away from the concentration on high politics and on the personality of Hitler, the calls for identification with German troops fighting Communism in 1945, or the search for exculpatory parallels and circumstances that are the hallmarks of the neoconservatives. It suggests that in the end, the demand that history should form the basis for an entire national consciousness is misplaced. Such a demand overestimates the historian's influence by a considerable margin. And several contributors to the debate have also argued that it is no longer possible in a pluralistic society such as West Germany to impose a single interpretation of history on the popular consciousness.[18] Nor is it likely that nearly two decades of intensive research on social and economic history can simply be forgotten about and thrown away. In a democratic society, historical events are inevitably going to be understood in a variety of ways. Any overall understanding of the past in a free intellectual culture must take account of these different points of view. So no one is going to obtain a monopoly on the portrayal of Germany's past while the Federal Republic of Germany remains a relatively free society.

Of course, the debate within West Germany is taking place in a context in which Chancellor Kohl's conservative coalition has for some time been pursuing a policy of placing its own adherents in charge of the country's radio and television stations; the press is heavily dominated by supporters of the ruling coalition; and state control over the schools curriculum, over history text books, and over senior historical appointments, is extensive. A new generation of teachers and school directors is steering the teaching of recent German history back to the lamentable situation of the 1950s, and the critical history teachers who entered the profession after 1968 are slowly being muzzled by pressures from parents and politicians. But the federal system places strict limits on the ability of the conservatives to influence media policy in states such as Hamburg, Schleswig-Holstein, or the Saarland, which are ruled by the opposition Social Democrats and their partners. Printing technology allows critical dailies to be printed far more cheaply than was once the case, as the rise of the left-wing *Die Tageszeitung* has shown. No one has yet found a way to stop critical views of the past being written and sold in books with a very wide circulation. In 1985, 54 percent of West Germans questioned in an opinion poll said that they did not want to hear any more about the Third Reich in the media. But among eighteen-to-twenty-five-year-olds, 61 percent disagreed with the point of view and thought that they had not heard enough.[19] Conservative historians have certainly been taking the "long march through the institutions," and have gained considerably in influence recently in terms of academic politics. This is a worrying development for those who want to encourage a critical attitude to the

German past. But it is an exaggeration to suppose that conservatives have been getting all the plum jobs as a result of concerted maneuvers behind the scenes.

Moreover, German history does not simply belong to the Germans. The rest of the world has an intense and legitimate interest in German attitudes to the recent past and Germans' feelings about their national identity and purpose. After an initial slowness to react, historians and commentators in many countries have turned their attention to the present debate. In France, discussion centered on the issues raised by the trial of Klaus Barbie for crimes committed in France during the war. In Italy, Nolte's theses in particular aroused strong disapproval in the media, while reactions to the debate in Israel, the United States, and the Soviet bloc (especially East Germany) combined the language of moral outrage with a reaffirmation of the uniqueness of Auschwitz.[20] Even those few conservative commentators who were willing to go along with Nolte to some extent on the latter issue were unwilling to follow him down the road of justifying a putative "internment" of German Jews as prisoners of war in 1939.[21] International surprise and dismay at the conservative revisionists' attempt to trivialize Nazi crimes—as it has widely been seen outside Germany—has been general and strongly felt. Perhaps the reaction from other countries has concentrated too much on one issue and one historian and, therefore, neglected or passed over too many of the other issues involved. Perhaps also it has expressed itself too much in the language of moral outrage and not enough in the calmer tones of scholarly debate. But the fact that it has been overwhelmingly negative confirms the failure of the revisionists to achieve their aims in a wider international context.

Indeed, if we try to draw up a balance of gains and losses in the present dispute, there can be little doubt as to which side has come out the winner in the argument. The revisionists have not been able to put forward any convincing new interpretations, nor have their documentary finds been able to stand the test of scholarly scrutiny. Indeed, particularly in Stürmer's case, they have resurrected arguments long since discarded by serious scholarship without providing any reasonable case for doing so. The vast majority of historians in West Germany who have engaged these issues have come out clearly against the idea that

Auschwitz was a copy of the Gulag, or indeed that it has significant historical parallels anywhere. They have responded with
considerable skepticism to the idea that Germany's recent history was determined by the country's geopolitical position. And
while they have been generally less critical of Hillgruber than
of Nolte, they have found it impossible to accept his idea that
present-day West Germans should "identify" with the German
Army on the eastern front in 1944–45. The debate has done
some damage to the national, and in particular the international, scholarly standing of Hillgruber, considerably more to
that of Stürmer, and a great deal to that of Nolte. As far as the
world of historical scholarship and research is concerned, the
attempt to escape from Hitler's shadow has clearly failed. The
bid to forget about Auschwitz, if that is what it is, has resulted
simply in the most intensive discussion of the subject that has
taken place for years.[22]

The argument, however, has not simply been fought out
within the confines of learned journals and university conferences and seminars. It has also been carried on in the mass
media. Here the results have been less clear-cut. Even if—as
with the treatment of the "preventive-war" theory by the
Frankfurter Allgemeine Zeitung—the outcome in terms of the
strength of the various theses advanced has either been inconclusive or generally a defeat, once more, for the revisionists, the
fact remains that Nolte in particular, and perhaps other revisionists (such as Hoffmann and Stegemann) as well, have succeeded in lending a degree of respectability to arguments
which a few years ago were only to be found in the indecent
obscurity of the radical-right and neo-Nazi press. Discussion of
the preventive-war thesis, assertions of the priority of the Gulag
and the relativity of Auschwitz, and pleas for a new, sanitized
version of German history have become relatively commonplace in organs such as the *Frankfurter Allgemeine Zeitung,*
where they would not have found an outlet before the present
controversy.[23]

With the backing of the Kohl government and provincial
Christian Democrats when it comes to academic appointments
and careers too, revisionist historians have achieved positions of
influence from which they may well have an impact on the
theories and methods adopted by the younger generation of

German historians, especially now that academic jobs are hard to come by. We may, therefore, see a shift away from the recent broad approach to the past and the recent willingness to take in the methods and concerns of social, economic, and demographic history, sociological theory, and quantitative methodology, back to a narrower concentration on the history of high politics using the methodological tools of German historicism. But this too should not be exaggerated. Moreover, it is important to emphasize that German historians are not abandoning "the West" in seeking to contribute more positively to a sense of national identity. Since the end of the 1960s or thereabouts, the historical profession in the Federal Republic has become well integrated into the international community of historians, and the turn to a more nationalist understanding of history to a large extent reflects a current international trend.

For the emergence of a neoconservative historiography with pronounced historicist and nationalist tendencies is far from being a phenomenon peculiar to the Germans. Britain and the United States, in the decade of Prime Minister Thatcher and President Reagan, have also experienced a resurgence of conservative thought. Conservative British historians such as Hugh Thomas and G. R. Elton have been calling for a return to studying the past in order to help bring about a resurgence of national pride. Others, like David Cannadine, have lamented the alleged collapse of a coherent and positive vision of the nation's past or, like J. C. D. Clark, have attempted to reassert the centrality of Church and Crown in the making of modern Britain.[24] Such initiatives have been supported by Prime Minister Thatcher's crusading conservatism, which seeks to resurrect "Victorian values" such as "self-reliance . . . self-respect . . . pride in your country." Thatcher herself has inveighed against those who, as she sees it, "gnaw away at our national self-respect, rewriting British history as centuries of unrelieved gloom, oppression and failure—as days of hopelessness, not days of hope."[25] Her calls for a positive interpretation of the British past are clearly intended to be reflected in the incorporation of history in a "national curriculum" in the schools. Similarly, U.S. Secretary of Education William Bennett urged "the study of history" in order to "give our students a grasp of their nation, a nation that the study of history and current events will reveal is still, indeed, 'the last, best hope on earth,' " and he has been backed up by conservative historians such as Gertrude Himmelfarb, who has launched a sharp and politically loaded attack on the study of social history.[26]

Yet these pleas, powerful though they may be, inevitably come up very quickly against the limits of possibility. History can help us to gain identity, but that identity must necessarily transcend the past. Being German, or British, or American in the late twentieth century inevitably means something different from what it meant fifty years ago. National identity is always changing. In continually constructing and reconstructing it, we have to decide what we want to keep and what we want to jettison, what we agree is good and what we reject as bad. Within the same nation, people will always define their historical identity in different ways, and it is part of the richness of national feeling that they should do so. As former West German President Gustav Heinemann once pointed out, the Federal Republic owes more to the tradition of Bebel and Liebknecht, who were sitting in jail when the German Empire was founded, than to the example of Bismarck or Kaiser Wilhelm. Germany has been described as a postnational society;[27] local and regional traditions have proved more durable than national ones and in some cases are being created where they never existed before. Indeed, German art, music, and other cultural achievements owe a great deal to traditions of political disunity and decentralization.[28] It is no accident, therefore, that recent years have seen a tremendous upsurge of interest in history on a smaller, more intimate scale—one that can help people identify with smaller groupings such as the family, the street, the neighborhood, or the village. At a time when the negative aspects of living in an advanced industrial society—from mass unemployment to environmental pollution and the threat of nuclear catastrophe—have suddenly become more obvious, it is scarcely surprising that historians have begun investigating the human cost of industrialization and the nature of everyday life in the industrial and preindustrial past, not just in Germany, but in many other parts of the developed world as well.

The recent growth of "grass-roots" history in West Germany has mostly been carried on by local "initiatives" outside the arena of professional university history. Its focus has been on recovering the history of everyday life in Germany, above all during the Nazi and postwar periods, and especially though not exclusively by using oral-history interviews with those who have lived through the period. This is a very widespread and diverse movement which has produced work of varying quality. At its worst, it is open to the charge that it trivializes the phenomenon of Nazism by concentrating on private lives which—in the memories of those questioned—were barely touched by it. But there are a number of important points to be made in defense of this "alternative" history. Its thrust is overwhelmingly critical. Time and again, it has uncovered local complicity in Nazism and its crimes both in the form of the acts of individuals and in major, collective events, which official local tradition, preserved by politicians, official histories, archivists, and administrators, has for so long tried to suppress. Underlying much of this "alternative" work is the consciousness that everyday normality and Auschwitz were interdependent, that the Germans who conformed were doing so because they had been selected for survival, because they were not subject to the various forms of discrimination that governed life in Nazi Germany.

Local history of this kind has revealed, and treated in a positive sense, numerous forms of resistance to Nazism at a local level, and has consciously tried to use these as a means of demonstrating the possibilities and limitations of resistance to fascism to the inhabitants of today's German towns and cities. Although this has sometimes been at the cost of neglecting the history of collaboration and affirmation in the Third Reich, this has nonetheless constituted a real attempt to create traditions of resistance with which ordinary people can identify, in contrast to the remote and largely conservative and aristocratic figures of July 1944. Here too "identification," as with the rather different case of Hillgruber and the soldiers on the eastern front, has sometimes been naive and uncritical. But it does make it difficult to sustain the argument that ordinary people were not aware of the evils of Nazism, or that murder, brutality, and extermination happened only far away, somewhere in the East. For all its contradictions and its flaws, therefore, the popular movement for the recovery of the history of everyday life does in the end place an important barrier in the way of conservative attempts to manufacture a new German nationalist ideology on the basis of relativizing or forgetting about the crimes of Nazism. In the last few years, it has done an enormous amount to spread the recollection of those crimes and extend popular knowledge of their scope. Finally, those who associate this movement with the German Green Party (not entirely unjustifiably), and see both as the vehicles of a revived German nationalism in their own way, would be well to remember that the Green deputies were the only ones in the Federal German Parliament to vote to cancel the invitation to U.S. President Ronald Reagan to visit the military cemetery at Bitburg in 1985.[29]

Besides helping recover national or local identities, history can also contribute to our identity in the widest possible sense—as human beings. It illuminates the human condition by confronting us with ways of thinking and behaving that may seem alien because they are separated from us by time but that are nevertheless directly relevant because they are human. Thus history can illustrate the possibilities of human behavior in ways that no other discipline can. That is why the Third Reich remains of abiding interest not just to the Germans themselves but also to humankind as a whole. It continues, rightly, to be seen as the paradigm of the collapse of civilization into barbarism.[30] It stands as a dreadful warning of the destructive potential of technology. It shows the ultimate consequences of racism; indeed, this is one reason why racism has been condemned so universally since 1945 and why South Africa stands isolated in the world community today. The Third Reich's bureaucratic deformation of language, its exaltation of ideological fanaticism, its cult of unthinking obedience to orders—all this, and much more, confronts us with the meaning of the pale reflections of these things that sometimes find places in our own lives. In many ways, therefore, the experience of Nazism and its crimes is of universal significance. Yet this still leaves unanswered the original questions with which the neoconservative revisionists began: What has the significance of the Third Reich been for the growth and development of West German society? How should Germans regard their past, and in particular this episode within it, now that half a century has passed and most of those responsible are dead? And for those of us outside present-day Germany, what does it mean for the way we see Germany and the Germans now? What significance does it have for Germany's place and reputation in the community of nations?

III

The emotive language with which many of the arguments of the West German revisionists have been greeted, the storm of moral anathemas which has rained down upon their heads, the often personal tone of the attacks on their theses—all this may reflect to some extent the customary manner in which historical and political controversy is conducted in the Federal Republic. But since such responses have also been common among outside observers, it clearly also constitutes a phenomenon of a broader and more general nature. For just as positions have become entrenched in the debate itself, so attitudes toward Germans and their Nazi past have become deeply embedded in wide areas of international opinion as well. There is still a great deal of anxiety about Germany and the Germans in the world. This is understandable enough and, as some of the facts and arguments presented in this short book may indicate, in some ways it is defensible. Yet there can be no denying that in some respects, and on some occasions, it has led to overreaction. Just as Nazism has become a symbol for absolute evil, so too everyone who had any connection with it runs the risk of being regarded as an absolutely evil person. Yet to make reasonable and meaningful moral judgments, a careful degree of differentiation is required. Two recent examples might help to make this clear.

Take first the case of Austrian President Dr. Kurt Waldheim, former secretary-general of the United Nations. Like many Austrian men of his generation—he was born in 1918—Waldheim served in the German Army after Hitler's annexation of Austria in 1938. He was badly wounded in the Russian campaign in 1941, and, according to his autobiography and his many subsequent public statements, he spent the rest of the war in Vienna, convalescing and completing his doctorate in law. While he was running for president, however, his opponents discovered he had been lying. Not only had he recovered from his wounds, he also served later in the war with the German Army in Yugoslavia and Greece, where he had been attached to units which were heavily involved in war crimes such as the massacre of civilians and the deportation of Jews to Auschwitz. International reaction was immediate. "Waldheim Was SS Butcher," claimed the *New York Post;* and a flood of stories in the international press, as well as at least one booklength publication, accused Waldheim of having been a "war criminal."[31]

The truth, however, turned out to be more prosaic. A very thorough investigation by historian Robert Herzstein, commissioned by the World Jewish Congress, came to the conclusion that Waldheim was not guilty of any war crimes as defined by the Nuremberg Tribunal. He had not personally murdered civilians or ordered the deportation of Jews. An International Historians' Commission, appointed by Waldheim himself, but consisting of expert scholars of undoubted integrity, came to similar conclusions. But at the same time, there was ample evidence to show that, as an intelligence officer in Greece and Yugoslavia, Waldheim had been well aware of the crimes that were being committed. Indeed, on one occasion he had even ventured to pen a report to higher authority that questioned the wisdom of the savagery customarily shown by the German Army toward the occupied population in these countries, an act that required a considerable degree of courage. Waldheim was not a committed Nazi but an opportunist. In this sense, he went along with the Nazi regime, even, apart from the one instance just quoted, when it was engaged in committing crimes of great cruelty and barbarity. In covering up his past after the war—even more, in tacitly condoning the anti-Semitic undertones which were apparent in his election campaign—Waldheim demonstrated the complete failure of his country to come to terms with the past. In its stifling corporatism, its continuing tradition of popular anti-Semitism, and its national evasion of responsibility for its role in the crimes of the Third Reich, contemporary Austria has demonstrated disturbing continuities with the Austria of the "clerico-fascist" and National Socialist past, continuities the figure of Kurt Waldheim symbolized. It is for this reason, because of his thoroughly representative character, that Waldheim has not so far come under overwhelming pressure from his fellow Austrians to resign.[32]

If one were to ask whether an affair such as this would be possible across the border in West Germany, the answer would probably have to be in the affirmative, but with reservations. Individuals with far murkier pasts than Waldheim's have made it to the top of West German civil and political society. A recent example is that of Hans Filbinger, Christian Democratic minister-president of the southwest German state of Baden-Württemberg, and therefore, in West Germany's federal system, one of the most important politicians in the country. While in office, Filbinger was discovered to have been a military judge who passed death sentences on anti-Nazi German soldiers in the last days of the war. Filbinger, like Waldheim, insisted he had done nothing wrong. Unlike Waldheim, however, he had to go. Subsequently, he has been active in propagating the idea that Germans of his generation have been unjustly maligned.[33] But public opinion in West Germany is a good deal more hostile toward this point of view than it is in Austria. The collective amnesia of the reconstruction period in the 1950s has continued in Austria up to the present; in Germany during the 1960s and 1970s, however, there was at least a partial recovery of public memory. A figure like Waldheim might have become president of West Germany, but he would not have been able to continue in office after the discovery of his dubious past.

A very different case from that of President Waldheim is the unfortunate episode of Philipp Jenninger, who until November 1988 was Speaker of the West German Parliament, the Bundestag. It fell to Jenninger to deliver a speech to the German parliamentarians and invited guests on the fiftieth anniversary of the Nazi pogrom against the Jews, the "Night of Broken Glass," on November 9, 1938. The speech was a disaster. Several deputies walked out in protest shortly after it had begun, and uproar ensued in the news media after it had finished. Jenninger was accused of justifying Nazism and had to resign. The novelist Stefan Heym said that Jenninger would be described in literature as an advocate of the devil. The Israeli magazine *Maariv* headlined its story "Jenninger defends Nazi era." The East German news agency ADN more cautiously described the speech as "giving the impression of a justification of Nazi rule." The Italian daily newspaper *Corriere della Sera* had no such reservations: "Hitler gave us a fantastic time," was its summary of the speech, and its conclusion was that "anti-Semitism blows up again in the German parliament." A spokesman of the World Jewish Congress said, "We are shocked."

Reading the text of Jenninger's speech in cold print after the event, however, it is difficult to understand what all the fuss was about. Much of the criticism seemed either exaggerated or beside the point. Jenninger described the events of the pogrom accurately and made clear his condemnation of them. He went on to outline the anti-Semitic policies that preceded and followed it, culminating in the extermination at Auschwitz, Treblinka, and elsewhere. More than this, Jenninger located these events in German history, traced back the course of German anti-Semitism into the nineteenth century, and criticized the suppression of consciousness and memory in West Germany after 1945. And he explicitly rejected what he called the "senseless" demand to draw a line after fifty years and start afresh. "Our past," he said, in a direct reference to Nolte's article that had started off the debate on the place of Nazism in West German political culture in 1986, "will not rest, neither will it pass away." All this was far removed from the shibboleths of the neoconservatives. Even more remarkable was Jenninger's admission that the majority of Germans had supported or tolerated Hitler as he restored Germany's international position between 1933 and 1938. "Who would wish to deny," he asked rhetorically, "that the great majority of Germans stood behind him in 1938 and identified with him and his policies?"

Here, however, lay the essence of Jenninger's blunder. For he went on to describe the "triumphal political progress" during Hitler's first years of dictatorship in terms that failed to make it clear that Jenninger himself did not share this view of the Nazis' "achievements," terms that suggested, indeed, that he regarded them as real. Moreover, a careless choice of words repeatedly implied, particularly in the early passages of the speech, that present-day Germans should identify with the majority who supported Hitler in 1938, rather than with the minorities who suffered at his hands. Many commentators also found the balance of the speech offensive. "When one is delivering a funeral speech for a murder victim," one journalist commented, "one does not dwell on the good qualities of the murderer." Finally, those who watched the speech were dismayed by the routine tone of its delivery. It was as if Jenninger were reading a seminar paper, rather than trying to find words of atonement for a horrific crime. Nevertheless, for all its inadequacies, the speech was far more open and honest in its confrontation with the past than one has come to expect from the Kohl government and its supporters. And that, of course, is why the Kohl government found it so easy to let Jenninger go. Kohl's first choice as his successor was the right-wing politician Alfred Dregger, whose views on the Nazi past are much closer to those of Nolte and Hillgruber. Only the fact that Dregger eventually resisted being "kicked upstairs" in this manner prevented the post—with its duties including the delivery of a number of speeches on sensitive historical issues in the anniversary year of 1989—being filled by a man who really does believe in drawing a veil over Nazism.[34]

The Jenninger affair thus demonstrated that there is at least some truth in what Nolte and the other neoconservatives have been saying: West German and international opinion is indeed often oversensitive toward any event in the Federal Republic that, superficially at least, appears at first sight suggestive of a revival of the Nazi past. This is not to say, however, that there are no connections at all between present-day West Germany and Hitler's Third Reich—only that the continuities with the Nazi period are subtler and less obvious in West Germany than in Austria. There are of course legal continuities, as many of the legal decisions taken under the Third Reich continue for various reasons to be regarded as valid. The widespread official refusal to clear the names of Communists unjustly condemned under the Nazis, the continued official reluctance to compensate individuals subjected by the Nazis to compulsory sterilization, the persistent failure to bring the perpetrators of Nazi crimes, and the servants of Nazi "justice," to book—all these disgrace the name of the Federal Republic and give ammunition to those who regard it as a continuation of the Nazi state under other auspices. There are economic continuities too, as many of the great industrial and financial enterprises which flourished under the Third Reich continue to do so today: companies, for instance, such as Daimler-Benz, the makers of the

Mercedes car, which did very well under Nazism, thanks not least to the employment, under barbarous, inhuman, and often deadly conditions, of many thousands of slave laborers to whom effective individual compensation is still denied. In celebrating the centenary of its foundation in 1986, the company chose to ignore its role in Hitler's Germany almost completely. Only the intervention of a group of radical historians working outside the university system managed to remind the world of the true facts.[35]

But the point needs to be made equally strongly that West German society and politics consist of far more than continuities with the Nazi past. There are also continuities with a longer history, or histories; much of what is German about today's Germany derives from older traditions, not all of which led inevitably to the rise of Nazism. Nor are these traditions, whether they belong to areas of belief, like religion, or social action, like youth protest, or politics, like socialist ideology and organization, static and unchanging. They are inevitably affected by the historical context. And this has changed in many respects beyond recognition. Prosperity and affluence, although by no means evenly distributed across all areas of society, have been the central experiences of West Germans since the 1950s. They have done more than anything else to reconcile the population to democratic institutions. Indeed, so successful and so powerful has West German capitalism become that it has begun to undermine democracy through a lengthy and seemingly never-ending series of corruption scandals. Among these must be counted the fact that German firms have been supplying the chemicals necessary for chemical warfare to Libya, either with the connivance or through the negligence of West German government officials. To link this scandal directly to the use of gas in Auschwitz is grotesque. But there is no doubting the fact that money, as so often in West Germany, has won out over political rectitude and responsibility. Political morality in West Germany is not at a very high level at the moment. But worrying though this is, it has relatively little to do with the Nazi past.

Many of the travails of West German democracy are not untypical of the problems assailing democracies everywhere as the twentieth century draws to a close. For all its uncertainties,

West German democracy does seem to have found a way of surviving and strengthening itself over the last couple of decades. The chances of reverting to an authoritarian system, however desirable this may seem to neoconservative intellectuals, seem remote. There have always been democratic forces in German society, but while they were generally on the losing side up to 1945, they have clearly been in the ascendant at least over the last two decades. The legacy of the Third Reich and its crimes for present-day West Germany has been far from wholly negative.[36] Germany's place in the world today may be less prominent than it was between 1871 and 1945, but who is to say, in view of what happened between those two dates, that this is a bad thing? West Germany is mercifully free from the postimperial illusions that are deforming the foreign and domestic policies of other European countries such as Britain and France. The experience of Nazism's inhumanity to non-Germans has led the Federal Republic to adopt an official policy, admittedly not always carried out in the spirit in which it was intended, of giving asylum to political refugees. Public opinion in West Germany, unlike that in Great Britain, is firmly against the death penalty:[37] the sanctity of human life is anchored in the constitution not least as a reaction to its destruction during the Nazi period. West Germany thus avoids the degrading barbarities of capital punishment that are occurring with increasing frequency in the United States and elsewhere at the present time. The bitter experience of the destructive effects of war has left West Germans with a strong and healthy distaste for military adventurism, as the German public's critical reaction to the American bombing of Libya and their rejection of the modernization of nuclear weaponry has shown.[38] Knowledge of the possibilities for abuse inherent in an overmighty state has created an equally widespread fear of intrusive state information-gathering, has led to the enforced withdrawal of an overinquisitive population census, and has produced strong opposition to machine-readable identity cards.[39]

The tradition of the strong state lives on in West Germany, but it is encountering more widespread and more determined resistance than ever before. Democratic vigilance has exposed the corruption of politics by big business and has brought the culprits to account. Federalism and the respect for regional and local identities inherent in West Germany's constitution has much to teach centralizing states such as contemporary Britain. West Germany today is not a perfect society, but neither is it crippled by the legacy of the past. The recent debate about the Nazi past has in many ways been an inward-looking and rather parochial debate; those of us who concern ourselves from the outside with Germany's past history and present condition know that the image of the Germans in the world today is not as unfavorable as some German historians imagine: on the contrary, Germans are widely admired. If opinion polls have shown that Germans are less proud of their nationality than other European nations are and much less proud of being German than Americans are of being American, this should not be a cause for alarm—rather the reverse.[40] "Shrewd, sober, calculating, reliable, without illusions—these," according to the same opinion polls, "could be the adjectives for the political attitudes of the Germans."[41] There are worse things to be. There is little evidence in all this of a neurotic search for identity. If the Germans are more concerned than others about the dangers of war, the destruction of the environment, the perils of nuclear power, the discriminatory practices of a male-dominated society, this is not, as some commentators have maintained, because they are suffering from an inherited state of *Angst*,[42] but because they are more affected by these things than other peoples of Europe.

Nevertheless, while the legacy of the past does not determine everything in the Federal Republic, it remains crucially important for German political culture, and rightly so.[43] Joachim Fest has remarked that time is on the neoconservatives' side, and that as the generations with direct experience of the Nazi period disappear into history, so public memory too will fade. But in the postmodern world, history plays an increasingly important role in political culture, as the benefits of modern industrialization seem increasingly counterbalanced by problems ranging from unemployment to environmental pollution and the threat of nuclear war. Moreover, there are some contemporary political cultures which remain profoundly shaped by past traumas. Northern Ireland is a particularly striking example, in which the events of the year 1690 are burned into popular consciousness with the indelibility of a birthmark, polit-

ical organizations take their cue from which side they identify
with in the Battle of the Boyne, and the activists in the majority
Protestant community continue to take their colors and their
name from the seventeenth-century Anglo-Dutch monarch
William of Orange. There is every reason to suppose that the
years 1933–45 will continue, therefore, to play a central role in
West German political culture, in a rather different but no less
powerful way to that played by the past in the political culture
of modern Ireland.

West Germans, like Americans, may well take their primary
national identity from the constitution, or in their case the Basic
Law of 1949: there is no political or historical reason why this
should be any less powerful an integrating factor than a broader
sense of national identity based on an imagined linguistic or
cultural community stretching farther back in time. Americans
have no difficulty in distinguishing what they have in common
as Americans, defined first and foremost by the Constitution,
from what they have in common with other English-speaking
countries in the cultural sphere. In this sense, Goethe belongs
equally to the West Germans, the East Germans, and the Austrians, just as Shakespeare belongs equally to the British, the
Americans, the Australians, and other English-speaking peoples, without thereby diminishing the separate national identity
of any of them. This is not to say, of course, that the West
German constitution is a perfect document; but at least it provides a guarantee of democratic structures that, by and large,
has stood the test of time.

That is why the political repercussions of the present debate
are so worrying. For what Nolte and the other neoconservatives
have done is to make far-right thinking respectable in West
Germany again. As a result of the preaching of national pride
and the relativizing or trivializing of Nazi crimes by respected,
professional university historians, journalists and politicians are
finding it easier to adopt and proclaim ultraright views than
they did a decade or so ago. The first clear evidence for this has
come in the dramatic rise of West Germany's Republicans
(Republikaner), who gained 7.5 percent of the vote in the West
Berlin state elections at the beginning of 1989. Their leader,
former SS soldier Franz Schönhuber, has proclaimed German
reunification as his "God-given mission," and demands West

Germany's withdrawal from the European Community and NATO, followed by a merger with East Germany to form a neutral German state equipped with a full military arsenal, including atomic weapons. His party has won support on the basis of a strong pan-German nationalism which is directed not only against the United States and the West, but also against foreigners and immigrants within West Germany itself, whom Schönhuber accuses of importing criminality and taking away Germans' jobs; he wants the constitution amended to remove their rights, and although he denies accusations of racism, his supporters show no inhibitions in the use of the slogan "Foreigners out!" and display marked anti-Semitic prejudices.

Schönhuber's view of German history is very much in keeping with this kind of nationalism. He defends his role in the SS and says he has nothing to be ashamed of in his past. He describes the Third Reich as an "absolutely unjust state" and says its racism led to a frightful catastrophe, but when asked by a journalist whether West German president Richard von Weizsäcker should pay a formal visit to Warsaw to commemorate the fiftieth anniversary of the Nazi invasion of Poland, he replied that Weizsäcker should in that case also go to Bromberg (Bydgoszcz) to commemorate the massacre of Germans by Poles at the same time. His party's program states that "the war propaganda of the victorious powers has entered our history books, and our youth must believe their exaggerations and falsifications to a large degree, because an objective historiography is still not completely possible." Its journal has said that the notion of "the singularity of German crimes" has been used as a "tool against German interests for four decades." The weekly magazine *Der Spiegel* has compared Schönhuber to the characters of Dr. Jekyll and Mr. Hyde, created by Robert Louis Stevenson: to journalists and critics he shows a kindly, smooth, and relatively moderate face, but among his own supporters he is far less inhibited. The general secretary of Chancellor Kohl's CDU has described the Republicans as "an extremist party with Nazi slogans." Membership in this and other far-right parties in West Germany rose by 10 percent in 1988 to about 28,000, and there are already signs that Kohl's own party is moving to the right to try to prevent any further erosion of its support to the extremists.

It would be wrong to blame the rise of right-wing extremism in West Germany on the neoconservative historians; they themselves are in some measure a reflection of a broader development of the "New Right" in the Federal Republic. But there can be no doubt that they have made it a lot easier for such extremism to flourish; and in so doing, they are contributing substantially to the reorientation of West German politics along more nationalistic and authoritarian lines. This, then, is the ultimate political significance of the debate about Nazism. West German political culture in West and East is shaped not only by the legacy of postwar reconstruction but also by the events that preceded it. How people regard the Third Reich and its crimes provides an important key to how they would use political power in the present or future. That is why the neoconservatives' reinterpretation of the German past is so disturbing.

For many if not most of the arguments they are advancing are derived, consciously or unconsciously, from the propaganda of the Nazis themselves. The call for West Germans to identify with the soldiers who fought on in the East in 1944–45 echoes the Nazis' call for the troops to fight to the last ditch in defense of the "Fatherland" against what Goebbels called the "indescribable atrocities" committed by the Red Army in the German East. The thesis that Germany was fighting a preventive war by invading the Soviet Union in 1941 also appears in the Nazi propaganda of the time. The argument that fascist violence was always a response to prior violence from the left was the very argument that fascists themselves used in justification of their crimes. The use of the word "Asiatic," even with the limited distance lent it by its enclosure in quotation marks, to describe the misdeeds of the Bolsheviks, inevitably recalls years of racist scaremongering, in which communism was portrayed as the creed of slit-eyed subhumans threatening Germany from the East.

The allegation that the Poles were bent on exterminating the ethnic Germans in their territory in September 1939 resembles Nazi descriptions of the events in Bromberg as the "largest bloodbath of all time," supposedly part of the implementation of "the extermination of the German people openly proclaimed today by the Jewish plutocratic democracies," as Goebbels's propaganda machine put it. The claim that Nazi Germany was defending Western civilization in its fight against Communism goes back at least as far as Goebbels's speech to the Nuremberg Rally in September 1935, when he described the Third Reich as acting on a "world mission" in defense of "Western culture." The suggestion that the bombing of German cities by the Allies was a piece of gratuitous aggression, rather than retaliation, goes back to Nazi propaganda against "terror bombing," in which no reference was made to previous German terror bombing of Warsaw, Rotterdam, Coventry, and Guernica. The claim that Hitler may have been justified in his "internment" of the Jews because the Jews were Germany's enemies, brings to mind Hitler's notorious speech of January 1939, in which he threatened destruction upon the Jews should they—as he saw it—launch a war against Germany, and has a troubling affinity with the Nazi leaders' belief during the war that the Allied fight to defeat them was orchestrated by a Jewish conspiracy. It was, indeed, Adolf Eichmann, the orchestrator of the "Final Solution," who put forward at his trial in Jerusalem the view that "Weizmann declared war on Germany in 1939." The implied identification of Jews with partisans by a historian such as Nolte bears a disturbing similarity to the Nazis' own obsessions, in which partisan activity in the East was given a vastly overrated significance, blamed on the Jews, and met with repeated orders for "reprisals" of a scope and savagery that bore no relation at all to the reality of the military problem which partisan bands were posing. The assertion that Germany's international stability requires an authoritarian regime backed up by a strong national consciousness is too close to the slogans of the Nazis and their sympathizers in 1933 for comfort.[44]

As we have seen throughout this book, these ideas do not lack opponents in Germany. But neither did those of the Nazis. It is up to those in the rest of the world who care about Germany's future to do everything possible to encourage a sober and rational attitude to Germany's past. Germany, East and West, and Austria too, continues to bear a heavy responsibility for the crimes of Nazism. But responsibility is not the same as guilt. Nations conventionally accept a degree of historical responsibility for their past actions, as Britain does, for example, for the legacy of her empire. So too does West Germany, especially in relation to Jews and other victims of Nazi tyranny and genocide. This does not mean that every individual German needs to feel guilty about the crimes of the Third Reich, least of all if he or she was born after 1945, as most Germans now living were. Germans are entitled to object if they are all held equally and personally guilty, if they are treated as pariahs in the rest of the world, or if every minor outbreak of neo-Nazism, however offensive, is treated as a sign that nothing has changed. Nolte is right in saying that it is time to treat Germany and the Germans with calmness, rationality, and objectivity. But he is wrong in saying that this requires releasing them from Hitler's shadow. The survival and strengthening of West German democracy, and the continued stability and calculability of West Germany in European and world politics, require, now more than ever, a continuing, open, and honest confrontation with the Nazi past.

Notes

CHAPTER 1: THE BURDEN OF GUILT

1. The literature on the Second World War is obviously enormous. A very useful now updated and reissued one-volume survey is Peter Calvocoressi and Guy Wint, *Total War: Causes and Courses of the Second World War* (London, 1972; new ed., New York, 1989). Two recent, clearly written accounts of the war's origins are William Carr, *Poland to Pearl Harbor: The Making of the Second World War* (London, 1985) and P. M. H. Bell, *The Origin of the Second World War in Europe* (London, 1986). In the following notes, general introductory and background references are confined as far as possible to publications in English.

2. See Robert H. Abzug, *Inside the Vicious Heart: Americans and the Liberation of Nazi Concentration Camps* (New York, 1985), for the following account. For other eyewitness accounts, see Derrick Sington, *Belsen Uncovered* (London, 1946), Marcus J. Smith, *Dachau: The Harrowing of Hell* (Albuquerque, 1972), and Michael Selzer, *Deliverance Day: The Last Hours at Dachau* (Philadelphia, 1978).

3. Abzug, *Inside,* pp. 27–30, citing Omar N. Bradley, *A Soldier's Story* (New York, 1951), pp. 539. See also Charles R. Codman, *Drive* (Boston, 1957), pp. 281–82.

4. Abzug, *Inside,* pp. 31–33.

5. Ibid., pp. 127–40.

6. Among numerous accounts, see Konnilyn G. Feig, *Hitler's Death Camps: The Sanity of Madness* (New York, 1979), and Raul Hilberg, *The Destruc-*

tion of the European Jews, 3 vols. (2nd ed., New York, 1985). Among many memoirs written by camp inmates, see for example Primo Levi, *If this Is a Man* (2nd ed., London, 1960), and Wieslaw Kielar, *Anus Mundi: Five Years in Auschwitz* (London, 1981).

7. Robert Jay Lifton, *The Nazi Doctors: Medical Killing and the Psychology of Genocide* (New York, 1986) is a useful introduction in English.

8. Intensive research in this area has only recently begun. The most thorough and useful survey so far is Ulrich Herbert, *Fremdarbeiter: Politik und Praxis des "Ausländer-Einsatzes" in der Kriegswirtschaft des Dritten Reiches* (Bonn, 1985). However, see also E. L. Homze, *Foreign Labor in Nazi Germany* (Princeton, 1967).

9. Walter Laqueur, *The Terrible Secret: Suppression of the Truth About Hitler's "Final Solution"* (London, 1980), provides a meticulous documentation and analysis of the problem of acceptance and belief. Laqueur notes that "Holocaust" is a "singularly inappropriate" term for the genocidal policies of the Nazis toward the Jews. Its meaning—to bring a wholly burnt offering—is inapplicable. As Laqueur notes (p. 7, n.), "It was not the intention of the Nazis to make a sacrifice of this kind, and the position of the Jews was not that of a ritual victim." See also the account of the term's evolution in Geoff Eley, "Holocaust History," *London Review of Books,* March 3–17, 1982, pp. 6–9. Eley argues that the term's religious overtones remain in a transmuted form, now implying "a certain mystification, an insistence on the uniquely Jewish character of the experience." Saul Friedländer has noted "the growing centrality of the '*Shoah*' (Hebrew for Holocaust) among Diaspora Jewry, particularly in the United States. The "'*Shoah,*'" he notes, "is almost becoming a symbol of identification, for better or for worse, whether because of the weakening of the bond of religion or because of the lesser salience of Zionism and Israel as an identification element" (Saul Friedländer, "West Germany and the Burden of the Past: The Ongoing Debate," *Jerusalem Quarterly* 42 [Spring 1987], pp. 3–18, here p. 16.) As a non-Jewish, secular historian, I find Laqueur's reservations unanswerable, and for this reason avoid the use of the term "Holocaust" in the present work.

10. For an impressive synthesis of a large quantity of this material, see Martin Gilbert, *The Holocaust: The Jewish Tragedy* (Glasgow, 1986). Much of the original material is preserved at the Fred R. Crawford Witness to the Holocaust Project, Emory University, Atlanta, Georgia 30322, which has also published a number of extracts.

11. Internationaler Militärgerichtshof Nürnberg, *Der Nürnberger Prozess gegen die Hauptkriegsverbrecher, vom 14. November 1945–1. Oktober 1946* (Munich, reprint, 1984).

12. Some idea of the range and scale of the documentation available can be gained from Jeremy Noakes and Geoffrey Pridham, *Nazism 1919–1945: A Documentary Reader* (4 vols., Exeter, 1983–89), which, with its excellent summaries and linking commentaries by Noakes, forms the best and

most comprehensive documentary history of Nazism now available. In view of the mass of documentation extrant, the present book does not deal with neofascist attempts to deny the reality of Nazism's crimes. Such denials are the product of political fanaticism, not of serious investigation, and are not susceptible to rational argument. For a useful guide to some of this distasteful literature, see Gill Seidel, *The Holocaust Denial: Antisemitism, Racism and the New Right* (London, 1986).

13. Noakes and Pridham, *Nazism*, vol. I. For useful studies of Nazism up to 1933, see also W. S. Allen, *The Nazi Seizure of Power: The Experience of a Single German Town 1930–35* (2nd ed., New York, 1984); Richard Bessel, *Political Violence and the Rise of Nazism: The Storm Troopers in Eastern Germany 1925–1934* (New Haven, 1984); Thomas Childers, *The Nazi Voter: The Social Foundation of Fascism in Germany, 1919–1933* (Chapel Hill, 1983); Michael Kater, *The Nazi Party: A Social Profile of Members and Leaders 1919–1945* (Oxford, 1985); Jeremy Noakes, *The Nazi Party in Lower Saxony, 1921–1933* (London, 1971); and Dietrich Orlow, *The History of the Nazi Party, Volume 1, 1919–1933* (Pittsburgh, 1969). The best short introduction to the political history of the Weimar Republic is now Eberhard Kolb, *The Weimar Republic* (London, 1988). The most useful general introductory survey remains Georges Castellan, *L'Allemagne de Weimar, 1918–1933* (2nd ed., Paris, 1972), which has unfortunately neither been translated nor updated.

14. Karl Dietrich Bracher, *The German Dictatorship: The Origins, Structure, and Consequences of National Socialism* (New York, 1970), pp. 243–51 ("Reflection: The 'Legal Revolution' "). Bracher's book is still the best one-volume history of the subject.

15. Noakes and Pridham, *Nazism*, vol. 2; Bracher, *The German Dictatorship*, pp. 288–494.

16. On Nazi foreign policy, see Noakes and Pridham, *Nazism*, vol. 3; William Carr, *Arms, Autarky, and Aggression: A Study in German Foreign Policy 1933–1939* (2nd ed., London, 1979), and Gerhard L. Weinberg, *The Foreign Policy of Hitler's Germany* (2 vols., Chicago, 1970–80).

17. Noakes and Pridham, *Nazism*, vol. 3, pp. 755–875; see also the works cited in n. 1, above.

18. Noakes and Pridham, *Nazism*, vol. 3, pp. 997–1208. As with other references in the present chapter, this is intended simply to point to a useful introductory text; more detailed discussion of some of the controversies surrounding the events summarized here, together with fuller references, is reserved for later.

19. Tony Sharp, *The Wartime Alliance and the Zonal Division of Germany* (London, 1975); Peter H. Merkl, *The Origin of the West German Republic* (New York, 1963); J. Schechtmann, *Postwar Population Transfers in Europe, 1945–1955* (London, 1962). For a general account of the peace settlement, see J. W. Wheeler-Bennett and Anthony Nicholls, *The Semblance of Peace* (London, 1972).

20. For a lively account by a journalist, see Norman Gelb, *The Berlin Wall* (London, 1986). Useful background histories include Volker R. Berghahn, *Modern Germany* (2nd ed., London, 1987), and Alfred Grosser, *Germany in Our Time: A Political History of the Postwar Years* (London, 1974).

21. See the indictment of Allied policy by Tom Bower, *Blind Eye to Murder: Britain, America, and the Purging of Nazi Germany—A Pledge Betrayed* (London, 1981).

22. The failure in West Germany to come to terms with the Nazi past during the first two postwar decades has perhaps received insufficient attention in the present debate. For exceptions, see William E. Paterson, "From *Vergangenheitsbewältigung* to the *Historikerstreit*" (unpubl. typescript, July 1988); Geoff Eley "Nazism, Politics, and the Image of the Past: Thoughts on the West German *Historikerstreit* 1986–87" *Past and Present* 121 (1988), pp. 171–208; and Wolfgang Benz, "Die Abwehr der Vergangenheit: Ein Problem nur für Historiker und Moralisten?" in Dan Diner (ed.), *Ist der Nationalsozialismus Geschichte? Zur Historisierung und Historikerstreit* (Frankfurt, 1987), pp. 17–33. A key critique of the silences of the 1950s was Alexander and Margarethe Mitscherlich, *The Inability to Mourn* (London, 1975). Useful texts on Allied policy in postwar Germany include Constantine Fitzgibbon, *Denazification* (London, 1969); J. Tent, *Mission on the Rhine: Re-education and Denazification in American-occupied Germany* (Chicago, 1982); N. Pronay and K. Wilson (eds.), *The Political Re-education of Germany and Her Allies After World War II* (London, 1985). A. Rückerl, *The Investigation of Nazi Crimes, 1945–1978* (London, 1979), provides an introduction to the later period.

23. For critical accounts of the historical writings of this period, see Richard J. Evans, *Rethinking German History: Nineteenth-Century Germany and the Origins of the Third Reich* (London, 1987), pp. 23–54; and Pierre Ayçoberry, *The Nazi Question: An Essay on The Interpretations of National Socialism, 1922–1975* (New York, 1981), esp. pp. 109–148. There is a differentiated account of the development of West German attitudes toward the Nazi past in Eckard Jesse, " 'Vergangenheitsbewältigung' in der Bundesrepublik Deutschland," *Der Staat* 26 (1987), pp. 539–65. See also Bernd Faulenbach, "NS-Interpretation und Zeitklima," *Aus Politik und Zeitgeschichte: Beilage zur Wochenzeitung "Das Parlament"* 22 (1987), pp. 19–30.

24. Classic texts include Carl Friedrich, *Totalitarianism* (Cambridge, Mass., 1954); Carl Friedrich and Zbigniew Brzezinski, *Totalitarian Dictatorship and Autocracy* (2nd ed., New York, 1966); and Hannah Arendt, *The Origins of Totalitarianism* (New York, 1951). In Germany, the main applications of the term to the history of Nazism were by Karl Dietrich Bracher (n. 14 above). See his *The Age of Ideologies: A History of Political Thought in the Twentieth Century* (London, 1982), for a recent defense of this approach.

25. See B. H. Liddell Hart, *The Other Side of the Hill* (London, 1948), p. 29; Heinz Guderian, *Panzer Leader* (London, 1952).

26. Irmgard Wilharm (ed.), *Deutsche Geschichte 1962–1983: Dokumente in zwei Bänden* (Frankfurt, 1985), vol. 2, p. 27 (Brandt's government declaration of October 18, 1969).

27. For a more detailed exposition of this interpretation, see below. Useful guides to the reinterpretations of the 1960s and 1970s include Hans-Ulrich Wehler, "Historiography in Germany Today," in Jürgen Habermas (ed.), *Observations on "The Spiritual Situation of the Age,"* (Cambridge, Mass., 1984), pp. 221–59; Georg Iggers, "Introduction," in Georg Iggers (ed.), *The Social History of Politics: Critical Perspectives in West German Historical Writing since 1945* (Leamington Spa, 1985), pp. 1–48; Kenneth D. Barkin, "From Uniformity to Pluralism: German Historical Writing Since World War I," *German Life and Letters* 34 (1981), pp. 234–47; David Blackbourn, "Introduction," in David Blackbourn, *Populists and Patricians: Essays in Modern German History* (London, 1987), pp. 1–32; and Geoff Eley, *From Unification to Nazism: Reinterpreting the German Past* (London, 1986), pp. 1–18.

28. For the background to this event, see Günter Berndt and Reinhard Strecker (eds.), *Polen—ein Schauermärchen, oder: Gehirnwäsche für Generationen* (Reinbek bei Hamburg, 1971), with useful criticisms of textbook accounts of the history of Polish-German relations current in the 1960s.

29. Thus the key word of the period, *Vergangenheitsbewältigung*—"mastering the past." The public debate can be followed through the essays of Martin Broszat, *Nach Hitler: Der schwierige Umgang mit unserer Geschichte*, ed. H. Graml, K.-D. Henke (Munich, 1986), esp. pp. 42–49, 230–33, 271–86.

30. See Martin Broszat et al., *Deutschlands Weg in die Diktatur* (Berlin, 1983), for the proceedings of one of the largest such conferences; for a characteristically vigorous summing-up, see Hans-Ulrich Wehler, *Aus der Geschichte lernen?* (Munich, 1988), pp. 44–60.

31. James Wald, "German History Backwards," *New German Critique* 21 (1980), pp. 154–80; Hellmut Diwald, *Geschichte der Deutschen* (Frankfurt, 1978).

32. Diwald, *Geschichte*, pp. 15–16. See also the same author's "Deutschland—was ist es?" in Wolfgang Venohr (ed.), *Die deutsche Einheit kommt bestimmt* (Bergisch Gladbach, 1983), and Hellmut Diwald, *Mut zur Geschichte* (Bergisch Gladbach, 1983). Venohr is a prominent figure in the West German "New Right."

33. Karl Otmar, Freiherr von Aretin, quoted in Wald, "German History," p. 157, n. 8. Other straws in the wind could be found in the writings of Hermann Lübbe, "Der Nationalsozialismus im Bewusstsein der deutschen Gegenwart," *Frankfurter Allgemeine Zeitung*, January 24, 1983, and "Der Nationalsozialismus im deutschen Nachkriegsbewusstsein," *Historische Zeitschrift* 236 (1983), pp. 579–99; see also his contribution and the ensuing discussion in Broszat et al., *Deutschlands Weg* (esp. pp. 329–49), and the commentary by H. Dubiel and G. Frankenberg,

"Entsorgung der Vergangheit," *Die Zeit*, March 18, 1983, p. 44. See also Alfred Heuss, *Versagen und Verhängnis: Vom Ruin deutscher Geschichte und ihres Verständnisses* (Berlin, 1984), for another relatively early example of the same tendency.

34. Geoffrey Hartman (ed.), *Bitburg in Moral and Political Perspective* (Bloomington, 1986), pp. xiii–xiv; Bernd Faulenbach, " 'Sinnstiftung' durch Geschichte?" *Links*, November 1986, pp. 48–49.

35. Ibid., p. 11. For the popular resonance of this event in Germany, see Hajo Funke, "Bitburg, Jews, and Germans: A Case Study of Anti-Jewish Sentiment in Germany During May, 1985," *New German Critique* 38 (1986), pp. 57–72.

36. Hartman, *Bitburg*, pp. 182–83, reprinting Arthur Schlesinger, Jr., "The Rush to Reconcile," *Wall Street Journal*, May 9, 1985.

37. Timothy Garton Ash, "Germany After Bitburg," *New Republic* (July 15–22, 1985) pp. 15–17, reprinted in Hartman, *Bitburg*, pp. 199–203. The *Washington Post*, on May 6, 1985, also complained that at Bitburg "our president was in that eight minutes forever being cued, nudged, positioned—stage-managed—by the Chancellor" (Hartman, *Bitburg*, p. 177). Among the analyses printed in Hartman's volume, Saul Friedländer, "Some German Struggles with Memory" (pp. 27–42) and Jürgen Habermas, "Die Entsorgung der Vergangenheit: Ein Kulturpolitisches Pamphlet," *Die Zeit*, May 24, 1985, pp. 43–45, an attack on Lübbe (see n. 33 above), are particularly noteworthy.

38. *The Times* (London, April 8, 1987). See also Kohl's speech at Belsen (Hartman, *Bitburg*, pp. 244–50). Weizsäcker's speech is reprinted on pp. 262–72 of the same volume. Jewish leaders refused to attend the ceremony at Belsen because of the politicians' insistence in going straight on to hold a similar ceremony at Bitburg. Jewish protesters were barred from the camp memorial by police and afterward held their own ceremony there to "reconsecrate" the memorial after its "desecration" by Kohl and Reagan (John Tagliabue, "The Two Ceremonies at Bergen-Belsen," *New York Times*, May 6, 1985, in Hartman, *Bitburg*, pp. 141–43.)

39. Richard von Weizsäcker, *A Voice from Germany* (London, 1985).

40. *Der Spiegel* 46 (November 10, 1986), pp. 17–30. See also Hans Mommsen, "Aufarbeitung und Verdrängung des Dritten Reiches im westdeutschen Geschichtsbewusstsein," *Gewerkschaftliche Monatshefte* 3 (1987), pp. 129–41.

41. See Heinrich August Winkler, "Auf ewig in Hitlers Schatten? Zum Streit über das Geschichtsbild der Deutschen," *Frankfurter Rundschau*, November 14, 1986. Like many of the contributions to the debate which is the subject of this book, this has been reprinted in R. Piper (ed.), *"Historikerstreit": Die Dokumentation der Kontroverse um die Einzigartigkeit der nationalsozialistischen Judenvernichtung* (Munich, 1987), pp. 256–63. In the following notes, the original place of appearance of such contributions is given on first appearance, together with the reference to the

Piper volume in parentheses; subsequent references to the same piece also cite the Piper volume. A second collection, often reprinting the same pieces again, is less comprehensive: Reinhard Kühnl (ed.), *Vergangenheit, die nicht vergeht: Die NS-Verbrechen und die Geschichtsschreibung der Wende* (Cologne, 1987). This was then withdrawn for legal reasons and replaced by a similar collection under a different title. Some of the main participants have reprinted their own contributions yet again in short collections of their own works. Reference is made to these mainly where they contain material not reprinted in the Piper volume.

42. Martin Broszat, "Zur Errichtung eines 'Hauses der Geschichte der Bundesrepublik Deutschland' in Bonn," in Broszat, *Nach Hitler,* pp. 304–9; Michael Stürmer, "Berlin und Bonn: Suche nach der Deutschen Geschichte," *Museumskunde* 3 (1984), pp. 142–53, reprinted in Michael Stürmer, *Dissonanzen des Fortschritts: Essays über Geschichte und Politik in Deutschland* (Munich, 1986), pp. 289–304. See also Ulrich Rose, "Geschichte, zur Schau gestellt in Vitrinen: Die Diskussion um zwei Museen und ein Mahnmal," in Gernot Erler et al., *Geschichtswende? Entsorgungsversuche zur deutschen Geschichte* (Freiburg, 1987), pp. 35–61; Hans Mommsen, "Verordnete Geschichtsbilder: Historische Museumspläne der Bundesregierung," *Gewerkschaftliche Monatshefte* 1 (1986), pp. 13–24; Karl-Heinz Janssen, "Die Qual mit der Geschichte: Streit um zwei Deutschland-Museen," *Die Zeit* (January 10, 1986); Freimut Duve (ed.), *Anhörung der SPD-Bundestagsfraktion zum "Haus der Geschichte der Bundesrepublik": Protokoll vom 9. Mai 1984* (Bonn, 1984); Geschichtswerkstatt Berlin (ed.), *Die Nation als Ausstellungsstück: Planungen, Kritik, und Utopien zu den Museumsgründungen in Bonn und Berlin* (Geschichtswerkstatt no. 11, Hamburg, 1987); and Die Grünen (ed.), *Wider die Entsorgung der deutschen Geschichte: Streitschrift gegen die geplanten historischen Museen in Berlin (W) und Bonn* (Bonn, 1986). Although they form an important part of the Kohl government's strategy for the presentation of a positive view of German history, and therefore play a role in the present debate, the planned museums are not in existence at the time of writing, so detailed comment would be premature.

43. Broszat, *Nach Hitler,* pp. 304–9. See also the various contributions in *Die Nation als Ausstellungsstück* (n. 42, above).

44. Broszat, *Nach Hitler,* p. 304. See also Lothar Gall, Klaus Hildebrand et al., *Überlegungen und Vorschläge zur Errichtung eines Hauses der Geschichte der Bundesrepublik Deutschland in Bonn* (Bonn, 1984); Jürgen Kocka, "Die deutsche Geschichte soll ins Museum," *Geschichte und Gesellschaft* 11 (1985), pp. 59–66; and the special issue of *Das Parlament* 36, nos. 20–21 (1986) on this subject.

45. *Die Nation als Ausstellungsstück* provides a variety of examples; see for example the feminists' contribution, "Nicht Kohl und nicht Wirsing—Brot und Rosen wollen wir!" pp. 109–10.

46. *Die Welt,* January 19, 1987; further, *Frankfurter Rundschau,* January 14, 1987; *Süddeutsche Zeitung,* January 16, 1987. The quotations are from Franz Josef Strauss, *Rede des Bayerischen Ministerpräsidenten*

Franz Josef Strauss beim Festkommers aus Anlass des 130jährigen Beste-hens des Cartellverbandes der Katholischen Deutschen Studentenverbin-dungen am 19, Juni 1987 (Munich, 1987). Some of Strauss's speeches are collected in Franz Josef Strauss, *Verantwortung vor der Politik: Beiträge zur deutschen und internationalen Politik 1978–1985* (Munich, 1985). The phrase is also used in Michael Stürmer, "Braucht die Republik eine Mitte? Von den geistigen Tauschplätzen einer Zivilisation," in Stürmer, *Dissonanzen des Fortschritts,* pp. 265–77, here p. 267, and discussed in Ernst Nolte, *Das Vergehen der Vergangenheit: Antwort an meine Kritiker im sogenannten Historikerstreit* (2nd ed., Berlin, 1988), p. 41. See also the discussion in Erler et al., *Geschichtswende?,* pp. 32–33 (Thomas Schnabel, "Geschichte und Wende: Vom heutigen Gebrauch der Vergangenheit bei konservativen Politikern und Publizisten," pp. 9–34).

47. Karl Carstens, "Demokratie und Vaterland," *Die politische Meinung* 31 (1986), pp. 34–41; see also Erler et al., *Geschichtswende?,* pp. 142–44 (Rolf-Dieter Müller, "Geschichtswende? Gedanken zu den Ursachen, Di-mension und Folgen des 'Historikerstreits,'" pp. 128–47).

48. See below, pp. 35, 43–45, and 123.

49. Müller, "Geschichtswende?" in Erler et al., *Geschichtswende?,* pp. 141–42. For the central role of the *Frankfurter Allgemeine Zeitung* in the encouragement and orchestration of neoconservative historical revision-ism in the Federal Republic, see Hermannus Pfeiffer (ed.), *Die FAZ: Nach-forschungen über ein Zentralorgan* (Cologne, 1988), esp. the contributions by Otto Köhler ("Die FAZ und der Historikerstreit," pp. 144–63) and Wilfried Meisen (" 'Beispielhafte Feldherrnkunst'—Der Mythos von Hitlers Generälen," pp. 164–73). Unfortunately, in their cri-tique of the apologetic account of the *FAZ*'s history in the Third Reich and before which has been published by *FAZ* editor Günther Gillessen (*Auf verlorenem Posten—Die Frankfurter Zeitung im Dritten Reich* [Berlin, 1986]), the authors ignore the excellent, and devastating, account by Mo-dris Eksteins, *The Limits of Reason: The German Democratic Press and the Collapse of Weimar Democracy* (Oxford, 1975). For further points on the *FAZ*, see Imanuel Geiss, *Die Habermas-Kontroverse. Ein deutscher Streit* (Berlin, 1988), pp. 98–99.

50. Müller, "Geschichtswende?" in Erler et al., *Geschichtswende?,* pp. 141–44, and more generally Pfeiffer, *Die FAZ.* For further references to the role played by this newspaper, see index.

51. Printed in the Piper volume, pp. 39–47, and in Nolte, *Das Vergehen,* pp. 171–78. The full title is "Vergangenheit, die nicht vergehen will: Eine Rede, die geschrieben, aber nicht gehalten werden konnte." The sugges-tion that the speech was banned refers to the fact that the article was originally written in response to a request from the organizers of the annual Römerberg Colloquia organized by the city of Frankfurt in 1986 on the theme of political culture in West Germany. In the publication which emerged from the discussions, the organizers provided detailed evidence to demonstrate that Nolte himself refused to give the speech: there was no question of censorship. See Hilmar Hoffman (ed.), *Gegen den*

Versuch, Vergangenheit zu verbiegen: Eine Diskussion um politische Kultur in der Bundesrepublik aus Anlass der Frankfurter Römerberggespräche 1986 (Frankfurt, 1986), pp. 13–15, n. 8.

52. This is the burden of most of the articles collected in Stürmer, *Dissonanzen des Fortschritts.* See, for example, "Deutsche Identität: Auf der Suche nach der verlorenen Nationalgeschichte," pp. 201–9, or "Die Deutsche Frage: Kein Eigentum der Deutschen: zum 17. Juni 1953," pp. 223–34. But see his letter to the *Frankfurter Allgemeine Zeitung* of August 16, 1986, (in Piper, *Historikerstreit,* pp. 98–99).

53. Stürmer, *Dissonanzen,* p. 272.

54. Ibid.; see also p. 266.

55. Ibid., pp. 267, 269–70. Stürmer's recent writings are discussed in Volker R. Berghahn, "Geschichtswissenschaft und Grosse Politik," *Aus Politik und Zeitgeschichte: Beilage zur Wochenzeitung 'Das Parlament'* (March 14, 1987), pp. 25–37; and Hans-Jürgen Puhle, "Die Neue Ruhelosigkeit: Michael Stürmers nationalpolitischer Revisionismus," *Geschichte und Gesellschaft* 13 (1987), pp. 382–99.

56. Saul Friedländer, "West Germany and the Burden of the Past: The Ongoing Debate," *Jerusalem Quarterly* 42 (Spring 1987), pp. 3–18; Konrad Adam, "Wo bleiben die Verschwörer?" *Frankfurter Allgemeine Zeitung,* October 9, 1986; Klaus Hildebrand (ed.), *Wem gehört die deutsche Geschichte? Deutschlands Weg vom alten Europa in die europäische Moderne* (Cologne, 1987).

57. For some early adumbrations of the attack on these neoconservative positions, see Hans Mommsen, "Die Last der Vergangenheit," in Jürgen Habermas (ed.), *Stichworte zur "Geistigen Situation der Zeit"* (Frankfurt, 1979), Vol. 1, pp. 164–84; and idem, "Rückwärtsrevision des Gechichtsbildes?" *Die Neue Gesellschaft,* Vol. 32 (1985), pp. 366–86.

58. Gordon A. Craig, "The War of the German Historians," *New York Review of Books,* January 15, 1987.

59. Charles S. Maier, *The Unmasterable Past: History, Holocaust, and German National Identity* (Cambridge, Mass., 1988), gives an intelligent account of these complex problems. For my own reservations about some aspects of Maier's generally excellent book, see Richard J. Evans, "A 'Normal' Act of Genocide?" *New York Times Book Review,* January 29, 1989. For a brief guide to the literature, see the "Further Reading" section of this book. Commentaries and bibliographies written from various points of view include Konrad Repgen, "Der 'Historikerstreit' (I). Einige Anmerkungen zu den aktuellen Veröffentlichungen über kontroverse Grundprobleme unserer Geschichte," *Historisches Jahrbuch* 107 (1987), pp. 417–30; Stefan Melnik, "Annotierte ausgewählte Bibliographie zur Historikerdebatte," *Liberal* 29 (1987), pp. 85–95; Eckard Jesse, "Ist der 'Historikerstreit' ein 'historischer Streit'? Zugleich eine Auseinandersetzung mit der Literatur," *Zeitschrift für Politik* 35 (1988), pp. 163–97; Anson Rabinbach, "German Historians debate the Nazi Past," *Dissent*

(Spring, 1988), pp. 192–200; Andrei Markovits, "Related to the *Historikerstreit,*" *German Politics and Society* 13 (February, 1988), pp. 41–42; Barbara Menke, "Auswahlbibliographie," in *Streitfall Deutsche Geschichte, Geschichts- und Gegenwartsbewusstsein in den 80er Jahren* (Landeszentrale für politische Bildung Nordrhein-Westfalen, Essen, 1988), pp. 251–67.

CHAPTER 2: "ASIATIC DEEDS"

1. See the entry for Nolte in *Wer ist Wer?,* vol. 25, (Lübeck, 1986), p. 963.

2. Ernst Nolte, *Three Faces of Fascism: Action Française, Italian Fascism, National Socialism* (New York, 1965; originally published in German in 1963). References below are to the Mentor paperback edition, published in 1969.

3. Hans Rogger and Eugen Weber (eds.), *The European Right: A Historical Profile* (Berkeley, 1966); Walter Laqueur and George L. Mosse (eds.), "International Fascism 1920–1945," *Journal of Contemporary History* I, no. 1 (1966); F. L. Carsten, *The Rise of Fascism* (London, 1967); John Weiss, *The Fascist Tradition* (New York, 1967); S. J. Woolf (ed.), *European Fascism* (London, 1968) and *The Nature of Fascism* (London, 1968); A. James Gregor, *The Ideology of Fascism* (New York, 1969); Eugen Weber, *Varieties of Fascism* (New York, 1964).

4. For a good survey of the historiography, see Walter Laqueur (ed.), *Fascism: A Reader's Guide—Analyses, Interpretations, Bibliography* (New York, 1976). S. U. Larsen et al. (eds.), *Who Were the Fascists?: Social Roots of European Fascism* (Bergen, 1980), provides a comprehensive account, together with critiques of totalitarianism theory (e.g., B. Hagtvet, "The Theory of Mass Society and the Collapse of the Weimar Republic: A Reexamination," pp. 66–117).

5. Nolte, *Three Faces,* pp. 539–40, explaining that the book's purpose is to integrate philosophy and history in the Hegelian manner.

6. See the useful critique by Zeev Sternhell, 'Fascist Ideology,' in Laqueur (ed.), *Fascism,* pp. 325–406, esp. pp. 396–99. Nolte's method of reducing complex historical phenomena and processes to pairs of philosophical opposites and then manipulating these as if they were real is subjected to a devastating critique by Hans Mommsen, "Das Ressentiment als Wissenschaft. Anmerkungen zu Ernst Noltes 'Der europäische Bürgerkrieg 1917–1945. Nationalsozialismus und Bolschewismus,'" *Geschichte und Gesellschaft* 34 (1988), pp. 495–512. It is usefully related to Nolte's philosophical premises by Charles Maier, *The Unmasterable Past: History, Holocaust, and German National Identity* (Cambridge, Mass., 1988), pp. 26–27, 86–87.

7. Thus Sternhell notes that "Nolte is clearly floundering in problems of methodology"; his concentration on ideas misleads him into elevating

Action Française into "the status of a fascism equivalent to Nazism." Sternhell suggests that Nolte's focus on the individual leaders implies "that it was almost by accident, by a mere conjunction of political circumstances, that the Nazis arose in Germany" (pp. 396–97). As George L. Mosse noted (*Journal of the History of Ideas* 27 [1966], p. 624), Nolte's statement, made apparently without any sense of irony, that "after the führer's death the core of leadership of the National Socialist state snapped back, like a steel spring wound up too long, to its original position and became a body of well-meaning and cultured Central Europeans," (*Three Faces*, p. 504), reduced Nazism to the individual figure of Hitler. By implication it exculpated everyone else. As Sternhell remarks (p. 397), "This sort of statement casts doubt on Nolte's understanding of Nazi ideology as well as on his analysis of bourgeois society." Moreover, Nolte's definition of fascism ("Fascism is anti-Marxism which seeks to destroy the enemy by the evolvement of a radically opposed and yet related ideology and by the use of almost identical, and yet typically modified, methods, always, however, within the unyielding framework of national self-assertion and autonomy" [*Three Faces*, p. 40]) comes close to being a restatement of totalitarianism theory and now reads rather differently in the light of Nolte's later work, which develops this view more consistently than some of his critics maintain (Hans-Ulrich Wehler, *Entsorgung der deutschen Vergangenheit? Ein polemischer Essay zum "Historikerstreit"* [Munich, 1988], pp. 13–20). As Sternhell already pointed out in 1976, "Fascism was not . . . as Nolte would have us believe, simply a shadow of Marxism. It was an entirely separate phenomenon and had a reality of its own which Nolte, transported into other realms by the phenomenological method, does not always perceive" ("Fascist Ideology," p. 399).

8. *Deutschland und der Kalte Krieg* (Munich, 1974). Neither this nor any of Nolte's more recent books has appeared in English. However, a sample of his shorter pieces is available in his *Marxism, Fascism, Cold War: Essays and Lectures 1974–1976* (New York, 1982).

9. Felix Gilbert, in *American Historical Review* 81 (1976), pp. 618–20; Nolte's protest and Gilbert's reply appeared in the same journal, vol. 82 (1977), pp. 235–36.

10. Peter Gay, *Freud, Jews, and Other Germans: Masters and Victims in Modernist Culture* (New York, 1978), pp. xi–xiv.

11. Ibid., citing Nolte, *Deutschland*, pp. 528, 159–60.

12. *Marxismus und Industrielle Revolution* (Stuttgart, 1983).

13. See *Marxism, Fascism, Cold War*, for a sample of this work; also Nolte, *Was ist bürgerlich?* (Stuttgart, 1979).

14. *Der europäische Bürgerkrieg 1917–1945: Nationalsozialismus und Bolschewismus* (Berlin, 1987). See Heinrich August Winkler, "Ein europäischer Bürger namens Hitler: Ernst Noltes Entlastungsoffensive geht weiter," *Die Zeit*, December 4, 1987, for a review. Further reviews are listed in the notes on Further Reading at the end of this book.

15. Nolte, "Vergangenheit" (Piper, pp. 39–47).

16. Alexander Solzhenitsyn, *The Gulag Archipelago 1918–1956: An Experiment in Literary Investigation* (3 vols., London, 1974–78); Nolte, "Vergangenheit." E. Klug, "Das 'Asiatische Russland': Über die Entstehung eines europäischen Vorurteils," *Historische Zeitschrift* 245 (1987), pp. 265–89, casts an interesting light on these questions. For a detailed consideration of Nolte's position on the uniqueness and comparability of Nazi exterminism, which is more complex than the article's emphasis on the technical procedure of gassing would imply, see Chapter 4.

17. Nolte, *Bürgerkrieg*, p. 517, and "Vergangenheit."

18. Nolte, *Bürgerkrieg*, pp. 147–48.

19. Ibid., pp. 181–85, 190, 204–9, 240, 317–18, 393. Nolte admits that the Communists wanted only to *expropriate* the bourgeoisie in Germany, but at the same time persists in referring to their *Vernichtungskonzept* (p. 182).

20. Nolte, *Bürgerkrieg*, pp. 317–18; also, Nolte, "Vergangenheit." Nolte has attempted to distance himself from some of these views by using the subjunctive *("müssten")* when discussing whether the Nazis should (might) have interned the Jews, and now prefers the use of the term "civil internees" to "prisoners of war" (Nolte, *Das Vergehen*, pp. 109, 145, 185). His convoluted reasoning and language seem almost intended to enable him to dispute whatever interpretation his critics put on these statements, and so to avoid confronting the real substance of the issue (*Das Vergehen*, passim). The inescapable implication of the arguments advanced by Nolte, however, seems to me to be a justification of, or an excuse for, the Nazis' mass murder of German and European Jews. If this is not the case, then it is impossible to see why Nolte is making these points. This is particularly the case since a number of these arguments have for long been common currency among far-right and neofascist publicists. For his original discussion of the argument, see Piper, *Historikerstreit*, pp. 24–25.

21. Nolte, "Vergangenheit"; Piper, *Historikerstreit*, pp. 25–26, 42.

22. Nolte, *Das Vergehen*, p. 90.

23. Nolte, "Vergangenheit."

24. "Between Myth and Revisionism?: The Third Reich in the Perspective of the 1980s," in H. W. Koch (ed.), *Aspects of the Third Reich* (New York, 1985), pp. 17–38. The arbitrariness of the book's construction extends to the editor's parenthetic intervention in his authors' texts and his abridgement of contributions without the authors' permission. These procedures make the volume generally unreliable as a source (see Nolte's own critique of Koch's procedures in Nolte, *Das Vergehen*, p. 129). Nolte's essay was also reworked by the editor; the original, full version is in Piper, *Historikerstreit*, pp. 13–32. Here he also puts forward many of the views familiar from his essay ("Vergangenheit") and subsequent book *(Bürgerkrieg)*, and makes clear the source of more than one of them in the writings of the far-right British publicist and admirer of Adolf Hitler,

David Irving. The article was not, as Koch stated, specially written, but had in fact first appeared in a shorter version as "Die negative Lebendigkeit des Dritten Reiches," *Frankfurter Allgemeine Zeitung*, July 24, 1980. For Irving, see below, pp. 166–68. For the "PLO" argument, see "Between Myth and Revisionism?," pp. 19–22; like many of Nolte's other speculations, the reference to the PLO has a suggestive power which makes it easily open to misinterpretation, and so it is, to say the least, unfortunate; *Bürgerkrieg*, pp. 554, n. 26, and 593–94, n. 29.

25. Imanuel Geiss, *Die Habermas-Kontroverse. Ein deutscher Streit* (Berlin, 1988), pp. 55–57; Helmut Müller, in *Das Parlament*, March 25, 1988.

26. In particular, Geiss and Müller (n. 25 above), Joachim Fest (n. 27 below), and Eckhard Jesse (page 177, n. 6, below). In English, see in particular the editorial remarks of Koch, an exiled German now teaching at the University of York, England, in *Aspects of the Third Reich*. Koch argues that the Weimar Republic was destroyed above all by the hostility of Germany's opponents in the Treaty of Versailles (p. 461), and that "Hitler achieved power by perfectly legal means" (p. 54). He attacks those who have argued that Hitler intended a war of European conquest as being ignorant of proper historical methods (pp. 181–95). He portrays Hitler's launching of the war against Russia as an unplanned response to Soviet ambitions for predominance in East-Central Europe, which became clear to Hitler in the course of 1940. Thus the Nazi invasion of Russia in 1941 was in part "a preventive stroke" (p. 319, also pp. 320–22). German rearmament in the 1930s, he says, was a "myth" (pp. 325–30). *Mein Kampf* is, in Koch's view, not a reliable guide to Hitler's early life or later views: he denies there is evidence that Hitler was anti-Semitic before September 1919. Koch says that Hitler became an anti-Semite because "it was in the revolutionary upheaval in Germany in 1918–19, and in Bavaria, in particular, that Jews played a very prominent part in the Bavarian Soviet Republic" (pp. 374–75). Koch goes on: "It seems to have been completely forgotten that the boycott of Jewish businesses in Germany on April 1, 1933, was in retaliation for a boycott against German goods and businesses in the United States and, to a lesser extent, in Great Britain" (p. 376). He endorses Nolte's view that Nazi anti-Semitism was further radicalized in response to the Weizmann declaration and other attacks on Germany from abroad (pp. 378–79). The Waffen-SS were, according to Koch, ordinary soldiers (pp. 380–85), and their war crimes in Poland in 1939 "took place against the background of mass murder by Poles of the German minority immediately after the outbreak of war" (p. 385). British war crimes, Koch adds (p. 385), have conveniently been forgotten. Koch excuses the destruction of the French village of Oradour by the Waffen-SS as a normal act of war, justifiable according to the terms of the Franco-German armistice in 1940 (pp. 386–89). The factual accuracy of these arguments is as dubious as their moral status. They are dealt with in more detail in the following chapters. Here it may be noted that Jewish shopkeepers in Germany were not responsible for a boycott on German goods in Britian and the United States, and that burning women and children alive in church, which is what happened at Oradour, hardly qualifies as

a normal act of war. Koch's views may be pursued further through his books *Der Deutsche Bürgerkrieg: Eine Geschichte der deutschen und österreichischen Freikorps* (Berlin, 1978); *The Hitler Youth: Origins and Development 1922–45* (London, 1978); *A History of Prussia* (London, 1978); and *A Constitutional History of Germany in the 19th and 20th Centuries* (London, 1984).

27. Joachim C. Fest, "Die geschuldete Erinnerung: Zur Kontroverse über die Unvergleichbarkeit der nationalsozialistischen Massenverbrechen," *Frankfurter Allgemeine Zeitung,* August 29, 1986, (Piper, pp. 100–112). See also Fest's *The Face of the Third Reich: Portraits of the Nazi Leadership* (London, 1970; first published in German, 1963); *Hitler* (London, 1974, first published in German, 1973); and *Hitler, eine Karriere* (film, 1977). Fest's film was widely criticized as too favorable toward Hitler. It made only the briefest of references to the murder of the Jews.

28. Koch's sweeping dismissal of *Mein Kampf* (n. 26, above) on these points cannot be sustained. See Fest, *Hitler,* for example; also Eberhard Jäckel, 'Die elende Praxis der Untersteller: Das Einmalige der nationalsozialistischen Verbrechen lässt sich nicht leugnen," *Die Zeit,* September 12, 1986 (Piper, *Historikerstreit,* pp. 115–22). For a more general critique of the "Asiatic deed" argument, see Hans Heinrich Nolte, " 'Die Qualen ihr erdachtet nach Barbaren Art.' Der 'Historikerstreit,' die 'Asiatische Tat' und die Sowjetunion," *Widerspruch. Münchner Zeitschrift für Philosphie* 10 (1987), pp. 10–16.

29. For a discussion of Nolte's tenuous chain of reasoning on this point, see Wehler, *Entsorgung?,* pp. 40–46.

30. Eberhard Jäckel and A. Kuhn (eds.), *Hitler, Sämtliche Aufzeichnungen 1905–1924* (Stuttgart, 1980); Jäckel, *Hitler's Weltanschauung* (Middletown, Conn., 1972); H. R. Trevor-Roper (ed.), *Hitler's Table Talk 1941–1944* (London, 1953).

31. Adolf Hitler, *Mein Kampf,* trans. Ralph Manheim, with an introduction by D. C. Watt (London, 1969).

32. Nolte, *Bürgerkrieg,* pp. 88–89. J. P. Nettl, *Rosa Luxemburg* (Oxford, 1966), pp. 766–80, provides a detailed description of the murders, which were carried out in a context of revolutionary defeat and vindictive reactionary triumphalism. For a suggestive study of the mentality of the Freikorps, see Klaus Theweleit, *Male Fantasies* (Minneapolis, 1987). For the general point behind these cases, see Wolfgang J. Mommsen, "Waren die Bolschewisten an allem schuld? Ein Buch vereinfacht Geschichtsdeutung," *Kölner Stadtanzeiger,* January 12, 1988.

33. Heinrich Hillmayr, *Roter und Weisser Terror in Bayern nach 1918* (Munich, 1974). The revolutionaries' murder of the hostages on April 30, 1919, although absolutely indefensible, was the product of embitterment and outrage at the numerous murders and acts of violence already committed by the Freikorps. See the account in *Die Münchner Tragödie: Entstehung, Verlauf, und Zusammenbruch der Räte-Republik München* (Berlin, 1919), p. 25, and the balanced assessment in Heinrich August Winkler,

Von der Revolution zur Stabilisierung: Arbeiter und Arbeiterbewegung in der Weimarer Republik 1918 bis 1924 (Berlin and Bonn, 1984), pp. 184–90. For the Tucholsky quotation, see Wolfgang Schieder, "Der Nationalsozialismus im Fehlurteil philosophischer Geschichtsschreibung. Zur Methode von Ernst Noltes 'Europäischem Bürgerkrieg,'" *Geschichte und Gesellschaft* 15 (1989), pp. 89–114, esp. pp. 102–3.

34. Hans-Ulrich Wehler, *Entsorgung der deutschen Vergangenheit? Ein polemischer Essay zum "Historikerstreit"* (Munich, 1988), pp. 147–54, and pp. 237–38, nn. 77, 78; Jürgen Kocka, "Hitler sollte nicht durch Stalin und Pol Pot verdrängt werden: Über Versuche deutscher Historiker, die Ungeheuerlichkeit von NS-Verbrechen zu relativieren," in Piper, *Historikerstreit*, pp. 132–42, here p. 142 (originally in *Frankfurter Rundschau*, September 23, 1986, but without this point). The "rat-cage" argument assumes more prominence in Nolte's article, and hence in the controversy, than it does in his book, and it must be pointed out that Nolte succeeds in establishing overall that the Bolsheviks committed many acts of brutality, terror, and murder, in 1917 and subsequently, during the Civil War, and that the early Nazis, including Hitler, knew about these from right-wing radical and Russian émigré circles in 1920–21 (Nolte, *Bürgerkrieg*, p. 115). However, see also the discussion in Niels Kadritzke, "Zweierlei Untergang in düsterer Verflechtung: Zur politischen Dimension der 'Historiker-Debatte,'" *Probleme des Klassenkampfs*, no. 66 (March, 1987), pp. 169–84, Wolfgang Schieder, "Der Nationalsozialismus im Fehlurteil," esp. pp. 99–102, and Heinrich August Winkler, "Ein europäischer Bürger namens Hitler: Ernst Nolte's Entlastungsoffensive geht weiter," *Die Zeit*, December 4, 1987.

35. Nolte, *Bürgerkrieg*, pp. 359–60, 370. Nolte points out that the pogrom of 1938 was less serious than the Stalinist purges or the tsarist pogroms, and argues that before 1938 the Jewish position in the German economy had been "scarcely affected" by Nazi hostility (*Bürgerkrieg*, pp. 294–95). There is certainly no denying that plenty of larger-scale pogroms than that of 1938 can be found in history, though this again belongs to Nolte's technique of "comparative trivialization." Nolte's emphasis on what he sees as the moderation of the Reichskristallnacht, rather than what it actually did to those who were its victims, is one-sided. As for the Jews' economic position, this was surely affected from the very start of the Third Reich, with mass dismissals from the civil service, the universities, hospitals, and other areas of the economy on racial grounds, and expropriations of department stores, publishing houses, and similar actions. Nolte, however, appears to condone anti-Semitic policies in the early years of the Third Reich, by pointing out that British Ambassador Sir Horace Rumbold referred to "the ostentatious kind of lifestyle of Jewish bankers and monied people" which "inevitably aroused envy, as unemployment spread generally." Rumbold, notes Nolte, went on to refer to "the sins of the Russian and Galician Jews" who came to Germany in 1918 (Nolte, *Bürgerkrieg*, p. 556, n. 17). For a brief summary of the events of Reichskristallnacht, see Noakes and Pridham, *Nazism*, vol. 3, p. 554. For a more extended treatment, see Walter H. Pehle (ed.), *Der Judenpogrom 1938:*

Von der "Reichskristallnacht" zum Völkermord (Frankfurt, 1988). For the Weizmann declaration, see *Letters and Papers of Chaim Weizmann, Series A: Letters, Vol. XIX, January 1935–June 1940* (Jerusalem, 1977), p. 145. A secondary dispute has arisen over whether Nolte actually argues that Weizmann "declared war" on Germany on behalf of Jews everywhere, or whether he has merely critically summarized this argument in a discussion of the support which it has received from David Irving (Imanuel Geiss, *Die Habermas-Kontroverse. Ein deutscher Streit* [Berlin, 1988], pp. 55–57, 70–71). As the "original" source for this idea, however, Geiss cites an account in a Nazi magazine dating from September 1939, without noting the propagandistic manipulation of Weizmann's statement by the magazine in question (p. 200, n.5). The fact that Nolte used the ideologically neutral term "the Jews in the whole world" and not, as Habermas implied, the Nazi term "World Jewry," seems beside the point in view of Nolte's original and quite unjustifiable extrapolation of Weizmann's statement onto a global basis. The very notion of such an entity as "the Jews in the whole world" was Nazi in its essence. The overall thrust of Nolte's argument, Hans Mommsen has noted, is to hint that the Jews were somehow to blame for their own destruction (Mommsen, "Das Ressentiment als Wissenschaft," p. 501).

36. Wehler, *Entsorgung*, p. 15; Gay, *Freud, Jews, and other Germans*, p. xiii; Nolte, *Deutschland und der Kalte Krieg*, p. 360. In *Bürgerkrieg*, p. 370, Nolte returns to this argument and suggests that Germany was "liberal" in 1939 in comparison to the USSR: the concentration camps were liberal in comparison to Soviet labor camps; and the judicial system was relatively independent, as were the churches, the economy, and the Army. These points are disputable. For example, Nolte takes Hitler's continuing attacks on German judges as evidence that the latter were still acting as guarantors of legal norms (*Bürgerkrieg*, pp. 427–48), whereas in fact the rule of law had been undermined from the very start of the Third Reich; large areas of the law were increasingly governed by Nazi ideological criteria and subjected to direct or indirect political interference. See Noakes and Pridham, *Nazism*, vol. 2. pp. 471–567. Nolte has received support on these points from Hans Koch, whose book *Der Volksgerichtshof. Politische Justiz im Dritten Reich* (Munich, 1988) argues somewhat unconvincingly that there was nothing more to Nazi justice than the simple application of the rule of law.

37. See p. 16 above. Sherman made the point during an unsuccessful attempt to invite French right-wing radical Jean-Marie Le Pen to a fringe meeting at the British Conservative Party Conference in 1987.

38. Helmut Krausnick et al., *Anatomy of the SS State* (London, 1968), esp. pp. 303–96 (Hans Buchheim, "Command and Compliance"). As Buchheim remarks, opportunities to avoid carrying out criminal orders "were both more numerous and more real than those concerned are generally prepared to admit today" (p. 373).

39. See Detlev Peukert, *Die Weimarer Republik: Krisenjahre der klassischen Moderne* (Frankfurt, 1987).

40. Nolte, *Bürgerkrieg,* pp. 211, 218, 251.

41. Klaus Hildebrand, "Krieg im Frieden und Frieden im Krieg: Über das Problem der Legitimität in der Geschichte der Staatengesellschaft 1931–1941," *Historische Zeitschrift* 244, no. 1 (1987), pp. 1–28 (quotations on pp. 23–26; see also his n. 21). See also Wolfram Wette, "Über die Wiederbelebung des Antibolschewismus mit historischen Mitteln, oder: Was steckt hinter der Präventivkriegsthese?," in Erler et al., *Geschichtswende?,* pp. 86–115, esp. pp. 91–95. For Hildebrand's earlier works in English translation, see his *Foreign Policy of the Third Reich* (London, 1973) and *The Third Reich* (London, 1984).

42. Ernst Topitsch, *Stalin's War: A Radical New Theory of the Origins of the Second World War* (New York, 1987); Joachim Hoffmann, "Stalin wollte den Krieg," *Frankfurter Allgemeine Zeitung,* October 16, 1986; Günther Gillessen, "Der Krieg der Diktatoren: Wollte Stalin im Sommer 1941 das Deutsche Reich angreifen?"; Gillessen, "Der Krieg der Diktatoren: Ein erstes Resumée der Debatte über Hitlers Angriff im Osten," *Frankfurter Allgemeine Zeitung,* February 25, 1987; Viktor Suvorov, "Who Was Planning to Attack Whom in June 1941, Hitler or Stalin?" *Journal of the Royal United Services Institute for Defence Studies* 130 (1985), pp. 50–55; Suvorov, "Yes, Stalin Was Planning to Attack Hitler in June 1941," ibid., 131 (1986), no. 2, pp. 73–74; Joachim Hoffmann, "Hitler or Stalin? A German View," ibid., p. 88; D. Kunert, *Ein Weltkrieg wird programmiert* (Frankfurt, 1986); Ernest Topitsch, "Psychologische Kriegsführung–einst und heute," *Allgemeine Schweizerische Militärzeitschrift* 152, no. 7–8 (1986), pp. 415–20; Topitsch, "Perfekter Völkermord," *Rheinischer Merkur (Christ and Welt),* January 16, 1987, p. 20; Bernd Stegemann, "Geschichte und Politik: Zur Diskussion über den deutschen Angriff auf die Sowjetunion 1941," *Beiträge zur Konfliktforschung: Psycho-politische Aspekte* 17, no. 1 (1987), pp. 73–97; Joachim Hoffmann, "Die Sowjetunion bis zum Vorabend des deutschen Angriffs," in *Das Deutsche Reich und der Zweite Weltkrieg, Vol. 4: Der Angriff auf die Sowjetunion* (Stuttgart, 1983); Max Klüver, *Präventivschlag 1941: Zur Vorgeschichte des Russlandfeldzuges* (Berg, 1986); Gerd-Klaus Kaltenbrunner, "Angst vor einem Raubtier, das absolut tot ist: Streit um die deutsche Geschichte: Eine Antwort an den Politologen Kurt Sontheimer," *Rheinischer Merkur (Christ und Welt),* December 12, 1986; Adolf von Thadden, "Der Russlandfeldzug—Überfall oder Präventivschlag?" *Nation Europa,* no. 3 (1987). The last-named author, Adolf von Thadden, was leader of the neo-Nazi National Democratic Party (NPD) in West Germany in the late 1960s and early 1970s, and was quick to take up the preventive-war thesis once it had been publicized in the press. The NPD's own view of history in the 1960s emphasized what its leaders saw as the innate terrorism and violence of Communism and the justifiable nature of Nazism as the only viable response to the Communist threat in 1933. According to this view, the Nazi takeover of Czechoslovakia was in the Czechs' own interest, to protect them against the Russian threat; the invasion of Poland in 1939 was defensive; America was mainly to blame not only for the Second World War, inspired by Jewish influence, and in an unholy alliance with

Britain and Russia, but also for the First World War; and the German invasion of the Soviet Union in 1941 was a "counteroffensive." See the analysis of the NPD press, and interviews with von Thadden, in Reinhard Kühnl et al., *Die NPD: Struktur, Ideologie, and Funktion einer neofaschistischen Partei* (Frankfurt, 1969), esp. pp. 131–44. More generally, see Lutz Niethammer, *Angepasster Faschismus: Politische Praxis der NPD* (Frankfurt, 1969).

43. Andreas Hillgruber, *Hitlers Strategie: Politik und Kriegführung 1940–1941* (2nd ed., Munich, 1982); Hillgruber, "Das Russland-Bild der führenden deutschen Militärs vom Beginn des Angriffs auf die Sowjetunion," in A. Fischer et al. (eds.), *Russland–Deutschland–Amerika* (Wiesbaden, 1978), pp. 296–310; Hillgruber, "Der Angriff auf die Sowjetunion," *Frankfurter Allgemeine Zeitung*, November 28, 1984; Hillgruber, "Noch einmal: Hitlers Wendung gegen die Sowjetunion 1941," *Geschichte in Wissenschaft und Unterricht* 33 (1982), pp. 214–26.

44. For an informative account of this affair, see Wehler, *Entsorgung*, pp. 192–96. The book in question is Wolfram Wette, *Gustav Noske: Eine politische Biographie* (Düsseldorf, 1987). For the background, Volker Berghahn, "Das Militärgeschichtliche Forschungsamt in Freiburg," *Geschichte und Gesellschaft* 14 (1988), pp. 269–74. Nolte, however, cites Hoffmann's work (and that of Ernst Topitsch) in support of his view that the validity or otherwise of the preventive-war thesis has not yet been determined by historical scholarship (*Bürgerkrieg*, p. 459).

45. Bianka Pietrow, "Deutschland im Juni 1941—ein Opfer sowjetischer Aggression? Zur Kontroverse über die Präventivkriegsthese," *Geschichte und Gesellschaft* 14 (1988), pp. 116–35; Gabriel Gorodetsky, "Was Stalin Planning to Attack Hitler in June 1941?" *Journal of the Royal United Services Institute for Defence Studies*, no. 2 (1986), pp. 72–79; Gerd Ueberschär, " 'Historikerstreit' und 'Präventivkriegsthese,' " *Tribüne* 103 (1987), pp. 108–16; Ueberschär, "Zur Wiederbelebung der 'Präventivkriegsthese': Die neuen Rechtfertigungsversuche des deutschen Überfalls auf die UdSSR 1941 im Dienste 'psychopolitischer Aspekte' und 'psychologischer Kriegführung,' " *Geschichtsdidaktik* 1987, pp. 331–42; John Erickson, *The Road to Stalingrad: Stalin's War with Germany* (London, 1975); Bianka Pietrow, *Stalinismus–Sicherheit–Offensive: Das Dritte Reich in der Konzeption der sowjetischen Aussenpolitik 1933–1941* (Melsungen, 1983); Wolfram Wette (ed.), *"Unternehmen Barbarossa": Der deutsche Überfall auf die Sowjetunion 1941* (Paderborn, 1984); Wolfram Wette, "Verteidigungslügen. Warum die Mär vom Präventivkrieg gegen Russland neubelebt wird," *Die Zeit*, August 7, 1988.

46. Willi A. Boelcke (ed.), *The Secret Conferences of Dr. Goebbels, October 1939–March 1943* (London, n.d.), pp. 176–77; Noakes and Pridham, *Nazism*, vol. 3, pp. 798–818 (including the initial directive for "Operation Barbarossa" issued by Hitler on December 18, 1940, pp. 809–10); Fred Taylor (ed.), *The Goebbels Diaries 1939–1941* (London, 1982) (not always reliable, however); Omer Bartov, *The Eastern Front, 1941–1945: German Troops and the Barbarization of Warfare* (London, 1985), pp. 84–85; H.

R. Trevor-Roper (ed.), *Hitler's War Directives, 1939–1945* (London, 1964); Ueberschär, "Hitlers Entschluss," p. 109; Wette, "Über die Wiederbelebung," p. 109. For a recent, carefully argued account of the genesis of "Operation Barbarossa," see William Carr, *Poland to Pearl Harbor: The Making of the Second World War* (London, 1985), pp. 112–27.

CHAPTER 3: BULWARK AGAINST BOLSHEVISM?

1. Andreas Hillgruber, *Hitlers Strategie;* Hillgruber (ed.), *Das Kriegstagebuch des Oberkommandos der Wehrmacht (Wehrmachtsführungsstab)*, vol. II, pts. 1 and 2 (Frankfurt, 1963); *Deutsche Geschichte 1945–1972: Die "deutsche Frage" in der Weltpolitik* (Berlin, 1974; 2nd ed., extended to 1982, Berlin, 1985); *Der Zweite Weltkrieg: Kriegsziele und Strategie der grossen Mächte* (Stuttgart, 1982). (Hillgruber died in May 1989, after this book was in press.)

2. Holger H. Herwig, "Andreas Hillgruber, Historian of 'Grossmachtpolitik,' 1871–1945," *Central European History* 15 (1982), pp. 186–98. For a rather less sympathetic account of Hillgruber's career, see Wehler, *Entsorgung,* pp. 20–24. For a sample of Hillgruber's work in English, see his *Germany and the Two World Wars* (Cambridge, Mass., 1981).

3. Hillgruber, *Zweierlei Untergang: Die Zerschlagung des Deutschen Reiches und das Ende des europäischen Judentums* (Berlin, 1986).

4. Ibid., pp. 9–10. The claim that these two events are comparable is thus advanced not simply on the dust jacket, as some of Hillgruber's defenders have maintained (e.g., Craig, "The War"); it is made explicitly in the text. The effect, as Martin Broszat has commented, borders on the apologetic (Martin Broszat, "Wo sich die Geister scheiden: Die Beschwörung der Geschichte taugt nicht als nationaler Religionsersatz," *Die Zeit,* October 3, 1986; also Piper, *Historikerstreit,* pp. 189–95).

5. Hillgruber, *Zweierlei,* pp. 18–19, 21, 24–25, 34–37, 40, 42. The claim that Hillgruber refers sympathetically to the local Nazi leaders (Jürgen Habermas, "Eine Art Schadensabwicklung: Die apologetischen Tendenzen in der deutschen Geschichtsschreibung," *Die Zeit,* July 11, 1986; also in Piper, *Historikerstreit,* pp. 62–63, and in Habermas, *Eine Art Schadensabwicklung* [Frankfurt, 1987], pp. 120–37, this last-named version being the fullest) is not borne out by the relevant text (Hillgruber, *Zweierlei,* p. 37), which Habermas manipulates in order to create this impression (Klaus Hildebrand, "Das Zeitalter der Tyrannen: Geschichte und Politik: Die Verwalter der Aufklärung, das Risiko der Wissenschaft und die Geborgenheit der Weltanschauung: Eine Entgegnung auf Jürgen Habermas," *Frankfurter Allgemeine Zeitung,* July 31, 1986; also in Piper, *Historikerstreit,* pp. 84–92). As Gordon A. Craig has pointed out ("The War"), the charge is misplaced. Hillgruber's text reads: "Some of the senior Nazi officials stood the test in the crisis of the last, desperate defense, of collapse and flight; others failed, some of them in a miserable way." Habermas creates out of this statement a quotation—"tested senior officials"—which

in the absence of the rest of the passage must give the impression that Hillgruber's attitude toward Nazi officials in the East is uncritical if not downright positive. This may appear a legitimate procedure to a polemicizing philosopher; to the historian, it looks like the manipulation of a source (see also Hillgruber, "Jürgen Habermas, Karl-Heinz Janssen, und die Aufklärung Anno 1986," *Geschichte in Wissenschaft und Unterricht,* 37 (1986), pp. 725–38, here p. 731; also in Piper, *Historikerstreit,* pp. 331–49.) Hans-Ulrich Wehler's defense of Habermas on this point rests somewhat insecurely on the ground that it is a matter of secondary importance (Wehler, *Entsorgung,* pp. 160–61). Habermas's defense of his procedure, which simply reaffirms that it was "justified," is equally unconvincing (Habermas, "Leserbrief," *Frankfurter Allgemeine Zeitung,* August 11, 1986; also in Piper, *Historikerstreit,* pp. 95–97, and "Anmerkung, 23. Februar 1987," in Piper, *Historikerstreit,* pp. 383–86, here p. 384; and in Habermas, *Eine Art,* pp. 149–58, here p. 150). Imanuel Geiss, in his *Die Habermas-Kontroverse. Ein deutscher Streit* (Berlin, 1988) devotes considerable space to Habermas's treatment of this quotation (pp. 52–55) and of other quotations from Hillgruber, Nolte, and others (pp. 55–72, 190–3); he also subjects Habermas's defenders to the same type of criticism (pp. 72–79). All this misses the overall context and thus the point of the controversy. This subdispute in the debate seems to me to indicate one of the many disadvantages of the polemical style, namely that its "no-holds-barred" approach detracts attention from the actual contest and diverts it onto the secondary issue of whether or not the rules are being adhered to.

6. Hillgruber, *Zweierlei,* pp. 47–48, 50–52, 55.

7. Ibid., pp. 56–57, 61–62, 64–65.

8. Ibid., pp. 66–67.

9. Ibid., pp. 68, 70–72, 74. Hillgruber's view that the "German question" is still an open one was given more extended treatment at a conference held in Augsburg in 1981, where he argued for a liberal nationalism linked to human rights as a means of keeping open links between East and West Germany and preventing either being permanently divided from the other. Hillgruber regarded this as more important than the constitutional form taken by reunification, and opposed it to a more right-wing approach which he rejected as arguing for the revival of Germany as a great power. The problem was, he said, convincing the younger generation of Germans that this "national-liberal" idea of reunification was worth supporting. See Otto Büsch and James J. Sheehan (eds.), *Die Rolle der Nation in der deutschen Geschichte und Gegenwart* (Berlin, 1985); Josef Becker and Andreas Hillgruber (eds.), *Die Deutsche Frage im 19. und 20. Jahrhundert* (Munich, 1983); and the discussion in Eley, "Nazism, Politics, and the Image of the Past," pp. 190–94.

10. Wehler, *Entsorgung,* is an exception. So too is Adelheid von Saldern, "Hillgrubers 'Zweierlei Untergang'—der Untergang historischer Erfahrungsanalyse?" in Heide Gerstenberger and Dorothea Schmidt (eds.),

Normalität oder Normalisierung? Geschichtswerkstätten und Faschismusanalyse (Münster, 1987), pp. 160–9. But see, on the other hand, Broszat, "Wo sich die Geister scheiden"; Craig, "The War"; Imanuel Geiss, "Auschwitz, 'asiatische Tat,'" *Der Spiegel,* October 20, 1986; Hans Mommsen, "Suche nach der 'verlorenen Geschichte'? Bemerkungen zum historischen Selbstverständnis der Bundesrepublik," *Merkur,* September-October 1986, pp. 864–74, esp. n. 7; Heinrich August Winkler, "Auf ewig in Hitlers Schatten? Zum Streit über das Geschichtsbild der Deutschen," *Frankfurter Rundschau,* November 14, 1986; Eberhard Jäckel, "Die elende Praxis der Untersteller: Das einmalige der nationalsozialistischen Verbrechen lässt sich nicht leugnen," *Die Zeit,* September 12, 1986; (all except Craig reprinted in Piper, *Historikerstreit,* pp. 189–95, 220–22, 156–73, 256–63, 115–22, as is Hildebrand, "Zeitalter," pp. 84–92). More recent contributions have been more willing to criticize Hillgruber. See for example Niels Kadritzke, "Zweierlei Untergang in düsterer Verflechtung: Zur politischen Dimension der 'Historiker-Debatte,'" *Probleme des Klassenkampfs,* no. 66 (March, 1987), pp. 169–84; Dieter Schellong, "Nationale Identität und Christentum," in Wieland Eschenhagen (ed.), *Die neue deutsche Ideologie: Einsprüche gegen die Entsorgung der Vergangenheit* (Darmstadt, 1988), pp. 139–62 (a theological critique); Friedländer, "West Germany and the Burden of the Past," pp. 6–8; also, for an earlier critique, Micha Brumlik, "Neuer Staatsmythos Ostfront: Die neueste Entwicklung der Geschichtswissenschaft der BRD," *Die Tageszeitung,* July 12, 1986 (also in Piper, *Historikerstreit,* pp. 77–83).

11. Hagen Schulze, "Fragen, die wir stellen müssen: Keine historische Haftung ohne nationale Identität," *Die Zeit,* September 26, 1986 (also in Piper, *Historikerstreit,* pp. 143–50).

12. Compare Hans Mommsen, "Suche," p. 871 (Piper, *Historikerstreit,* p. 168). See also Hillgruber's statement that the mass murder of the Jews was a unique crime in the "Western" world but "cannot qualitatively be judged different" from the murder of the kulaks and others by the Russians ("Für die Forschung gibt es Kein Frageverbot: Ein Gespräch mit dem Kölner Historiker Andreas Hillgruber, der eine Bilanz der Revisionismus-Debatte zieht," *Rheinischer Merkur (Christ und Welt),* October 31, 1986; also in Piper, *Historikerstreit,* pp. 232–240, here p. 236). Support for Hillgruber and Nolte is also provided by Klaus Hildebrand, "Wer dem Abgrund entrinnen will, muss ihn aufs genaueste ausloten: Ist die neue deutsche Geschichtsschreibung revisionistisch?" *Die Welt,* November 22, 1986, and Joachim C. Fest, "Die geschuldete Erinnerung: zur Kontroverse über die Unvergleichbarkeit des nationalsozialistischen Massenverbrechens," *Frankfurter Allgemeine Zeitung,* August 29, 1986 (also in Piper, *Historikerstreit,* respectively pp. 281–92 and 100–112). For counterarguments, see Hans Mommsen, "Neues Geschichtsbewusstsein und Relativierung des Nationalsozialismus," *Blätter für deutsche und internationale Politik* 31, no. 10 (1986), pp. 5–18 (Piper, *Historikerstreit,* pp. 174–88), concentrating on Fest, Hildebrand, and Nolte.

13. Alfred Dregger, "Im Wortlaut: 'Beleidigung meines Bruders': Offener Brief an 53 US-Senatoren," *Frankfurter Rundschau,* April 23, 1985; Dreg-

ger, "Aus der Rede zum Volkstrauertag: 'Alle Toten verdienen die gleiche Ehrfurcht,'" *Frankfurter Allgemeine Zeitung*, November 17, 1986; Thomas Schnabel, "Geschichte und Wende," in Erler, *Geschichtswende?*, pp. 24–25, 27–28; the full version of Dregger's speech can be found in *Bulletin des Presse- und Informationsamts der Bundesregierung*, no. 140, November 18, 1986, pp. 1164–72. These views also reflect a widely held belief among conservatives that Germany was fighting two wars in the 1941–45 period, and that in the East, it was, as it were, on the right side. Such was the implication of Bitburg (see above). Such is also the explicit argument of Major-General J. F. C. Fuller, in *The Conduct of War 1789–1961: A Study of the Impact of the French, Industrial, and Russian Revolutions on War and its Conduct* (London, 1961), a book that has been highly praised by the Regius Professor of History at Oxford, Michael Howard, (see his comments on the back cover), and used as a set book by Britain's Open University. Fuller wrote: "There can be no doubt whatsoever that in 1939 the best policy for France and Great Britain would have been to keep out of the war, let the two great dictatorial Powers cripple each other, and in the meantime have re-armed at top speed. Had they done so, a time would have come when they could profitably intervene. Should Russia then be winning, Hitler would be discredited, and support could be given to Germany" (p. 264). Fuller is thus heavily critical of Churchill ("Blinded by his hatred of Hitler," p. 266) and Roosevelt (whom he describes, quoting U.S. General Albert C. Wedemeyer, as "surrounded by intrigues and soft-on-Communism eggheads," pp. 268–69). Russian foreign-policy aims, Fuller wrote, were more dangerous to the democracies than German (p. 249).

14. Bartov, *Eastern Front*, pp. 2, 142. For Nolte's arguments on these points, see Nolte, *Bürgerkrieg*, pp. 502–3, 465–67, 470, 485, 499. Mention should be made here of the American lawyer Alfred de Zayas, who in a series of publications has drawn attention to Allied war crimes (and there were undoubtedly violations of the rules of war committed by Allied troops) without, however, balancing this out by situating them in the context of the far more widespread and serious war crimes committed by the Germans. See Alfred de Zayas, *Die Wehrmacht-Untersuchungsstelle: Deutsche Ermittelungen über alliierte Völkerrechtsverletzungen im Zweiten Weltkrieg* (4th ed., Munich, 1984), a book which Nolte describes as showing "happy evidence of the will to objectivity on the part of a foreigner" (*Bürgerkrieg*, pp. 512–13, n. 26). See also the favorable review of *Bürgerkrieg* by de Zayas in *Die Welt*, November 20, 1987, and further comments below, p. 172, n. 4.

15. Michael Burleigh, *Germany Turns Eastwards: A Study of Ostforschung in the Third Reich* (Cambridge, 1988), pp. 181–85; Martin Broszat, *Nationalsozialistische Polenpolitik 1919–1945* (2nd ed., Frankfurt, 1965), pp. 119–122; Helmut Krausnick, *Hitlers Einsatzgruppen. Die Truppe des Weltanschauungskrieges 1936–1942* (Frankfurt, 1985), pp. 45–50.

16. Bartov, *Eastern Front*, pp. 152–54, 106. See also Christian Streit, *Keine Kameraden: Die Wehrmacht und die sowjetischen Kriegsgefangenen*,

1941–1945 (Stuttgart, 1978); and Theo Schulte, *The German Army and Nazi Policies in Occupied Russia* (Deddington, 1988).

17. Bartov, *Eastern Front*, pp. 142–49.

18. Ibid., pp. 80, 83, 85, 94, 112, 117.

19. Ibid., pp. 121, 134.

20. See Martin Gilbert, *The Holocaust: The Jewish Tragedy* (London, 1986), pp. 20–21, 141–42, 154, 289, 304, 509; however, for examples of ethnic Germans helping Jews, see ibid., pp. 253, 776, 808 (the last two at the very end of the war).

21. Bartov, *Eastern Front*, pp. 27, 29, 116, 153–54, and Streit, *Keine Kameraden*.

22. Bartov, *Eastern Front*, p. 104. For Bartov's own comments on Hillgruber, see Bartov, "Historians on the Eastern Front: Andreas Hillgruber and Germany's Tragedy," *Jahrbuch des Instituts für deutsche Geschichte, Tel-Aviv* 16 (1987), pp. 325–45. See also Kadritzke, "Zweierlei." It is unfortunate that the conduct of the German Army on the Eastern front is nowhere alluded to in Imanuel Geiss's defense of Hillgruber (Geiss, *Die Habermas-Kontroverse*, pp. 44–46).

23. Hillgruber, *Zweierlei*, pp. 20, 47. That Hillgruber's own advocacy of a Central Europe dominated by a strong and united Germany is shared by Nolte is also noted by Hans Mommsen, "Das Ressentiment als Wissenschaft. Anmerkungen zu Ernst Noltes 'Der europäische Bürgerkrieg 1917–1945. Nationalsozialismus und Bolschewismus,'" *Geschichte und Gesellschaft* 14 (1988), pp. 495–512, here p. 499.

24. For popular attitudes toward Hitler, see Ian Kershaw, *"The Hitler Myth": Image and Reality in the Third Reich* (Oxford, 1987); for the plotters' attitudes to the extermination program, see Sarah Gordon, *Hitler, Germans, and the Jewish Question* (Princeton, 1984), pp. 273–77, 282.

25. Wehler, *Entsorgung*, pp. 54–57 and Schnabel, "Geschichte und Wende," in Erler et al., *Geschichtswende?*, p. 25.

26. Schnabel, "Geschichte und Wende," p. 27; F. L. Carsten, "Stauffenberg's Bomb," *Encounter*, September 1964, pp. 64–67; there is a useful discussion of the aims of the 1944 opposition movement in J. C. G. Röhl (ed.), *From Bismarck to Hitler: The Problem of Continuity in German History* (London, 1970), pp. 164–82.

CHAPTER 4: AUSCHWITZ AND ELSEWHERE

1. Hillgruber, *Zweierlei*, p. 77, following in particular Hans-Günter Zmarzlik, "Antisemitismus im Deutschen Kaiserreich, 1871–1918," in Bernd Martin and Ernst Schulin (eds.), *Die Juden als Minderheit in der Geschichte* (Munich, 1981).

2. Hillgruber, *Zweierlei*, pp. 79–81, 83–85, 89, 90–91, 97–99.

3. Such oversimplifications are often present in inevitably brief introductions to standard works on the fate of the Jews under the Third Reich—for example Lucy Dawidowicz, *The War Against the Jews 1933–45* (London, 1975), chap. 2.

4. Hans-Georg Stümke, " 'Wo nix is, hett de Kaiser sien Recht verlor'n' oder 'Der Stein auf dem Sofa der Frau Senatorin': Die Hamburger Unruhen vom 31. August bis 5. September 1830," in Jörg Berlin (ed.), *Das andere Hamburg: Freiheitliche Bestrebungen in der Hansestadt seit dem Spätmittelalter* (Cologne, 1981), pp. 48–68. It is difficult to understand why this article on anti-Semitic disturbances should appear in a volume devoted to "progressive and democratic movements" in the city. See also Mosche Zimmermann, "Antijüdische Sozialproteste von Unter- und Mittelschichten 1819–1835," in Arno Herzig et al. (eds.), *Arbeiter in Hamburg* (Hamburg, 1983), pp. 89–94.

5. See the useful survey in Eleonore Sterling, *Judenhass: Die Anfänge des politischen Antisemitismus in Deutschland (1815–1850)* (Frankfurt, 1969).

6. See Geoff Eley's comments, reviewing (among other books) Richard S. Levy, *The Downfall of the Anti-Semitic Political Parties in Imperial Germany* (New Haven, 1975), in *Social History* 2, no. 2 (1977), pp. 691–95; Blackbourn, *Populists and Patricians*, pp. 168–87; Hans-Jürgen Puhle, *Agrarische Interessenpolitik und preussischer Konservatismus im Wilhelminischen Reich, 1893–1914* (Bonn, 1975), pp. 111–42, 274–92; Röhl, *Bismarck to Hitler*, pp. 39–53. For the Social Democrats, see Rosemarie Leuschen-Seppel, *Socialdemokratie und Antisemitismus im Kaiserreich* (Bonn, 1978), comprehensively demolishing the thesis of "socialist anti-Semitism" advanced by E. Silberner, *Sozialisten zur Judenfrage* (Berlin, 1962) and others. Further evidence on this point is presented in Richard J. Evans, *Kneipengespräche im Kaiserreich: Die Berichte der Hamburger Politischen Polizei 1892–1914* (Reinbek, 1989), pp. 302–21.

7. Donald Niewyk, *The Jews in Weimar Germany* (Baton Rouge, 1980); Niewyk, *Socialist, Anti-Semite, and Jew* (Baton Rouge, 1971); Peter Pulzer, *The Rise of Political Anti-Semitism in Germany and Austria* (New York, 1964).

8. Gordon, *Hitler*, pp. 88–90, W. S. Allen, *The Nazi Seizure of Power: The Experience of a Single German Town 1922–1945* (rev. ed., New York, 1984), p. 84.

9. Ian Kershaw, *Popular Opinion and Political Dissent in the Third Reich: Bavaria 1933–1945* (Oxford, 1983), pp. 224–77, esp. p. 277; Gordon, *Hitler;* Ian Kershaw, "How Effective Was Nazi Propaganda?" in David Welch (ed.), *Nazi Propaganda: The Power and the Limitations* (London, 1983), pp. 180–205.

10. Rudolf Augstein, "Die neue Auschwitz-Lüge," *Der Spiegel*, October 6, 1986 (also in Piper, *Historikerstreit*, pp. 196–203). On the genesis of the

"Final Solution," there is a balanced survey of the arguments in Ian Kershaw, *The Nazi Dictatorship* (2nd ed., London, 1989), pp. 82–105. Hillgruber's own account is available in greater detail in his articles "Die ideologisch-dogmatische Grundlage der nationalsozialistischen Politik der Ausrottung der Juden in den besetzten Gebieten der Sowjetunion und ihre Durchführung, 1941–44," *German Studies Review* 2 (1979), pp. 264–96, and "Die 'Endlösung' und das deutsche Ostimperium als Kernstück des rassenideologischen Programms des Nationalsozialismus," in Manfred Funke (ed.), *Hitler, Deutschland, und die Mächte* (Düsseldorf, 1975), pp. 94–114. The emphasis placed in the 1970s by conservative historians such as Bracher and Hildebrand on the determining influence of Hitler is usefully discussed by Tim Mason, "Intention and Explanation: A Current Controversy About the Interpretation of National Socialism," in Gerhard Hirschfeld and Lothar Kettenacker (eds.), *The "Führer State": Myth and Reality* (Stuttgart, 1981), pp. 23–40.

11. Hillgruber, *Zweierlei*, pp. 97–98; Habermas, "Eine Art Schadensabwicklung" (Piper, *Historikerstreit*, p. 66); Craig, "The War," p. 16. Peter Steinbach, "Unbestechlich und unabhängig: Andreas Hillgrubers Essay über 'Zweierlei Untergang,' " *Frankfurter Allgemeine Zeitung*, July 8, 1986, also notes the contrast. Geiss, *Die Habermas-Kontroverse*, pp. 66–69, misses the point once more.

12. Hillgruber, *Zweierlei*, pp. 97–98; Albert Speer, *Inside the Third Reich* (London, 1979); Manfred Schmidt, *Albert Speer: Das Ende eines Mythos* (Munich, 1982); Kershaw, *Nazi Dictatorship*, pp. 82–105. The evidence for the anti-Semitic convictions of many leading and second-rank Nazis is extensive: for a sample, see Joachim C. Fest, *The Face of the Third Reich* (London, 1970). See also the account in Ian Kershaw, *The Hitler Myth: Image and Reality in the Third Reich* (Oxford, 1987), pp. 229–52, presenting evidence of the enthusiastic anti-Semitism of Nazi officials at least down to the level of *Kreisleiter*.

13. See the remarks of Kershaw, *Nazi Dictatorship*, pp. 61–81. Failure to distinguish between propagandistic and rhetorical statements on the one hand and genuine statements of belief and intent on the other is a major weakness in Nolte's analysis, perhaps reflecting a more general weakness of the philosophical, "phenomenological," or history-of-ideas approach.

14. Kershaw, *Nazi Dictatorship*, pp. 61–81; Mason, "Intention"; Klaus Hildebrand, "Nationalsozialismus ohne Hitler?" *Geschichte in Wissenschaft und Unterricht* 31 (1980), pp. 284–305, and the following acrimonious debate in ibid., 32 (1981), pp. 197–98, 738–42, and *Geschichtsdidaktik* 5 (1980), pp. 325–57, and 6 (1981), pp. 233–38. See also Martin Broszat, "Soziale Motivation und Führer-Bindung des Nationalsozialismus," *Vierteljahrshefte für Zeitgeschichte* 18 (1970), pp. 392–409; and Hans Mommsen, "National Socialism: Continuity and Change," in Laqueur (ed.), *Fascism*, pp. 151–92, for criticisms of the more conservative point of view; for a classic exposition of the latter, see Bracher, *The German Dictatorship*.

15. Martin Broszat, *The Hitler State: The Foundation and Development of the Internal Structure of the Third Reich* (New York, 1981). This work has not been invalidated by Henry Ashby Turner, Jr., *German Big Business and the Rise of Hitler* (New York, 1985), although Turner does succeed in disposing of many of the more colorful legends about the role of big business. See the review by F. L. Carsten in *Bulletin of the German Historical Institute London* (1986), pp. 20–23. The objections raised to Turner's work by David Abraham, "Big Business, Nazism, and German Politics at the End of Weimar," *European History Quarterly* 17 (1987), pp. 235–46, are overstated, to say the least.

16. See above, pp. 50, 63–65.

17. Bartov, *Eastern Front,* pp. 155–56.

18. Hans Mommsen, "The Realization of the Unthinkable: The 'Final Solution of the Jewish Question' in the Third Reich," in Hirschfeld, *Policies,* pp. 93–144, here pp. 134–35, n. 36.

19. *German History* 6, no. 1 (1988), p. 109; also Kershaw, *Hitler Myth,* pp. 229–52.

20. Broszat, "Wo sich die Geister scheiden"; Broszat, "Hitler und die Genesis der 'Endlösung': Aus Anlass der Thesen von David Irving," in Hermann Graml and Klaus-Dietmar Henke (eds.), *Nach Hitler: Der Schwierige Umgang mit unserer Geschichte: Beiträge von Martin Broszat* (Munich, 1986), pp. 187–229—a convincing analysis of Irving's work. In his books *Hitler's War* (London, 1977) and *The War Path* (London, 1978), Irving seeks to argue that Hitler had no aggressive intentions toward Western Europe, and only "mundane" territorial ambitions in Central Europe and the East (*The War Path,* pp. xii–xiv). Irving also claims that the *Kommissarbefehl,* Hitler's order that political commissars in the Red Army should be shot if captured, was a response to the Soviet intention of exterminating the ruling classes in Western Europe. As this suggests, Irving also supports the preventive-war thesis. In a number of respects, indeed, these arguments are now taken up by Nolte in his book *Der europäische Bürgerkrieg.* In 1982 Irving temporarily abandoned his writing in order to try to unify various splinter groups of the ultraright in Britain under the aegis of an organization called Focus (Paul Wilkinson, *The New Fascists* [2nd ed., London, 1983], p. 169). Irving was reported as admitting to the *Oxford Mail* that he had "links at a low level" with the National Front. He was also reported as referring to *Spotlight,* the magazine of the neo-Nazi "Liberty Lobby" in the United States, as "an excellent fortnightly paper." Correspondents to *Focal Point,* the magazine of Irving's organization, included John Tyndall, of the British National Party, perhaps the most significant of postwar British neofascists; and the magazine carried advertisements for *Excalibur,* the journal of the Nationalist Party, a spinoff from the National Front (Gill Seidel, *The Holocaust Denial,* [London, 1980], pp. 54–56). This move into politics, regarded at the time as highly important by Irving himself and very significant by observers of the neofascist scene such as Martin Walker, author of the standard work on postwar British fascism, failed for lack of funds. However, Irving continued to be observed

speaking regularly at fascist and neofascist meetings on the Continent, including those of the Deutsche Volks-Union, at which a number of members of the Wikinger Jugend, described by author Robert Harris as "a fanatical sect of young neo-Nazis," were present. See Robert Harris, *Selling Hitler: The Story of the Hitler Diaries* (London, 1986), esp. pp. 338–39 and 344, recounting Irving's conversion to the belief that the forged "Hitler diaries," "discovered" in 1983, were genuine. Harris's excellent and very entertaining book, however, seriously underplays the political motives behind the diaries' emergence from Nazi and neo-Nazi circles in the Federal Republic. Despite his denial that Hitler knew about the extermination of the Jews, Irving admitted that he had, pinned to his wall, a copy of Hitler's January 1939 speech in which he said that if the Jews provoked a world war, it would end with their destruction (Seidel, *The Holocaust Denial*, pp. 122–23). See also B. Smith, "Two Alibis for the Inhumanities: A. R. Butz, *The Hoax of the Twentieth Century*, and David Irving, *Hitler's War*," *German Studies Review*, October 1978, pp. 327–35; and Charles W. Snydor, Jr., "The Selling of Adolf Hitler: David Irving's *Hitler's War*," *Central European History* 12, no. 2 (1979), pp. 169–99. Irving's political beliefs can also be gauged from his book *Uprising* (London, 1981), in which he apparently suggests that the Stalinist regime in Hungary was run by Jews, and the 1956 uprising was anti-Semitic, the latter implicitly therefore being understood in a positive sense, with the implication, as Seidel (*Holocaust Denial*, pp. 127–28) points out, that anticommunists should be anti-Semitic too.

21. Kershaw, *Nazi Dictatorship*, pp. 99–100. See also Christopher Browning, *The Final Solution and the German Foreign Office* (New York, 1978), and Gerald Fleming, *Hitler and the Final Solution* (London, 1986).

22. For a sample of this work, see Projektgruppe für die vergessenen Opfer des NS-Regimes (ed.), *Verachtet—verfolgt—vernichtet: Zu den "vergessenen" Opfer des NS-Regimes* (Hamburg, 1986); also, Angelika Ebbinghaus et al. (eds.), *Heilen und Vernichten im Mustergau Hamburg* (Hamburg, 1984); Hans-Georg Stümke and Rudi Finkler (eds.), *Rosa Winkel, Rosa Listen: Homosexuelle und "Gesundes Volksempfinden" von Auschwitz bis heute* (Reinbek, 1981); Tilman Zülch (ed.), *In Auschwitz vergast, bis heute verfolgt: Zur Situation der Roma (Zigeuner) in Deutschland und Europa* (Reinbek, 1979).

23. Detlev Peukert, "Alltag und Barbarei: Zur Normalität des Dritten Reiches," in Dan Diner (ed.), *Ist der Nationalsozialismus Geschichte? Zur Historisierung und Historikerstreit* (Frankfurt, 1987), pp. 51–61. Traces of the same argument can also be found in Geoff Eley, "Nazism, Politics, and the Image of the Past: Thoughts on the West German *Historikerstreit* 1986–1987," *Past and Present* 121 (1988), pp. 177–208. For the contribution of the German History Workshop to the current debate, see Heide Gerstenberger and Dorothea Schmidt (eds.), *Normalität oder Normalisierung? Geschichtswerkstätten und Faschismusanalyse* (Münster, 1987). However, as Jürgen Kocka has pointed out, the contributions mostly concentrate on local research and fail to address the central issues in the debate ("Geschichtswerkstätten und Historikerstreit," *Die Tages-*

zeitung, January 26, 1988). Nevertheless, the contribution by Barbara Hahn and Peter Schöttler, "Jürgen Habermas und das ungetrübte Bewusstsein des Bruchs," pp. 170–77, does provide an interesting critique of Habermas's identification with "the West" from a left-wing point of view. And for another discussion of the view from the left, see Mary Nolan, "The *Historikerstreit* and Social History," *New German Critique* 44 (1988), pp. 51–80.

24. See above, and Nolte, *Bürgerkrieg*, pp. 502–4.

25. Ibid., pp. 297–98. Nolte goes on to ask whether Hitler might not have been about to realize the "main tenet" of Marxism by eliminating the "dying bourgeoisie" in the interests of the "rising proletariat." The speculation is characteristic of Nolte's style of argument. It rests solely on an anecdote told in a speech by Hitler, who reported that as he had seen motorcars full of well-off bourgeois Germans passing a gang of roadworkers, he had said to himself that the two groups should really change places. Quite apart from its inadequacy as evidential support for a speculation as far-reaching as that which Nolte bases on it, the story also has to be understood as an aspect of Nazi rhetoric rather than a genuine statement of intent; here as elsewhere, Nolte does not distinguish properly between the two. Pseudo-egalitarian rhetoric of this kind was a commonplace in the public utterances of Hitler and the other Nazi leaders, and has been extensively discussed in the literature, although Nolte seems unaware of this historiography. See for example David Schoenbaum, *Hitler's Social Revolution: Class and Status in Nazi Germany 1933–1939* (London, 1967), esp. pp. 77–118; Kershaw, *Popular Opinion*, pp. 66–110; Kershaw, *Nazi Dictatorship*, pp. 130–148. When defending Nolte, the Bremen historian Imanuel Geiss also frequently resorts to speculation, claiming, for instance, to know how Nolte would stand on points which he has not in fact discussed in his writings at all (Geiss, *Die Habermas-Kontroverse*, pp. 101, 105).

26. Nolte, *Bürgerkrieg*, pp. 515–16. For the comparable attempts by Hillgruber and others to isolate Hitler, see above, pp. 71–74.

27. Nolte, *Bürgerkrieg*, pp. 509–13, 500. It is worth noting in this context the claim of the "revisionist" Arthur Butz, in his *Hoax of the Twentieth Century* (1976), that the concentration camps mostly contained people detained "for punitive or security reasons" (G. Seidel, *The Holocaust Denial*, p. 72). The resemblances between Nolte's arguments and right-wing extremist "revisionism" are also noted in Hans Mommsen, "Das Ressentiment als Wissenschaft. Anmerkungen zu Ernst Noltes 'Der europäische Bürgerkrieg 1917–1945. Nationalsozialismus und Bolschewismus,' " *Geschichte und Gesellschaft* 14 (1988), pp. 495–512, esp. pp. 502, 509.

28. Nolte, *Bürgerkrieg*, pp. 592–93, nn. 26, 29. It is characteristic of Nolte's procedures that he should simultaneously cover himself against criticism by explicitly conceding the reality of the "Final Solution." However, the novelty, and the emphasis, of Nolte's account clearly lie in his willingness to take seriously the neofascist "revisionists" on this subject, and to lend support, however qualified, to some of their arguments. Nolte's insistence that those who deny the reality of the "Final Solution" have to be taken

seriously as objective scholars follows the line taken by another neoconservative writer, Armin Mohler, in *Criticon: Zeitschrift für Konservatives Denken* 56 (November-December 1979). Mohler is a Swiss journalist, former secretary of the writer Ernst Jünger, and, like Nolte, a recipient of the Adenauer Prize. As Gill Seidel has remarked, "His contention that 'revisionist' arguments represent a respectable, academic interpretation of history is entirely consonant with the pseudoobjective, pseudoacademic stance favored by Butz. . . . It is exemplified as a whole in the *Journal of the Institute for Historical Review*, the magazine of the anti-Semitic propagandists" (Seidel, *The Holocaust Denial*, pp. 52–53). Arthur Butz, in *The Hoax of the Twentieth Century* (1976), one of the most influential attempts to deny the reality of the "Final Solution," has, as Seidel points out, a pseudoacademic style, and adorns his book with 450 footnotes, 5 appendices, and 32 plates and diagrams. Butz maintains that the professional historians who assert the reality of the "Final Solution" are Jews. In this context, it is also relevant to note the resemblance between Nolte's self-proclaimed status as an outsider to the German historical profession (see the jacket blurb to *Bürgerkrieg*) and Butz's attack on "academic historians" and "established scholarship" for allegedly avoiding a critical examination of what he regards as the "Holocaust hoax" (Seidel, *The Holocaust Denial*, pp. 74–75). For further resemblances, see Hans-Georg Betz, "*Deutschlandpolitik* on the Margins: On the Evolution of Contemporary New Right Nationalism in the Federal Republic," *New German Critique* 44 (1988), pp. 127–58. The contradictions of Nolte's various arguments are also noted by Mommsen, "Das Ressentiment." Nolte's *Bürgerkrieg* received a critical review from Mohler ("Missverständnisse um Ernst Nolte. Über sein Buch 'Der europäische Bürgerkrieg 1917–1945,' " *Criticon* 17 [1987], pp. 104, 267–70) and a positive one from Adolf von Thadden ("Der europäische Bürgerkrieg 1917–1945," *Nation Europa* 38 [1988], pp. 4–10). Mohler evidently took Nolte's gestures in the direction of the "uniqueness of Auschwitz" view too seriously. It is impossible to take seriously, however, Eckard Jesse's statement that Nolte fails to deliver any ammunition for extreme right-wing propaganda (Jesse, "Ist der 'Historikerstreit . . . ?' " p. 177). For evidence to the contrary, see Rolf Kosiek, *Historikerstreit und Geschichtsrevision* (Tübingen, 1987).

29. See Hilberg, *Destruction;* and Walter Laqueur, *The Terrible Secret: Suppression of the Truth About Hitler's "Final Solution"* (London, 1980). For Geiss's views on Nolte's general procedures, which he expresses with a restraint and delicacy which he altogether fails to show toward Nolte's opponents, see Geiss, *Die Habermas-Kontroverse*, p. 39. Geiss disqualifies Habermas as a competent historian and accuses him of arbitrary methods of citation, instrumentalization of the past for political purposes, and procedures that have no connection with rational scholarship (p. 83). These criticisms should, however, more properly be directed at Nolte. See Mommsen, "Das Ressentiment," pp. 497, 509.

30. Jäckel, "Elende Praxis" (trans. in Craig, "The War").

31. Wehler, *Entsorgung*, pp. 167–71; Jäckel, "Elende Praxis"; Jürgen Kocka, "Hitler sollte nicht durch Stalin und Pol Pot verdrängt werden: Über Ver-

suche deutscher Historiker, die Ungeheuerlichkeit von NS-Verbrechen zu relativieren," *Frankfurter Rundschau*, September 23, 1986 (Piper, *Historikerstreit*, pp. 123–31). See also Hildebrand, "Das Zeitalter der Tyrannen" (in Piper, *Historikerstreit*, pp. 84–92), with an equation of Auschwitz and the Gulag along similar lines to those laid down by Hillgruber.

32. William Shawcross, *Sideshow: Kissinger, Nixon, and the Destruction of Cambodia* (London, 1979).

33. Wehler, *Entsorgung*, pp. 169–70; Stefan Merl, " 'Ausrottung' der Bourgeoisie und der Kulaken in Sowjetrussland? Anmerkungen zu einem fragwürdigen Vergleich mit Hitlers Judenvernichtung," *Geschichte und Gesellschaft* 13 (1987), pp. 368–81; M. Lewin, *Russian Peasants and Soviet Power: A Study of Collectivization* (London, 1968); Merle Fainsod, *Smolensk Under Soviet Rule* (Cambridge, Mass., 1950). Robert Conquest's *The Harvest of Sorrow: Soviet Collectivization and the Terror Famine* (New York, 1986), argues that the "dekulakization" of the early 1930s led to the deaths of 6,500,000 people. But this estimate is arrived at by extremely dubious methods, ranging from reliance on hearsay evidence through double counting to the consistent employment of the highest possible figures in estimates made by other historians. The most conservative estimate of the numbers of victims of this terrible and criminal policy gives a figure of about 300,000. See Stephen Merl, "Wie viele Opfer forderte die 'Liquidierung der Kulaken als Klasse'? Anmerkungen zu einem Buch von Robert Conquest," *Geschichte und Gesellschaft* 14 (1988), pp. 534–40; and more generally, on Conquest's overestimation of the numbers of victims of Stalin's purges, S. G. Wheatcroft, "On Assessing the Size of Forced Concentration Camp Labour in the Soviet Union, 1929–1956," *Soviet Studies* 33 (1981), pp. 265–95; idem, "Towards a Thorough Analysis of Soviet Forced Labour Statistics," ibid. 35 (1983), pp. 223–37; and the contributions by Conquest and others to the same debate in *Slavic Review* 39 (1980), pp. 559–611; ibid., 43 (1984), pp. 83–88; ibid., 44 (1985), pp. 505–36; and *Soviet Studies* 34 (1982), pp. 434–9; 36 (1984), pp. 277–81; and 39 (1987), pp. 292–313. Further downward revision of Conquest's figures, on the basis of documentation in the Smolensk Archive, is provided by J. Arch Getty, *Origins of the Great Purges: The Soviet Communist Party Reconsidered, 1933–1938* (Cambridge, 1985). Charles S. Maier, in *The Unmasterable Past* (Cambridge, Mass., 1988), pp. 74–75, estimates that Stalinism was responsible for 20 million deaths up to 1953, Nazism 8 million. But these figures include deaths indirectly caused by Stalinism, through famines, deportations, etc., and accept Conquest's implausible and inflated estimates without question, while omitting deaths caused by Nazi aggression in the East (which also, apart from military and exterminatory action, led to famines and deportations). The number of deaths caused by Nazism's eastward drive may itself have been as many as 20 million. As Maier remarks, however, the issue of numbers, though important, is not relevant to the issue of uniqueness. It is perhaps just worth noting that Habermas, in his critique of Nolte, initially described Stalin's policy toward the kulaks as an "expulsion," and admitted later that "extermination" would have been a better word. But this point scarcely deserves the importance accorded it by

Geiss (*Die Habermas-Kontroverse*, p. 69), who altogether fails to tackle the central point of comparison at issue.

Finally, none of this of course excuses the appalling barbarity of Stalinism; it merely exposes the limitations of attempts to equate it with the barbarity of Nazism by mathematical means.

34. For Maier's stress on the unpredictability of Stalinist terror, see *The Unmasterable Past,* pp. 74–84.

35. Fest "Die geschuldete Erinnerung" (Piper, *Historikerstreit,* pp. 100–112). Kershaw, *Nazi Dictatorship,* p. 82; Hagen Schulze, "Fragen, die wir stellen müssen: Keine historische Haftung ohne nationale Identität," *Die Zeit,* September 26, 1986 (Piper, *Historikerstreit,* pp. 143–50); Beatrice Heuser, "*The Historikerstreit:* Uniqueness and Comparability of the Holocaust," *German History* 6, no. 1 (1988), pp. 69–78, here pp. 72–73; Helmut Fleischer, "Die Moral der Geschichte: Zum Disput über die Vergangenheit, die nicht vergehen will," *Nürnberger Zeitung,* September 20, 1986 (Piper, *Historikerstreit,* pp. 123–31); Yehuda Bauer, *The Holocaust in Historical Perspective* (London, 1978), p. 31. The argument that Auschwitz's uniqueness means that it cannot be "historicized" because it stands outside history (Dan Diner, "Zwischen Aporie und Apologie. Über Grenzen der Historisierbarkeit des Nationalsozialismus" in Diner [ed.], *Ist der Nationalsozialismus Geschichte?,* p.73) seems to me to mystify the event in a manner more appropriate to a theologian than a historian.

36. Hillgruber, *Zweierlei,* p. 98; cf. the comments of Habermas, "Eine Art," (Piper, *Historikerstreit,* p. 17); Fest, "Die geschuldete Erinnerung"; Kocka, "Hitler"; Bartov, *Eastern Front,* p. 155.

37. Bartov, *Eastern Front,* pp. 155–56. For further comments on these issues, see Julius Schoeps, "Treitschke redivivus? Ernst Nolte und die Juden," *Der Tagesspiegel,* January 10, 1988 (reply by Nolte in *Das Vergehen,* pp. 204–14 [full version: edited original in *Der Tagesspiegel,* February 21, 1988]).

38. Maier, *The Unmasterable Past,* p. 82. See also, Heinz Galinski, "Beweiszwang für die Opfer, Freispruch für die Täter," *Blätter für deutsche und internationale Politik* 32 (1987), pp. 20–24.

CHAPTER 5: RESHAPING CENTRAL EUROPE

1. See Wolfgang Benz (ed.), *Die Vertreibung der Deutschen aus dem Osten: Ursachen, Ereignisse, Folgen* (Frankfurt, 1985), for a recent, balanced survey of these events, including an extensive critical bibliography. The official West German account was published in five volumes: *Dokumentation der Vertreibung der Deutschen aus Ost-Mitteleuropa* (Bonn, 1953–64; repr., Munich, 1984). The editors included respected West German historians Theodor Schieder, Hans Rothfels, and Werner Conze; their assistants, who did much of the actual research, included Martin Broszat and Hans-Ulrich Wehler. For the numbers involved in the expulsions and murders, see Benz, *Die Vertreibung,* pp. 12, 226.

2. Nolte, *Bürgerkrieg*, p. 504.

3. Robert L. Koehl, *RKFDV: German Resettlement and Population Policy 1939–1945. A History of the Reich Commission for the Strengthening of Germandom* (Cambridge, Mass., 1957); Noakes and Pridham, *Nazism 1919–1945* Vol. 3 (Exeter, 1988), pp. 940–6.

4. Klaus-Dietmar Henke, in Benz, *Vertreibung*, pp. 51–52 (Henke, "Der Weg nach Potsdam—Die Alliierten und die Vertreibung," pp. 49–69); Ibid., See also Delef Brandes, *Grossbritannien und seine osteuropäischen Alliierten 1939–1943. Die Regierungen Polens, der Tschechoslowakei und Jugoslawiens im Londoner Exil vom Kriegsausbruch bis zur Konferenz von Teheran* (Munich, 1988). This work makes clear the numerous and varied weaknesses of Alfred M. de Zayas, *Die Anglo-Amerikaner und die Vertreibung der Deutschen* (Munich, 1977). For further notes on de Zayas, see above, p. 162, n.14.

5. Henke, in Benz, *Vertreibung*, p. 55.

6. See in particular Rudolf Jaworski, "Die Sudetendeutschen als Minderheit in der Tschechoslowakei 1918–1978," in Benz, *Vertreibung*, p. 29–38; Norbert Krekeler, "Die deutsche Minderheit in Polen und die Revisionspolitik des Deutschen Reiches 1919–1933," ibid., pp. 15–28; and Wolfgang Benz, "Der Generalplan Ost: Zur Germanisierungspolitik des NS-Regimes in den besetzten Ostgebieten 1939–1945," ibid., pp. 39–48.

7. See also Martin Broszat, *Zweihundert Jahre deutsche Polenpolitik* (Munich, 1963).

8. Nolte, *Bürgerkrieg*, p. 211. See, more generally, Peter Bender, "Mitteleuropa—Mode, Modell oder Motiv?" *Die neue Gesellschaft* 34 (1987), pp. 297–304.

9. Winkler, "Auf ewig"; Wolfgang J. Mommsen, "Weder Leugnen noch Vergessen befreit von der Vergangenheit," *Frankfurter Rundschau*, December 1, 1986 (Piper, *Historikerstreit*, pp. 300–321); and the summary of Wolfgang Mommsen's contribution to the debate in Hilmar Hoffmann (ed.), *Gegen den Versuch, Vergangenheit zu verbiegen: Eine Diskussion um politische Kultur in der Bundesrepublik aus Anlass der Frankfurter Römerberggespräche 1986* (Frankfurt, 1987), pp. 116–17. See also James J. Sheehan, "What Is German History? Reflections on the Role of the *Nation* in German History and Historiography," *Journal of Modern History* 53 (1981), pp. 1–23. On Austrian national consciousness, see Robert Knight, "The Waldheim Context: Austria and Nazism," *Times Literary Supplement*, October 3, 1986, pp. 1003–4. On West and East Germany, see Gebhard Schweigler, *National Consciousness in Divided Germany* (London, 1975).

10. See below, pp. 136–7.

11. See Jäckel, "Die elende Praxis" (Piper, *Historikerstreit*, p. 119).

12. Schulze, "Fragen" (Piper, *Historikerstreit*, p. 145).

13. Schulze, "Fragen"; see also Hagen Schulze, *Wir sind, was wir geworden sind: Vom Nutzen der Geschichte für die deutsche Gegenwart* (Munich, 1987), pp. 189–95 (reprinting "Auf der Suche nach einer deutschen Identität: Ein Gespräch mit Adelbert Reif," *Börsenblatt für den deutschen Buchhandel* 42 [1986], pp. 690–95).

14. Unlike Nolte, Stürmer did not decline the invitation to attend, but he did refuse to allow his contribution to be printed in the colloquium proceedings, complaining of the "defamations and denunciations" to which he had allegedly been subjected by the other participants. The published version of his contribution ("Weder verdrängen noch bewältigen: Geschichte und Gegenwartsbewusstsein der Deutschen," *Schweizer Monatshefte* 66 [1986], pp. 689–94) is heavily amended to remove many of the more controversial statements. Even so, Stürmer did not give his permission for it to be reprinted in Piper, *Historikerstreit*. The tape-recorded account of the colloquium is therefore used as the basis for the account of Stürmer's contribution given here (Dieter Kramer, "Die Diskussion der "Römerberg-Gespräche 1986," in Hoffmann [ed.], *Gegen den Versuch*, pp. 105–39). The advisory committee on the Römerberg Colloquia has a well-established tradition of producing a politically "balanced ticket," with invited speakers from both right and left. For an independent account, see Verena Auffermann, "Fragen nach politischer Kultur: Zu den 13. Römerberg-Gesprächen in Frankfurt," *Süddeutsche Zeitung*, June 13, 1986 (Stürmer criticized this account, however, in a letter to the newspaper on June 25). For the quotations here, see Hoffmann (ed.), *Gegen den Versuch*, pp. 122–23, 116. See also the account in Craig, "The War," who rightly comments on the declamatory obscurity of Stürmer's style.

15. Hoffmann (ed.), *Gegen den Versuch*, p. 112. See also the critiques of Stürmer by Hans Mommsen in ibid., pp. 118–19, and Michael Schneider, ibid., p. 120, and the quotation in Michael Wildt, "Instandsetzung der Zitadelle: Beim Deutschen Historischen Museum geht's um kulturelle Hegemonie," in Geschichtswerkstatt Berlin (ed.), *Die Nation als Ausstellungsstück: Planungen, Kritik, und Utopien zu den Museumsgründungen in Bonn und Berlin* (Geschichtswerkstatt No. 11, Hamburg, 1987), pp. 25–28, here p. 26.

16. Michael Stürmer, *Das ruhelose Reich: Deutschland 1866–1918* (Berlin, 1980). Stürmer's historical essays are collected in his *Dissonanzen des Fortschritts: Essays über Geschichte und Politik in Deutschland* (Munich, 1986).

17. Hagen Schulze, *Weimar. Deutschland 1917–1933* (Berlin, 1982), pp. 16, 22.

18. Klaus Hildebrand, "Deutscher Sonderweg und Drittes Reich," in Wolfgang Michalka (ed.), *Die nationalsozialistische Machtergreifung* (Paderborn, 1984), pp. 388–90, 392.

19. Thus the argument of Stürmer, *Das ruhelose Reich*. For a jaundiced view of Stürmer's career and writings, see Wehler, *Entsorgung*, pp. 28–36, 138–45. In addition, see Heinrich August Winkler, "Bismarcks Schatten.

Ursachen und Folgen der deutschen Katastrophe," *Die Neue Gesellschaft* 35 (1988), p. 121. Perhaps the strongest criticism of Stürmer is advanced in Hans-Jürgen Puhle, "Die neue Ruhelosigkeit. Michael Stürmers nationalpolitischer Revisionismus," *Geschichte und Gesellschaft* 13 (1987), pp. 382–99. See further, Hans Mommsen, "Rückwärtsrevision des Geschichtsbildes?" *Die Neue Gesellschaft* 32 (1985), p. 364.

20. See my review of Schulze, *Weimar*, in *Journal of Modern History* 58 (1986), pp. 363–66.

21. Michael Stürmer, "Nation und Demokratie," *Die politische Meinung* 230 (1987), p. 22.

22. See the discussion in Thomas Schnabel, "Geschichte und Wende," in Erler, *Geschichtswende?*, pp. 22–23.

23. Alfred Dregger, "Der Friede ist das Werk der Gerechtigkeit," *Bulletin des Presse- und Informationsamts der Bundesregierung* 140 (November 18, 1986), pp. 1169–72.

24. Timothy Garton Ash, "Germany After Bitburg," *New Republic*, July 15–22, 1985, pp. 15–17, reprinted in Geoffrey Hartman (ed.), *Bitburg in Moral and Political Perspective* (Bloomington, Indiana, 1986), pp. 199–203.

25. Peter Pulzer, "Germany Searches for a Less Traumatic Past," *The Listener*, June 25, 1987, pp. 16–18.

26. See Winkler, "Auf ewig," and more generally, Hermannus Pfeiffer (ed.), *Die FAZ: Nachforschungen über ein Zentralorgan* (Cologne, 1988).

27. See for example Paul Kennedy, *The Rise of the Anglo-German Antagonism 1860–1914* (London, 1980); D. C. B. Lieven, *Russia and the Origins of the First World War* (London, 1983); John F. V. Keiger, *France and the Origins of the First World War* (London, 1983); and Zara S. Steiner, *Britain and the Origins of the First World War* (London, 1977).

28. See Geoff Eley, *Reshaping the German Right: Radical Nationalism and Political Change After Bismarck* (New Haven, 1980); Roger Chickering, *We Men Who Feel Most German: A Cultural Study of the Pan-German League* (Winchester, Mass., 1984); and the critique of Stürmer in Bernd Faulenbach, " 'Sinnstiftung' durch Geschichte?" *Links*, November 1986, pp. 48–49.

29. Fritz Fischer, *Germany's Aims in the First World War* (London, 1967); Schnabel, "Geschichte," in Erler, *Geschichtswende?*, pp. 22–23.

30. Schnabel, "Geschichte." The literature on the collapse of Weimar is obviously immense. A starting-point may be made with Eberhard Kolb, *The Weimar Republic* (London, 1988), which includes a useful guide to the literature.

31. Heinrich August Winkler, *Von der Revolution zur Stabilisierung* (Bonn, 1984), *Der Schein der Normalität* (Bonn, 1985), and *Der Weg in die Katastrophe* (Bonn, 1987).

32. Bartov, *The Eastern Front,* citing Werner Maser, *Nuremberg* (London, 1979).

CHAPTER 6: GERMANY AND THE WEST

1. Pulzer, "Germany," pp. 16–18; Michael Stürmer, *Dissonanzen des Fortschritts: Essays über Geschichte und Politik in Deutschland* (Munich, 1986), pp. 766–76, 195–96, 266–67, 273, 293–94, 326–29 (Stürmer reprints here an unpublished speech from 1981, given at the opening of an exhibition; an article from *Neue Zürcher Zeitung,* May 3, 1986; a school speech delivered on October 28, 1984; a lecture, "Berlin und Bonn: Suche nach der deutschen Geschichte," first printed in *Museumskunde* [1984], pp. 142–53; and "Mitten in Europa: Versuchung und Verdamnis der Deutchen," first printed in a collection of essays presented to Franz Josef Strauss on his seventieth birthday [reference not given]). It is worth noting that the concept of "civil war" *(Bürgerkrieg)* runs right through Stürmer's collection; at various points he writes of Weimar as living in a state of civil war, of the years 1918–1945 as those of a European civil war, and of the present day as experiencing a world civil war. He thus engages in the same inflation of the concept that Nolte does. The implication of describing a country or a continent as existing in a state of "civil war" would seem to be a justification of emergency repressive measures, including the curtailment of civil liberties and possibly even violence, undertaken in the name of restoring order. Certainly this is the import of the claim that—for example in Argentina or El Salvador, or indeed in Northern Ireland—suppressing terrorism involves the state and the armed forces in a "war" rather than in the simple enforcement of the law of the land. Once more, Geiss, in concentrating on the manner in which Stürmer's assertions have been quoted by his critics, misses the broader, and surely more important issue at stake (Geiss, *Die Habermas-Kontroverse,* pp. 58–62). For further comments on Nolte's use of the "civil war" metaphor, see Hans Mommsen, "Das Ressentiment als Wissenschaft. Anmerkungen zu Ernst Noltes 'Der europäische Bürgerkrieg 1917–1945. Nationalsozialismus und Bolschewismus,'" *Geschichte und Gesellschaft* 14 (1988), pp. 495–512, here p. 495.

2. Habermas, "Eine Art" (Piper, *Historikerstreit,* pp. 62–76); Pulzer, "Germany." For a more extended discussion of the relation of the *Historikerstreit* to Habermas's thought, see Charles S. Maier, *The Unmasterable Past* (Cambridge, Mass., 1988), pp. 39–42. For Nolte's defense of the Freikorps, see above, p. 29.

3. For a useful, if rather one-sided, view of these events, see John A. Moses, *The Politics of Illusion* (London, 1975); also Imanuel Geiss, *Studien über Geschichte und Geschichtswissenschaft* (Frankfurt, 1972); and Arnold Sywottek, "Die Fischer-Kontroverse," in Imanuel Geiss and Bernd-Jürgen Wendt (eds.), *Deutschland in der Weltpolitik des 19. und 20. Jahrhun-*

derts (Düsseldorf, 1973), pp. 19–74; Hans-Ulrich Wehler, "Historiography in Germany Today," in Jürgen Habermas (ed.), *Observations on "The Spiritual Situation of the Age"* (Cambridge, Mass., 1984); Volker R. Berghahn, "West German Historiography Between Continuity and Change: Some Cross-Cultural Comparisons," *German Life and Letters* 34 (1980–81), pp. 248–59; Kenneth D. Barkin, "From Uniformity to Pluralism: German Historical Writing Since World War I," ibid., vol. 4, pp. 234–47.

4. For more detailed expositions of the following arguments, with full references, see David Blackbourn and Geoff Eley, *The Peculiarities of German History* (Oxford, 1984); Eley, *From Unification to Nazism* (London, 1985); Blackbourn, *Populists and Patricians* (London, 1987); Richard J. Evans, *Rethinking German History* (London, 1987).

5. However, these arguments should not be misunderstood. Recently, a group of American historians has produced a book which argues for a more positive picture of Wilhelmine Germany (Jack Dukes and Joachim Remak [eds.], *Another Germany: A Reconsideration of the Imperial Era* [Boulder, Colo.: 1987]). The book's contributors claim, for example, that Germany was justified in increasing the size of its Army in 1913 because it was encircled by foreign powers; that French, British, and Russian policies and politicians were "strident," "threatening," etc., while the Germans were "modest" and "moderate" and based their diplomacy on rational assessments of intelligence data; that the Great Powers should have been "mature" enough to give Germany equality on the international scene (Dukes, "Militarism and Arms Policy Revisited"); that service in the Prussian Army was a valuable experience for those who went through it, a "rite of passage" whose benefits have been underplayed by a generation of middle-class American historians blinded to the pleasures of the soldier's life by overreaction to the Vietnam War (D. Showalter, "Army, State, and Society"); and that Wilhelmine Germany was a progressive society dominated by modern attitudes, with a powerful, free press and a go-ahead educational system which encouraged scientific research. As many of the authors (e.g., Charles McLelland, Andrew Lees, Alan Beyerchen, Konrad Jarausch, Ronald J. Ross), given the more balanced picture in their other writings, must know, this is as one-sided a view as the opposing perspective, which sees Wilhelmine Germany as a backward or semifeudal dictatorship. The claim advanced by the editor in his concluding remarks, that Wilhelm II's Germany resembles Ronald Reagan's America, casts a light on the latter in a way that perhaps was not intended (Remak, "Summing-Up"). It should be pointed out that the contributions on militarism and foreign policy in particular fail to take account of recent literature and fall well short of the normally high standards of modern American scholarship in this field.

6. Detlev Peukert, "Wer gewann den Historikerstreit? Keine Bilanz," in Peter Glotz et al. (eds.), *Vernunft riskieren: Klaus von Dohnanyi zum 60. Geburtstag* (Hamburg, 1988), pp. 38–50; A. Trus, "Die blinden Flecken des Historikerstreit: Über das kommunikative Beschweigen sogenannter Aussenseiterpositionen," *Arena* 8 (1988), pp. 4–6. For two (more or less

random) examples, see Ernst Nolte, *Das Vergehen der Vergangenheit: Antwort an meine Kritiker im sogenannten Historikerstreit* (2nd ed., Munich, 1988), p. 215, with its accusation that Nolte's opponents in the debate had encouraged acts of terrorism against him (his car was set on fire by left-wing political extremists on February 9, 1988, while it was parked outside his office); or Rudolf Augstein, writing in *Der Spiegel* on October 6, 1986, calling Hillgruber a "constitutional Nazi" and urging his dismissal from his university post (for what else can he mean by the statement that "any teacher who told his pupils this kind of thing would have to be dismissed from the education service"?)—even though Augstein himself on an earlier occasion wrote that "whether the anti-Hitler allies committed fewer crimes than Hitler is not at all certain. The one who initiated such crimes against humanity was, in any case, Stalin, in 1928" (Augstein, "Auf die schiefe Ebene zur Republik," *Der Spiegel*, 1985, no. 2, p. 32, quoted by Saul Friedländer, "Some German Struggles with Memory," in Hartman [ed.], *Bitburg*, p. 36). See also Augstein's review of Nolte, *Bürgerkrieg*, "Herr Noltes Umwälzung der Wissenschaft," *Der Spiegel*, 1988, no. 1, pp. 141–44. For some earlier, unhelpfully polemical overreactions to interpretations of German history which did not fit established categories, see Hans-Ulrich Wehler, " 'Deutscher Sonderweg' oder allgemeine Probleme des westlichen Kapitalismus? Zur Kritik einiger Mythen deutscher Geschichtsschreibung," *Merkur* 5 (1981), pp. 478–82; or Wehler's contribution to Franz-Josef Brüggemeier and Jürgen Kocka (eds.), *"Geschichte von unten—Geschichte von innen": Kontroversen um die Alltagsgeschichte* (Hagen, 1985). In this context it is also appropriate to note the contribution to the debate by Imanuel Geiss, *Die Habermas-Kontroverse. Ein deutscher Streit* (Berlin, 1988). Geiss argues, along similar lines, that the debate has been too polarized. He suggests that, despite the difficulties of advancing an intermediate position, it is time for a sober and calm approach to the questions at issue, time to start building bridges between the opposing camps (pp. 9–12). Geiss's criticism of the strong language used by Hillgruber and others in the debate (pp. 28–30) is well taken; but the language he uses against Habermas, Wehler, Hans Mommsen, and other opponents of Hillgruber and Nolte is every bit as strong as the language he criticizes in others (pp. 82–83). In a similar category is the attempt at a balance by Eckhard Jesse, who also criticizes the polemical style of Wehler and other supporters of Habermas, while saying little or nothing about the strong language used on the other side. Jesse's assertion that "the time is not yet ripe" for a full appreciation of Nolte's "great and bold work," the value of which will only be fully appreciated after several decades have passed, must surely rank as the most fatuous statement made by anyone during the entire controversy (Eckhard Jesse, "Ist der 'Historikerstreit' ein 'Historischer Streit'? Zugleich eine Auseinandersetzung mit der Literatur," *Zeitschrift für Politik* 35 (1988), pp. 163–97, here p. 176). For further comments on the polarization of opinion, see Karl-Ernst Jeismann, "Die deutsche Geschichte als Instrument im politischen Streit," *Die neue Gesellschaft* 34 (1987), pp. 362–9.

7. As suggested in Gordon A. Craig's characteristically learned and entertaining survey of the debate ("The War").

8. For an account of the role of controversy among British historians and philosophers in the 1950s and 1960s, see Ved Mehta, *Fly and the Fly-Bottle: Encounters with British Intellectuals* (London, 1963). The "Abraham Debate" (*Central European History* 17 [1984], pp. 159–293) is not, in my view, related to the discussion analyzed in the present book. The point at issue—the role of big business in the collapse of the Weimar Republic—has played no part in the present debate. The argument was fought out over issues of detailed historical scholarship and research, unlike the present one, where archival research does not feature at all.

9. To claim that the underlying purpose of the debate has been, on both sides, to achieve "cultural hegemony" in West Germany seems exaggerated on the one hand and neglectful of the international dimensions of the debate on the other ("Kampf um die kulturelle Hegemonie? Hans-Ulrich Wehler im Gespräch mit Rainer Erd über Ziel und Folgen des Historikerstreits," *Frankfurter Rundschau*, February 11, 1988). See the reasoned contribution to the debate by Christian Meier, in his capacity as president of the West German Historians' Association ("Eröffnungsrede zur 36. Versammlung deutscher Historiker in Trier, 8 October 1988," in Piper, *Historikerstreit*, pp. 204–14); and Geiss, "Zum Historiker-Streit," *Evangelische Kommentare*, February 1987 (Piper, *Historikerstreit*, pp. 373–80). Wehler's description of Geiss's criticism of Habermas, which forms part of a seven-page article, as *schier endlos*, seems rather inappropriate in a book which takes up 249 pages in Habermas's defense, (Wehler, *"Entsorgung,"* p. 234, n. 69). However, it has now been retrospectively justified by the appearance of Geiss's book, *Die Habermas-Kontroverse. Ein deutscher Streit* (Berlin, 1988).

10. Craig, "The War"; Thomas Nipperdey, "Unter der Herrschaft des Verdachts: Wissenschaftliche Aussagen dürfen nicht an ihrer politischen Funktion gemessen werden," *Die Zeit*, October 17, 1986, (Piper, *Historikerstreit*, pp. 215–19). ; Geiss, *Die Habermas-Kontroverse*, pp. 14–16. Geiss attacks the critic Volker Ullrich for making this point without alluding to the fact that Hillgruber had been the first to advance it (Volker Ullrich, "Die Fronten sind geklärt. Zwei Dokumentationen des 'Historiker-Streits' und ein Nachwort von Jürgen Habermas," *Frankfurter Rundschau*, September 5, 1987). But this is mere polemics, as is Geiss's criticism of Ullrich for failing to provide (in a review printed in a daily newspaper!) proper references for the views he puts forward (Geiss, *Die Habermas-Kontroverse*, pp. 195–6, n.3). Geiss himself admits (p.9) that his own study of the controversy "makes no claim even to come near being a comprehensive account of the arguments."

11. Broszat, *Nach Hitler*, pp. 305–6 ("Zur Errichtung eines 'Hauses der Geschichte der Bundesrepublik Deutschland' in Bonn"); Broszat, "Die Ambivalenz der Forderung nach mehr Geschichtsbewusstsein," in Hoffmann (ed.), *Gegen den Versuch*, pp. 67–82, (also in Broszat, *Nach Hitler*, pp. 310–23, here p. 315).

12. Hillgruber, *Zweierlei Untergang*, pp. 23–24; Habermas, "Eine Art"; Wolfgang J. Mommsen, "Weder Leugnen noch Vergessen befreit von der Vergangenheit," *Frankfurter Rundschau*, December 1, 1986 (Piper, *Historikerstreit;* pp. 300–21); Paul M. Kennedy. "The Decline of Nationalistic History in the West, 1900–1970," *Journal of Contemporary History* 6 (1973), pp. 77–100. For an illuminating example of the disturbing lengths to which nationalist history can go, see Michael Burleigh, *Germany Turns Eastward: A Study of Ostforschung in the Third Reich* (Cambridge, 1988).

13. Schulze, *Weimar;* Michael Stürmer, *Bismarck—Die Grenzen der Politik* (Munich, 1987). See the devastating review by Hans-Ulrich Wehler, "Bismarck—der Durchbruch zur 'eigentlichen' Biographie? Michael Stürmer's Versuch über den ersten Reichskanzler oder: Die Nemesis der Hektik," *Die Zeit,* April 10, 1987.

14. Hillgruber, *Zweierlei,* pp. 98–99 (cf. the remarks on this point in Habermas, "Eine Art").

15. Richard Bessel, in *Bulletin of the German Historical Institute London,* issue 9 (1982), pp. 3–5, reviewing Karl Dietrich Erdmann and Hagen Schulze (eds.), *Weimar: Selbstpreisgabe einer Demokratie* (Düsseldorf, 1980). Bessel adds: "This volume appears in many places to be less about the fate of Weimar than about attitudes of influential historians towards political developments in the Federal Republic." The view of Mary Nolan, that the neoconservatives have manipulated social history and *Alltagsgeschichte* to their own ends, seems to me entirely misplaced and without convincing foundation (Mary Nolan, "The *Historikerstreit* and Social History," *New German Critique* 44 [1988], pp. 51–80).

16. Broszat, *Nach Hitler,* pp. 305–6, 311–13; W. J. Mommsen, "Weder Leugnen"; Rolf Bade, "Die Wende im Verständnis des Nationalsozialismus: Von der Harmonisierung zur Verharmlosung," *Bremer Lehrer-Zeitung,* February 1987, pp. 23–25; Martin Broszat, Saul Friedländer, "A Controversy about the Historicization of National Socialism," *New German Critique* 44 (1988), pp. 85–126.

17. Broszat, *Nach Hitler,* pp. 239–44, 159–73; Saul Friedländer, "West Germany and the Burden of the Past: the Ongoing Debate," *Jerusalem Quarterly* 42 (Spring 1987), pp. 3–18, here p. 10; Saul Friedländer, "Überlegungen zur Historisierung des Nationalsozialismus," in Diner (ed.), *Ist der Nationalsozialismus Geschichte?,* p. 34–50.

18. "Wir können jetzt durchregieren," *Der Spiegel,* April 21, 1987. Stürmer writes: "In geschichtslosem Land, die Zukunft gewinnt wer die Erinnerung füllt, die Begriffe prägt und die Vergangenheit deutet"—"In a land without history, he who fills the memory, defines the concepts, and interprets the past, wins the future" (from Stürmer, "Weder Verdrängen" translation from Craig, "The War"). The phrase deliberately or coincidentally echoes the Party slogan called to mind by O'Brien in Orwell's *1984:* "Who controls the past controls the future: who controls the present controls the past" (George Orwell, *1984* [Harmondsworth, 1965], p. 199).

Compare the discussion of recent events at the Military History Research Office in Freiburg, above, pp. 44–45 and 158, n. 44. Moreover, the claim that there has been a concerted policy of making politically conservative but otherwise undistinguished appointments to the directorships of the German Historical Institutes in London, Paris, and Washington loses some of its force when the general lack of applications for these posts is taken into consideration (Wehler, *Entsorgung*, pp. 190–91). See further Claus Leggewie, "Der Geist denkt rechts," *Die Zeit*, October 16, 1987. Ernst Nolte has recently had a government-funded grant for a joint project with Israeli historians withdrawn as a result of Israeli disapproval of his views (see Nolte, *Das Vergehen*, pp. 90–150, but also "Der Umgang des Historikers Ernst Nolte mit Briefen aus Israel: Otto Dov Kulka, Professor für Neuere Geschichte an der Jerusalemer Universität, schlägt ein neues Kapitel im 'Historikerstreit' auf," *Frankfurter Rundschau*, November 5, 1987).

19. The opinion-poll figures were reported in *Die Zeit*, February 15, 1985, p. 10. See also Schnabel, "Geschichte und Wende," in Erler *et al.*, *Geschichtswende?*, p. 19.

20. Gian Enrico Rusconi, "Italien und der deutsche 'Historikerstreit,' " in Diner (ed.), *Ist der Nationalsozialismus Geschichte?*, pp. 102–19; Claus Leggewie, "Frankreichs kollektives Gedächtnis und der Nationalsozialismus," ibid., pp. 120–40; A. Bolaffi, "Polemiche Storiche: Hitler l'asiatico," *L'Espresso*, December 21, 1986; Ian Kershaw, "Nuova Inquietudine Tedesca? Le Reazioni Internazionali," *Passato a presente* 16 (1988), pp. 159–64;Alfred Cattani, "Die Last des Bösen," *Neue Zürcher Zeitung*, September 26, 1986; André Gisselbrecht, "Le Débat des historiens sur le Nazisme," *Allemagnes d'aujourd' hui* 99 (1987), pp. 233–64; Gernot Erler, "Ohne Rücksicht auf Verluste: Der deutsche 'Historikerstreit' im Spiegel des Auslands," in Erler et al., *Geschichtswende?*, pp. 116–27; Walter Grab, "Kritische Bemerkungen zur nationalen Apologetik Joachim Fests, Ernst Noltes, und Andreas Hillgrubers," *1999: Zeitschrift für Sozialgeschichte des 20. und 21. Jahrhunderts* 2 (1987), pp. 151–57; G. Lozek, "Der Streit geht weiter: Zum Versuch einer apologetischen Revision des Faschismusbildes durch rechtskonservative Historiker der BRD," *Zeitschrift für Geschichtswissenschaft* 36 (1988), pp. 5–12; Kurt Pätzold, "Wider die 'neue Auschwitzlüge,' " *1999: Zeitschrift für Sozialgeschichte des 20. und 21. Jahrhunderts* 2 (1987), pp. 158–69; Pätzold, "Wo der Weg nach Auschwitz begann", *Blätter für deutsche und internationale Politik* 32, (1987), pp. 160–72; Pätzold, "Von Verlorenem, Gewonnenem, und Erstrebtem: Wohin der 'neue Revisionismus' steuert," ibid., 31 (1986), pp. 1452–63; H. Freeden, "Eine Debatte unter Deutschen: Wie israelische Geschichtsforscher auf die 'neue Unbefangenheit' reagieren," *Frankfurter Rundschau*, November 14, 1986; P. Stadler, "Rückblick auf einen Historikerstreit. Versuch einer Beurteilung aus nichtdeutscher Sicht," *Historische Zeitschrift* 247 (1988), pp. 15–26. Some of the contributions to the debate have been published in *Germania: il passatio che non passa* (Turin, 1987). The Piper volume on the *Historikerstreit* has been published in a French

translation. Gustavo Corni, "Neue deutsche Unruhe? Das Ausland und der innerdeutsche Streit um die National- und Zeitgeschichte aus italienischer Sicht," in *Streitfall Deutsche Geschichte. Geschichts- und Gegenwartsbewusstsein in den 80er Jahren* (Landeszentrale für politische Bildung, Nordrhein-Westfalen, Essen, 1988), pp. 131–40. Accounts of the debate in English include Geoff Eley, "Nazism, Politics, and the Image of the Past: Thoughts on the West German *Historikerstreit,* 1986–87" *Past and Present* 121 (November 1988), pp. 171–208; William E. Paterson, "From *Vergangenheitsbewältigung* to the *Historikerstreit*" (unpubl. typescript, July 1988); James H. Markham, "German Book Sets Off New Holocaust Debate," *New York Times,* September 6, 1986; Judith Miller, "Erasing the Past: Europe's Amnesia About the Holocaust," *New York Times Magazine,* November 16, 1986; Charles S. Maier, "Immoral Equivalence: Revising the Nazi Past for the Kohl Era," *New Republic,* December 1, 1986, pp. 36–41; Gordon A. Craig, "The War of the German Historians," *New York Review of Books,* January 15, 1987, pp. 16–19; Jane Kramer, "Letter from Europe," *New Yorker,* October 12, 1987, pp. 130–44; Peter Schneider: "Hitler's Shadow: On Being a Self-Conscious German," *Harper's,* September 1987, pp. 49–54; Saul Friedländer, "West Germany and the Burden of the Past: The Ongoing Debate," *Jerusalem Quarterly* 42 (Spring 1987), pp. 3–18; Konrad H. Jarausch, "Removing the Nazi Stain? The Quarrel of the German Historians," *German Studies Review* 11 (1988), pp. 285–301; Dan Diner, "The Historians' Controversy: Limits to the Historicization of National Socialism," *Tikkun* 2 (1987), pp. 74–78; Karen J. Winkler, "German Scholars Sharply Divided Over Place of Holocaust in History," *The Chronicle of Higher Education,* May 27, 1987, pp. 4–7; Amity Shlaes, "More History," *The American Spectator,* April 1987, pp. 30–32; Hagen Schulze, "The *Historikerstreit* in Perspective: Report on a Conference About 'The Unresolved Past,' " *German History* 6 (1988), pp. 65–69; Beatrice Heuser, "The *Historikerstreit:* Uniqueness and Comparability of the Holocaust," ibid., pp. 69–78; Peter Pulzer, "Germany: Whose History?" *Times Literary Supplement,* October 2–8, 1987, pp. 1076–88; Peter Pulzer, "Germany Searches for a Less Traumatic Past," *The Listener* 117, no. 3017 (June 25, 1987), pp. 16–18; Omer Bartov, "Historians on the Eastern Front: Andreas Hillgruber and Germany's Tragedy," *Jahrbuch des Instituts für deutsche Geschichte, Tel-Aviv* 16 (1987), pp. 375–45.

21. Erler, "Ohne Rücksicht," in Erler *et al., Geschichtswende?,* p. 124, citing articles by Lothar Höbelt in *Die Presse* (Vienna) on October 18, 1986, by Alfred de Zayas in *Die Welt* on December 13, 1986, and by an anonymous writer for *Le Monde* on January 22, 1987. But see the outline of the views of Hans Koch given above, pp. 153–54, n. 26.

22. Saul Friedländer, "West Germany and the Burden of the Past: The Ongoing Debate," *Jerusalem Quarterly* 42 (Spring 1987), pp. 3–18, here p. 4; Peukert, "Wer gewann," p. 45; also, Gerd R. Ueberschär, "Deutsche Zeitgeschichte in Hitlers Schatten: Ein Überblick zum 'Historikerstreit' über die Ursprünge und Vergleichbarkeit der NS-Verbrechen," in Erler et al., *Geschichtswende?,* pp. 62–85. The claim that Nolte and Hillgruber have encountered little opposition within the historical profession and have

somehow won the argument (Michael Buckmiller, "Vergangenheits-bemächtigung und die Gefahren für die Zukunft: Zur Auseinandersetzung über die Normalisierung der deutschen Geschichte," *Vorgänge* 25 [1986], pp. 47–59) is not borne out by the evidence, and rests on a number of faulty judgments (e.g., taking Joachim Hoffmann's views as representative of the Military History Research Office).

23. Ursula Homann, "Ein Ende ist noch nicht abzusehen: Historikerstreit: Chronologie, Fragen, und Probleme," *Tribüne*, 26 (1987), pp. 103–18.

24. David Cannadine, "British History: Past, Present—and Future?" *Past and Present*, no. 116, (August 1987), pp. 169–91; J. C. D. Clark, *English Society, 1688–1832: Ideology, Social Structure, and Political Practice During the Ancien Régime* (Cambridge, 1985); Clark, *Revolution and Rebellion: State and Society in England in the 17th and 18th Centuries* (Cambridge, 1986).

25. Harvey J. Kaye, "The Use and Abuse of the Past: The New Right and the Crisis of History," in Ralph Miliband et al., (eds.), *Socialist Register 1987* (London, 1987), pp. 332–64, for a general account of this trend; Margaret Thatcher, "Let Me Give You My Vision," (1975), in Thatcher, *Let Our Children Grow: Selected Speeches, 1975–1977* (London, 1977), p. 29, for the quotation. See also G. R. Elton, *The Future of the Past* (Cambridge, 1986); Elton, *The History of England* (Cambridge, 1984); Colin Hughes, "History Teaching Should Foster Pride in Britain, Joseph Says," *The Times*, August 24, 1984 (referring to the views of the then secretary of state for education); Keith Joseph, "Why Teach History in School?" *The Historian* 2 (1984), p. 12 (*The Historian* is the history teachers' magazine of the British Historical Association); Hugh Thomas, *History, Capitalism, and Freedom* (London, 1985); Hugh Thomas, *An Unfinished History of the World* (London, 1979); Paul Johnson, *The Recovery of Freedom* (London, 1986); Johnson, *A History of the Modern World* (London, 1983).

26. William J. Bennett, "Lost Generation: Why America's Children Are Strangers in Their Own Land," *Policy Review* 33 (1985), p. 43; Gertrude Himmelfarb, *The New History and the Old* (Cambridge, Mass., 1987); Theodore Draper, "Neo-conservative History," *New York Review of Books*, January 16, 1986.

27. Winkler, "Auf ewig"; W. J. Mommsen, "Weder Leugnen noch Vergessen."

28. Mommsen, "Weder Leugnen"; also Lutz Niethammer et al. (eds.), *Die Menschen machen ihre Geschichte nicht aus freien Stücken, aber sie machen sie selbst: Einladung zu einer Geschichte des Volkes in Nordrhein-Westfalen* (Bonn, 1984), for a recent example of the "history" of a newly created *Land.*

29. See above, and, for work directly related to the current debate, Lutz Niethammer, " 'Normalisierung' im Westen: Erinnerungsspuren in die 50er Jahre," in Diner (ed.), *Ist der Nationalsozialismus Geschichte?*, pp. 153–84; Peukert, "Alltag und Barbarei," ibid., pp. 51–61; Gerstenberger and Schmidt, *Normalität.* For a sample of *Alltagsgeschichte*, see Hannes

Heer and Volker Ullrich (eds.), *Geschichte entdecken* (Reinbek bei Hamburg, 1985) or Detlev Peukert and Jürgen Reulecke (eds.), *Die Reihen fast geschlossen: Beiträge zur Geschichte des Alltags unterm Nationalsozialismus* (Wuppertal, 1987). Most of this work is focused on urban or big-city communities. It should not be confused with the nostalgic recovery of the rural past exemplified in the film *Heimat* (see Kenneth D. Barkin, "Modern Germany: A Twisted Vision," *Dissent,* Spring 1987, pp. 252–55).

30. Broszat, *Nach Hitler,* p. 321.

31. Luc Rosenzweig and Bernard Cohen, *Waldheim* (New York, 1987).

32. Robert E. Herzstein, *Waldheim: The Missing Years* (New York, 1988) is the most thorough and balanced treatment of the subject. Michael Palumbo, *The Waldheim Files* (London, 1988), is an attempt to exonerate Waldheim; it is unbalanced in its treatment and highly speculative in its theories about the role of various national intelligence agencies in the affair. Richard Bassett, *Waldheim and Austria* (New York, 1988), is a superficial, journalistic account. For connections to the present debate, see Gerhard Botz, "Österreich und die NS-Vergangenheit: Verdrängung, Pflichterfüllung, Geschichtsklitterung," in Diner (ed.), *Ist der Nationalsozialismus Geschichte?,* pp. 141–52. More generally, see Anton Pelinka and Erika Weinzierl (eds.), *Das grosse Tabu. Österreichs Umgang mit seiner Vergangenheit* (Vienna, 1987).

33. Hans Filbinger, *Die geschmähte Generation* (Munich, 1987). Filbinger welcomes the neoconservative reinterpretation of recent German history (pp. 249–55), and expresses the hope that critical histories of Nazi crimes will be balanced by information on the "terror bombing" of Dresden and the expulsion of Germans from Eastern Europe after the war. For a recent critical study of the military justice system under the Nazis, which Filbinger portrays as an area of resistance to Nazism (pp. 86–88), see Manfred Messerschmidt and F. Wüllner, *Die Wehrmachtsjustiz im Dienste des Nationalsozialismus* (Baden-Baden, 1987). Messerschmidt was a member of the Historians' Commission appointed by Waldheim to investigate the Austrian president's war career.

34. The sources for this account of the Jenninger affair, including the full text of the speech, are in *Die Zeit* 47 (November 18, 1988), pp. 1–7. Here again, however, most of the journalists who comment on the speech are at a loss to find convincing reasons for the uproar. The most sensible commentary is by Walter Jens, "Ungehaltene Worte über eine gehaltene Rede," ibid., p. 3.

35. Jörg Friedrich, *Die kalte Amnestie: NS-Täter in der Bundesrepublik* (Frankfurt, 1985); see also Niels Kadritzke, "Zweierlei Untergang in düsterer Verflechtung: Zur politischen Dimension der 'Historiker-Debatte,' " *Probleme des Klassenkampfs,* no. 66 (March 1987), pp. 169–84; Angelika Ebbinghaus (ed.), *Das Daimler-Benz Buch: Ein Rüstungskonzern im "Tausendjährigen Reich"* (Nördlingen, 1987).

36. See the attempt at a balance in Eckhard Jesse, " 'Vergangenheitsbewältigung' in der Bundesrepublik Deutschland," *Der Staat,* 26 (1987), pp.

539–65. This is more sensible than Jesse's subsequent intervention (p. 177, n.6, above). For further reflections, see Arno Klönne, " 'Historiker-Debatte' " und " 'Kulturrevolution von rechts,' " in Reinhard Kühnl (ed.), *Vergangenheit, die nicht vergeht. Die "Historiker-Debatte." Darstellung, Dokumentation, Kritik* (Cologne, 1987), pp. 317–30.

37. Karl-Heinz Reuband, "Sanktionsverlangen im Wandel: Die Einstellung zur Todesstrafe in der Bundesrepublik Deutschland seit 1950," *Kölner Zeitschrift für Soziologie und Sozialpsychologie* 32 (1980), pp. 535–58.

38. H. Mommsen, "Suche nach der verlorenen Geschichte," p. 873.

39. Ibid.; see also above.

40. Elizabeth Noelle-Neumann and Renate Köcher, *Die verletzte Nation: Über den Versuch der Deutschen, ihren Charakter zu ändern* (Stuttgart, 1987).

41. Werner Weidenfeld, "Am Pulsschlag der verletzten Nation: Was die Bundesbürger hoffen und fürchten," *Die Zeit,* April 10, 1987 (reviewing Noelle-Neumann and Köcher).

42. Walter Laqueur, *Germany Today: A Personal Report* (London, 1985).

43. Some years ago, it seemed that this was not so, and that West Germany was losing its historical consciousness like other advanced industrial societies were. This view, which reflected the assumptions of modernist culture, no longer seems very plausible today. See Richard J. Evans, "Rethinking the German Past," in W. Paterson and G. Smith (eds.), *The West German Model: Perspectives on a Stable State* (London, 1981), pp. 134–48.

44. " 'Unser Endziel ist der Bundestag?' Der Parteivorsitzende Franz Schönhuber über die Zukunft der Republikaner," *Der Spiegel* 6 (1989), pp. 28–32; Hans-Georg Betz, *"Deutschlandpolitik* on the Margins: On the Evolution of Contemporary New Right Nationalism in the Federal Republic," *New German Critique* 44 (1988), pp. 127–57, here pp. 145, 148 (Betz's translations).

45. Thus, for example, Saul Friedländer notes that Nolte's claim, based on an argument advanced by David Irving, that Hitler would have been justified in "interning" the Jews because of Weizmann's alleged statement that they could fight on Britain's side in the war, derives ultimately from a pamphlet used by Goebbels in Nazi propaganda and employed repeatedly since 1945 in neo-Nazi literature denying the existence of the "Final Solution." See Friedländer, "West Germany," pp. 12–14; and Wolfgang Benz, "Judenvernichtung aus Notwehr? Die Legenden um Theodore N. Kaufman," *Vierteljahrshefte für Zeitgeschichte* 29 (1981), pp. 615–30. Gill Seidel (*The Holocaust Denial,* p. 95) notes that characteristic neofascist arguments, such as those advanced by the self-proclaimed fascist writer Maurice Bardèche, include the assertions that the Allies were also guilty of war crimes, that the Nazis were fighting a preventive war, that the Treaty of Versailles enslaved the Germans, and that a strong state is necessary to fight Communism. See also Arno J. Mayer, *Why Did the*

Heavens Not Darken?: The "Final Solution" in History (New York, 1988), esp. pp. 145–46, 246, 298, 321, 335–36, and 415, for the examples of Nazi propaganda referred to above. See also Hannah Arendt, *Eichmann in Jerusalem: A Report on the Banality of Evil* (New York, 1964). For Nazi claims about the "Bromberg massacre," see Burleigh, *Germany Turns Eastward*, pp. 182–3. For a characterization of Nolte's arguments as a "regression back to the brew of racist-nationalistic ideologies of the interwar period," see Hans Mommsen, "Das Ressentiment als Wissenschaft," p. 512. As Mommsen notes, Nolte deliberately seems to wipe out the distinction between Hitler's view of anti-Semitism and that of his interpreter (p. 502). For the relation of a number of Nolte's theses to Nazi propaganda, see Ian Kershaw, *The Nazi Dictatorship: Problems and Perspectives of Interpretation* (2nd ed., London, 1989), pp. 174–8.

FURTHER READING

Contributions to the debate which is the subject of this book now number well over a thousand, and the degree of repetition is such that no useful purpose would be served by providing a full bibliography. The following notes are intended merely as an introductory guide to the major and most representative publications, up to the end of 1988. The main contributions to the debate have been conveniently collected in R. Piper (ed.), *"Historiker-streit": Die Dokumentation der Kontroverse um die Einzigartigkeit der na-tionalsozialistischen Judenvernichtung* (Munich, 1987). This is the essential starting point. An English translation is in preparation. Charles S. Maier, *The Unmasterable Past: History, Holocaust, and German National Identity* (Cambridge, Mass., 1988) is a recent survey of the debate that is especially good on the theoretical and methodological aspects. A guide to the political background is provided by Geoffrey Hartman (ed.), *Bitburg in Moral and Political Perspective* (Bloomington, 1986).

The most useful general introduction to the way in which historians have approached the history of Nazi Germany is Ian Kershaw, *The Nazi Dictatorship: Problems and Perspectives of Interpretation* (2nd ed., London, 1989). This edition contains two new chapters on the *Historikerstreit* and the "historiciza-tion" of Nazism. The most comprehensive general introduction to Nazism itself is Jeremy Noakes and Geoffrey Pridham (eds.), *Nazism, 1919–1945: A Docu-mentary Reader,* 4 vols. (Exeter, 1984–91). The final volume in the set is still under preparation at the present time. When completed, it will, with excellent commentaries by Jeremy Noakes, constitute the best single history of Nazism in English. Older, but still valuable, is Karl Dietrich Bracher, *The German Dictatorship* (London, 1969). Michael Burleigh, *Germany Turns Eastwards: A Study of Ostforschung in the Third Reich* (Cambridge, 1988), is a brilliant and chilling study of how historians who play politics can become involved in mass murder; it also casts light on a number of points at issue in the present debate, as does Omer Bartov, *The Eastern Front 1941–45. German Troops and the Barbarization of Warfare* (London, 1985), a book which is, however, so badly written as to be scarcely readable at times.

The best account of the debate is by a group of historians associated with the Military History Research Office in Freiburg: Gernot Erler, Rolf-Dieter Müller, Ulrich Rose, Thomas Schnabel, Gerd Ueberschär, and Wolfram Wette, *Geschichtswende? Entsorgungsversuche zur deutschen Geschichte* (Freiburg, 1987). The authors' attempts to distinguish among the politicians between Kohl and Weizsäcker on the one hand, and Strauss and Dregger on the other, are not always very persuasive, however. Hans-Ulrich Wehler, *Entsorgung der deutschen Vergangenheit? Ein polemischer Essay zum "Historikerstreit"* (Munich, 1988), engages usefully with the central issues, but sees the debate too much in terms of individual personalities. Imanuel Geiss, *Die Habermas-Kontroverse. Ein deutscher Streit* (Berlin, 1988) is a painstaking and well-written attempt to redress the balance in favor of Nolte; essential reading, but concentrates too much on secondary issues. Stefan Melnik, "Annotierte ausgewählte Bibliographie zur Historikerdebatte" *Liberal* 29 (1987), pp. 85–95, is a good basic guide to the early literature. Reinhard Kühnl (ed.), *Vergangenheit, die nicht vergeht: Die "Historiker-Debatte": Darstellung, Dokumentation, Kritik* (Cologne, 1987), is a collection of the major contributions with commentaries from a point of view more or less identified with the West German Communist Party, but the contributions have in many cases been abridged, and the Piper volume is preferable.

Dan Diner (ed.), *Ist der Nationalsozialismus Geschichte? Zur Historisierung und Historikerstreit* (Frankfurt, 1987), is a very stimulating collection of articles, many of which reflect the international dimension of the debate. Hilmar Hoffmann (ed.), *Gegen den Versuch, Vergangenheit zu verbiegen: Eine Diskussion um politische Kultur in der Bundesrepublik aus Anlass der Frankfurter Römerberggespräche 1986* (Frankfurt, 1986), contains the proceedings, and some of the papers, of the conference which began the debate. *Streitfall Deutsche Geschichte. Geschichts– und Gegenwartsbewusstsein in den 80er Jahren* (hg. von der Landeszentrale für politische Bildung, Nordrhein-Westfalen, Essen, 1988) is an outstanding set of papers, broadly speaking by supporters of the Habermas line. The same source has also produced a thoughtful account of the debate in its broader historical and political context: Bernd Faulenbach and Rainer Bölling, *Geschichtsbewusstsein und historisch-politische Bildung in der Bundesrepublik Deutschland. Beiträge zum "Historikerstreit"* (Düsseldorf, 1988). Wieland Eschenhagen (ed.), *Die neue deutsche Ideologie: Einsprüche gegen die Entsorgung der Vergangenheit* (Darmstadt, 1988), a collection based on lectures delivered at Paderborn (with one exception) by nonhistorians, is less useful; the lectures either tend not to address themselves to the central issues, or, if they do, overshoot the mark. Helga Grebing et al., *Von der Verdrängung zur Bagatellisierung. Aspekte des sogenannten Historikerstreits* (Hanover, 1988), is preferable.

Wolfgang Fritz Haug, *Vom hilflosen Antifaschismus zur Gnade der späten Geburt* (Berlin, 1987) a markedly left-wing contribution to the debate, makes some provocative points, but buries them in a style that is so dense and so complex that it is often nearly impossible to tease them out. Heidi Gerstenberger and Dorothea Schmidt (eds.), *Normalität oder Normalisierung? Geschichtswerkstätten und Faschismusanalyse* (Münster, 1987), prints articles from the German "history workshop" movement that are mostly, at best, tangential to the debate. Eike Hennig, *Zum Historikerstreit: Was heisst und zu welchem Ende studiert man Geschichte?* (Frankfurt, 1988), like Haug's book, contains previously published work not directly relevant to the discussion, and is written in rather inaccessible language. Probably the most stimulating discussion of the debate from a position to the left of Habermas is Heinrich Senfft, *Der Blick zurück: Hinter den Fassaden des Historikerstreits* (Nördlingen, 1989). Geoff Eley, "Nazism, Politics and the Image of the Past: Thoughts on the West German *Historikerstreit* 1986–1987," *Past and Present* 121 (1988), pp. 171–208, is the best treatment from the left in English.

The original participants in the debate have mostly printed their contributions, with additional material, in books of essays: Hans Mommsen, *Auf der Suche nach historischer Normalität: Beiträge zum Geschichtsbildstreit in der Bundesrepublik* (Berlin, 1987), is one such collection. Another is Christian Meier, *40 Jahre nach Auschwitz: Deutsche Geschichtserinnerung heute* (Munich, 1987). Jürgen Habermas, *Eine Art Schadensabwicklung* (Frankfurt, 1987), contains the full versions of his contributions; Michael Stürmer, *Dissonanzen des Fortschritts: Essays über Geschichte und Politik in Deutschland* (Munich, 1986), omits some of his. Michael Stürmer, *Deutsche Fragen: Oder die Suche nach der Staatsräson* (Munich, 1988), is a collection of his more directly political pieces. *New German Critique*, one of the liveliest American journals covering German cultural life, devoted its issue number 44 (Spring/Summer 1988) to the debate; the issue contains an excellent selection of translated original contributions (including two of Habermas's articles) and commentaries (by Mary Nolan and Anson Rabinbach, among others). Of particular interest is the exchange between Martin Broszat and Saul Friedländer on the "Historicization of National Socialism" (pp. 81–126) originally published in the *Vierteljahrshefte für Zeitgeschichte* 36 (1988), pp. 339–72. Hagen Schulze, *Wir sind, was wir geworden sind: Vom Nutzen der Geschichte für die deutsche Gegenwart* (Munich, 1987), gives a broad-based selection of Schulze's views. Stürmer's *Das ruhelose Reich* and Schulze's *Weimar* are also essential; both volumes appear in the Siedler history series *Die Deutschen und ihre Nation*, and together are an important statement of some central themes of the neoconservatives.

Andreas Hillgruber has added to his original contribution, *Zweierlei Untergang: Die Zerschlagung des Deutschen Reiches und das Ende des europäischen Judentums* (Berlin, 1986), one new text, *Die Zerstörung Europas: Beiträge zur Geschichte der Weltkriegsepoche* (Berlin, 1988), which, however, is not always directly related to the central questions in the debate. Ernst Nolte has produced a major book, *Der europäische Bürgerkrieg 1917–1945: Nationalsozialismus und Bolshewismus* (Frankfurt, 1987), and a collection of essays and critiques, *Das Vergehen der Vergangenheit: Antwort an meine Kritiker im sogenannten Historikerstreit* (2nd ed., Berlin, 1988). The first book is perhaps the central text in the whole controversy: the second, unfortunately, contains numerous extracts from correspondence, interviews, and articles instead of the complete texts, has little of substance to add to Nolte's original exposition of his theses, and makes virtually no attempt at a direct reply to the criticisms which have been made on grounds of historical accuracy or persuasiveness. Some of Nolte's views are available in English in Ernst Nolte, "Between Myth and Revisionism?: The Third Reich in the Perspective of the 1980s," in H. W. Koch (ed.), *Aspects of the Third Reich* (New York, 1985), pp. 17–38 (abridged by the editor without the author's permission).

Among the more interesting reviews of Nolte's *Bürgerkrieg* are D. Beyrau, "Archipel Gulag und Auschwitz," *Geschichte, Politik und ihre Didaktik* 16 (1988), pp. 95–104; Heinrich Senfft, in *1999: Zeitschrift für Sozialgeschichte des 20. und 21. Jahrhunderts* 3 (1988), 134–7; the magisterial critique by Hans Mommsen, "Das Ressentiment als Wissenschaft. Anmerkungen zu Ernst Noltes 'Der europäische Bürgerkrieg 1917–1945. Nationalsozialismus und Bolschewismus,'" *Geschichte und Gesellschaft* 14 (1988), pp. 495–540; and the detailed account by Wolfgang Schieder, "Der Nationalsozialismus im Fehlurteil philosophischer Geschichtsschreibung. Zur Methode von Ernst Nolte's 'Europäischem Bürgerkrieg,'" *Geschichte und Gesellschaft* 15 (1989), 89–114, which usefully links Nolte to the recent controversy about the pro-Nazi sympathies of his teacher Martin Heidegger. Klaus Hildebrand (ed.), *Wem gehört die deutsche Geschichte? Deutschlands Weg vom alten Europa in die europäische Moderne* (Cologne, 1987) is a useful guide to the wider field of conservative thinking on modern German history.

The political and ideological background to the debate has also been the subject of some discussion. Claus Leggewie, *Der Geist steht rechts: Ausflüge in die Denkfabriken der Wende* (Berlin, 1987) and Hermannus Pfeiffer (ed.), *Die FAZ: Nachforschungen über ein Zentralorgan* (Cologne, 1988), are useful guides. A particularly significant text is the attempt by the right-wing extremist Rolf Kosiek to draw comfort from the dispute: *Historikerstreit und Geschichtsrevision* (Tübingen, 1987). Federal President Richard von Weizsäcker's moderate and conciliatory views are available in his *A Voice from Germany* (London, 1985). Finally, the most extreme manifestations of "revisionism" are discussed, against their contemporary background in the emergence of the New Right, by Gill Seidel, *The Holocaust Denial: Antisemitism, Racism, and the New Right* (London, 1986). Those who want to delve further into the debate are referred to the numerous articles and other contributions cited in the notes above.

INDEX

ABOUT THE AUTHOR

Richard J. Evans has been professor of European history at the University of East Anglia since 1983, and the author and editor of numerous books on modern German history. In 1989, he was appointed professor of history at Birkbeck College, University of London.